Confronting Intolerance

TRANSGRESSIONS: CULTURAL STUDIES AND EDUCATION
Volume 31

Series Editors
    Shirley Steinberg, *McGill University, Canada*
    Joe Kincheloe, *McGill University, Canada*

Editorial Board
    Heinz-Hermann Kruger, *Halle University, Germany*
    Norman Denzin, *University of Illinois, Champaign-Urbana, USA*
    Roger Slee, *McGill University, Canada*
    Rhonda Hammer, *University of California Los Angeles, USA*
    Christine Quail, *SUNY, Oneonta*

Scope

Cultural studies provides an analytical toolbox for both making sense of educational practice and extending the insights of educational professionals into their labors. In this context *Transgressions: Cultural Studies and Education* provides a collection of books in the domain that specify this assertion. Crafted for an audience of teachers, teacher educators, scholars and students of cultural studies and others interested in cultural studies and pedagogy, the series documents both the possibilities of and the controversies surrounding the intersection of cultural studies and education. The editors and the authors of this series do not assume that the interaction of cultural studies and education devalues other types of knowledge and analytical forms. Rather the intersection of these knowledge disciplines offers a rejuvenating, optimistic, and positive perspective on education and educational institutions. Some might describe its contribution as democratic, emancipatory, and transformative. The editors and authors maintain that cultural studies helps free educators from sterile, monolithic analyses that have for too long undermined efforts to think of educational practices by providing other words, new languages, and fresh metaphors. Operating in an interdisciplinary cosmos, Transgressions: Cultural Studies and Education is dedicated to exploring the ways cultural studies enhances the study and practice of education. With this in mind the series focuses in a non-exclusive way on popular culture as well as other dimensions of cultural studies including social theory, social justice and positionality, cultural dimensions of technological innovation, new media and media literacy, new forms of oppression emerging in an electronic hyperreality, and postcolonial global concerns. With these concerns in mind cultural studies scholars often argue that the realm of popular culture is the most powerful educational force in contemporary culture. Indeed, in the twenty-first century this pedagogical dynamic is sweeping through the entire world. Educators, they believe, must understand these emerging realities in order to gain an important voice in the pedagogical conversation.

Without an understanding of cultural pedagogy's (education that takes place outside of formal schooling) role in the shaping of individual identity--youth identity in particular--the role educators play in the lives of their students will continue to fade. Why do so many of our students feel that life is incomprehensible and devoid of meaning? What does it mean, teachers wonder, when young people are unable to describe their moods, their affective affiliation to the society around them. Meanings provided young people by mainstream institutions often do little to help them deal with their affective complexity, their difficulty negotiating the rift between meaning and affect. School knowledge and educational expectations seem as anachronistic as a ditto machine, not that learning ways of rational thought and making sense of the world are unimportant.

But school knowledge and educational expectations often have little to offer students about making sense of the way they feel, the way their affective lives are shaped. In no way do we argue that analysis of the production of youth in an electronic mediated world demands some "touchy-feely" educational superficiality. What is needed in this context is a rigorous analysis of the interrelationship between pedagogy, popular culture, meaning making, and youth subjectivity. In an era marked by youth depression, violence, and suicide such insights become extremely important, even life saving. Pessimism about the future is the common sense of many contemporary youth with its concomitant feeling that no one can make a difference.

If affective production can be shaped to reflect these perspectives, then it can be reshaped to lay the groundwork for optimism, passionate commitment, and transformative educational and political activity. In these ways cultural studies adds a dimension to the work of education unfilled by any other sub-discipline. This is what Transgressions: Cultural Studies and Education seeks to produce—literature on these issues that makes a difference. It seeks to publish studies that help those who work with young people, those individuals involved in the disciplines that study children and youth, and young people themselves improve their lives in these bizarre times.

CONFRONTING INTOLERANCE

Critical, Responsive Literacy Instruction with Adult Immigrants

Stephen G. Mogge
Towson University

SENSE PUBLISHERS
ROTTERDAM / NEW YORK/TAIPEI

A C.I.P. record for this book is available from the Library of Congress.

ISBN: 978-90-8790-487-6 (paperback)
ISBN: 978-90-8790-488-3 (hardback)
ISBN: 978-90-8790-489-0 (e-book)

Published by: Sense Publishers,
P.O. Box 21858
3001 AW Rotterdam
The Netherlands

Printed on acid-free paper

All Rights Reserved © 2008 Sense Publishers

No part of this work may be reproduced, stored in a retrieval system, or transmitted in any form or by any means, electronic, mechanical, photocopying, microfilming, recording or otherwise, without written permission from the Publisher, with the exception of any material supplied specifically for the purpose of being entered and executed on a computer system, for exclusive use by the purchaser of the work.

Dedication

This book is dedicated to Garry.

CONTENTS

Acknowledgements ix

Introduction: Our Time and Place in the Historical Struggle 1

Part I. Getting Started in a Critical, Responsive Literacy Classroom 15

    Chapter 1 Critical, Responsive Teaching and Generative Groundwork 17
    Chapter 2 "In English My Name Means Hope" 27

Part II. Naming Injustice 41

    Chapter 3 Race, Class, Gender and Literary Conversations 43
    Chapter 4 Justine: Searching for the Good Fight 53
    Chapter 5 Personal and Political Narratives 63

Part III. Language, Literacy, and Power 81

    Chapter 6 Agency and Discourse 83
    Chapter 7 Lucía: Sampling Rhetoric and Raising Her Voice 93
    Chapter 8 La Marcha 103

Part IV. Race and American Dreams 119

    Chapter 9 Critical Engagement with Race and Multiculturalism 121
    Chapter 10 Olivia: With Dreams of Elvis 133
    Chapter 11 The Skin is Talking 145

Part V. The Adult Literacy Education System for Latino/A Immigrants 163

    Chapter 12 Global Economy, Citizenship, and Educational Opportunity 165
    Chapter 13 Jacinta: Feeling Her Way Through 175
    Chapter 14 Education/*Educación* for Latinas in Chicago 189

Part VI. Reflections 217

    Chapter 15 Reflections on Confronting Intolerance 219

References 231

ACKNOWLEDGEMENTS

I am grateful to all of the teachers, administrators, and staff who welcomed me at Erie Neighborhood House, especially Tim Bell for having invited me to teach and conduct my research in Erie's Adult Education program. I was always treated with respect and kindness and as a member of the team. I have tremendous admiration for Tim and the staff at Erie, who have only to look into their students' faces to know that a more caring and just world is worth their efforts. They do look and they do offer us a more hopeful world.

Many mentors helped me to launch my academic career and pursue this work. Caroline Heller listened attentively when I expressed my longing to tell stories from the adult literacy classroom. She has been a good friend and colleague while keeping the hope alive for this project. Bill Ayers, Tim Shanahan, Irma Olmedo, Susan Lytle, Bill Schubert, David Hansen, and Marcia Farr were among the many teachers/scholars who helped me to think critically and deeply about literacy education.

I am grateful to Susan Lytle and Bill Ayers for their encouragement and support in trying to get this book published. I also thank Bess Altwerger for her support and for leading me eventually to Joe Kincheloe who championed this work. Finally, thank you to Michel Lokhorst at Sense for taking on this book.

Many friends and colleagues along the way read drafts and provided important, essential feedback. These include Ana Colomb, Cynthia Reyes, Sue Reynolds, Chris Worthman, Barbara Laster, Cynthia Hartzler-Miller, and Kate Power. I am tremendously grateful for your efforts and fortunate to have you as colleagues and friends. I thank all the graduate students—classroom teachers—who read various chapters and let me know these types of stories are important for teachers to read. Thanks to Teresa Coffin and Maureen Fern who provided focused and detailed support. Maureen's dedication to helping me tell the many stories in this book was invaluable.

I am grateful to George at Arte Publico Press, who thought my teaching project was worthwhile, went to the shelves of discarded books (they looked fine to me), and sent boxes of them to Erie Neighborhood House. They were read!

I deeply appreciate all the family members, especially Garrett and Penny, who helped me find the time for writing. Very special thanks to Kate and Garry for your constant encouragement and love.

I especially want to thank my Erie Neighborhood House students who helped me to appreciate their dreams and some of my own as well.

INTRODUCTION:

OUR TIME AND PLACE IN THE HISTORICAL STRUGGLE

"Are you Polish? Are you from Poland?" A middle aged woman with dark hair and brown skin turned and greeted me. I detected a Mexican accent but could barely hear the woman amidst all the cheering at the culmination of a union organizer's solidarity speech.

"No. I'm from Baltimore in Maryland," I responded, returning the woman's smile. My various ancestors immigrated to North America between 125 and 250 years ago from England, France, Ireland and Scotland. On this first day of May, 2006, I had come to Chicago to join tens of thousands of literacy teachers at the International Reading Association's annual conference. Earlier that morning I came away from a keynote speech by Jonathan Kozol (2006) feeling unsettled. Kozol's contempt for the policies of the No Child Left Behind education policies in the United States and his impassioned pleas for more humane educational policy and practice left me longing for something more compelling than what I expected to find at the conference that day in the scores of presentations on reading pedagogy. Fortunately, I knew where to look. That morning's Chicago Tribune forecasted hundreds of thousands of immigrant rights activists marching in the rain through the streets of Chicago to an assembly at the south end of Grant Park (Avila & Martinez, 2006). That afternoon the woman and I stood in the soggy Grant Park softball infield amidst the throng of immigrants rights demonstrators who persevered through the steady afternoon drizzle.

"I used to live in Chicago until about five years ago. I lived in Chicago for about 20 years. I lived in Logan Square for many of those years," I continued, wanting the woman to understand that even though I was not a Polish immigrant—an ethnic group that once comprised Chicago's largest immigrant community but had in recent decades been eclipsed by those of Mexican heritage—we might share something other than just the coincidence of standing side by side at the demonstration. Indeed, she informed me that she once lived in West Town near Logan Square but had recently moved out by O'Hare Airport where she and her husband were able to afford a house. I let her know that at one time I was a teacher in West Town. We talked some more and shared our enthusiasm for the tremendous numbers that turned out for the day's events. While I made my way from the conference on the lake front, she had marched with the hundreds of thousands from Union Park on the west side of the city. We agreed that it did not matter much whether we could hear the speakers clearly or that the rain appeared to have no end. It was good to be there. It felt good to be part of a demonstration that was linked with others across the nation.

INTRODUCTION

Several years earlier, from 1995-1997, I was a teacher at Erie Neighborhood House, a settlement house and community agency in the northwest Chicago neighborhood of West Town. I taught intermediate to advanced English language learners—mostly Mexican—many of whom were also active in Erie's efforts to confront a persistent, anti-immigrant fervor that had swept across the nation. Anti-immigrant policies had gained significant ground following California's Proposition 187 (to be discussed below) in the early 1990s and were being written into federal law, most notably in the immigration and welfare reforms of 1996. During my time at Erie Neighborhood House, the students and I examined immigrant experiences and the political issues that affected them. We also participated in a variety of public demonstrations. We joined dozens who marched in support of affordable housing at the local alderman's office, the mayor's residence, and at city hall (see chapter 14). We were among hundreds in August, 1996 who marched to the Democratic National Convention held in Chicago to voice opposition to immigration policies drafted in the Congress led by Georgia Republican Representative Newt Gingrich and signed into law by President Bill Clinton. We traveled to Washington, D.C. two months later on Columbus Day in October, 1996 to join 25,000 for *La Marcha*, a national demonstration for Latino and immigrant rights (see chapter 8). At the time, we could not have fathomed four hundred thousand taking to the streets of Chicago a decade later in 2006.

In fact, until the spring of 2006, the United States had never witnessed so many protesting for immigrant rights. Public demonstrations across the nation turned out tens of thousands in small cities and hundreds of thousands in Los Angeles, Chicago, New York and Washington, D.C. The mainstream U.S. media typically proclaimed surprise at the large and influential immigrant rights movement. It had seemingly arisen from nowhere and, the media often proclaimed, was focused on gaining amnesty for the millions of undocumented immigrants. This narrative pitted immigrant rights activists against those who railed against the flouting of the federal immigration laws and policies by people who crossed the U.S. southern border illegally. Concern over national security in the post-September 11, 2001 era had already escalated the clamor for immigration restrictions and dramatically increased border security. Amidst the public debate, President George W. Bush and bipartisan legislators agreed on a comprehensive immigration reform policy in 2007 that attempted to resolve, at least temporarily, the nation's immigration "crisis" through heightened border security and pathways to citizenship. However, organized groups on both sides, but primarily from the conservative right, wielded enough clout to thwart a consensus policy. The debate continued in the 2008 Presidential election campaigns while the new Homeland Security Administration escalated its policy of seizing undocumented workers and their employers.

TWENTIETH CENTURY POLICY: MEXICAN IMMIGRATION

Recent immigration debates often return to the 1986 Immigration Reform and Control Act, which included a form of amnesty and poorly enforced employer sanctions, to identify where immigration policy went awry. But we cannot understand current immigration without a more thorough historical perspective. Tichenor (2002) argues for greater appreciation of the political institutions, ideological traditions, and organized social interests that have contended for influence on immigration policy. Immigration has always fostered unexpected alliances in which conservatives and liberals have frequently abandoned their partisan coalitions. Some take free market positions that favor open immigration while others take nationalist or even isolationist positions favoring restricted immigration. Some argue for acceptance of highly educated immigrants to fill employer demands while others argue for support of poor, uneducated immigrants who have family connections or ethnic ties to particular communities. Tichenor asserts that nations continually define themselves through policies of official selection of foreigners who are permitted to enter their country. In the United States, he explains that every era has seen fierce debate over economic, social, cultural, and national security matters during which native born citizens "mythologize their sojourn past" (p. 1) while newcomers struggle for cultural acceptance and civil liberties. Amidst episodic debates, the history of U.S. immigration reveals a general acceptance of immigrants interrupted by periods of decisive restrictions. In recent years, the influx of millions of undocumented Mexican immigrants to the U.S. has brought another period, albeit a sustained one, of restriction advocacy.

Current debates over Mexican immigration, legal and illegal, reflect the consistently capricious and vacillating policies that have existed since 1848 when the Treaty of Guadalupe Hidalgo brought the Mexican-American War to an end. The Treaty severed most of the current U.S. western states from Mexico (roughly half of the nation of Mexico) and established a 1,950 mile long border from Texas to California which until recent decades was minimally patrolled and remained essentially porous (Ellingwood, 2004; Tichenor, 2002). Mexicans (and Americans) freely traversed the border, back and forth, often with the legislative and financial support from U.S. policy makers and employers. The lack of border enforcement reflected the tremendous desire for Mexican labor throughout the past century. Though their labor was promoted, Mexican immigrants were not encouraged to establish permanent residency. Ellingwood (2004) quotes the 1911 Dillingham Commission on Immigration: "The Mexican migrants are providing a fairly adequate supply of labor. . . . In the case of the Mexican, he is less desirable as a citizen than as a laborer" (p. 20). Such comments resonate nearly one hundred years later in contemporary discussions about immigration.

Throughout the twentieth century, western and southern U.S. employers, primarily in the agricultural sector but also in the transportation and manufacturing industries, continually lobbied for the cheap labor that Mexicans provided. Encouraged by U.S. demands for labor and fleeing the strife of the Mexican Revolution, Mexican immigration dramatically increased between 1910 and 1920. The U.S. Immigration Act of 1917, which for the first time required a literacy test and small fee, and the Immigration Act of 1924, which expressed concern about racial contamination by Mexicans were passed, in part, as a response to Mexican immigration. Despite such concerns, the encouragement of Mexican labor

INTRODUCTION

continued until the Depression of the 1930s, when one-half million Mexicans were repatriated in order to make space for U.S. citizen workers. Then during World War II, Mexican workers were encouraged to return in support of the war effort (Tichenor, 2002; Zolberg, 2006). The *Bracero* Program launched in 1942 and disbanded twenty years later formally brought Mexican workers to the U.S. as farm labor throughout the western region of the U.S. In establishing the *Bracero* Program, the U.S. pledged to the Mexican government—which because of a history of worker abuse by U.S. employers was reluctant to enter into an agreement—to enforce numerous human and civil rights provisions. However, these were not enforced and were habitually violated by employers (Tichenor, 2002). Fifty years later, many pro-immigrant advocates decried President George W. Bush's call for a guest worker program as a return to exploitative labor practices of the *Bracero* Program.

During the 1960s, two circumstances changed the course of immigration history, particularly for Latinos/Mexicans, in the United States. First, the Hart-Celler Act of 1965 dismantled the national origins quota system that had been in place for decades and replaced it with a new preference system that emphasized family reunification (Zolberg, 2006). The new policy permitted immigrants who had established permanent residency in the U.S. to bring family members for years and generations to come. The population of Mexicans in the United States increased. This change was accompanied by a new political activism influenced by the Civil Rights Movement and advanced in the United Farm Workers Movement led by César Chávez. The ensuing Chicano Rights Movement in the Southwest, centered in Los Angeles, California, ushered in an era of Mexican cultural and historical pride, academic studies, and eventually more sophisticated political and legislative participation in which immigrant rights advocates across the national-origins spectrum joined forces. The 1986 Immigration and Reform Act that included amnesty was greatly influenced by this new political lobby which in 1990 and 1996 policy debates continued to influence a pro-immigration policy and quell reactionary public fervor against immigrants (Tichenor, 2002; Zolberg, 2006).

The arrival of four hundred thousand immigrant rights demonstrators in Chicago's Grant Park in the spring of 2006 was no historical anomaly. Organizers and activists across the nation, like those I worked with at Erie Neighborhood House in the late 1990s, had been cultivating this movement for the previous four decades. Still, their motivations lay not just in flexing political muscle and advocating for amnesty or pathways to citizenship. The anti-immigrant fervor was strong as well and its vehemence, true to historical precedent, was being expressed through disparaging rhetoric. Clearly, this most recent anti-immigrant wave was taking aim at Mexicans specifically and Latin Americans more generally. Though the anti-immigrant zeal was clearly anti-Latino/Mexican it was understood by many ethnic immigrant communities as threatening to their rights and opportunities. It only made sense to stand and be counted, to confront those passions and polices that had arisen to threaten their American dreams. The throngs of demonstrators in Grant Park and across the nation in 2006 were exercising their firmly established rights to participate in American democracy and make their voices heard.

TWO DECADES OF DEBATE

At the outset of the 1990s, the U.S. still held to a fairly liberal immigration policy. Apprehension over illegal immigration was outweighed by concern for the nation's economic health and prosperity. The first Bush administration, the Clinton administration and the Congress supported policies that could solve labor shortages (both low and high skilled) and stimulate international competitiveness while continuing the family reunification agenda (Tichenor, 2002). The North American Free Trade Act (NAFTA) ushered in an era in which goods and capital would flow freely across the northern and southern U.S. borders though workers—legally— could not. Citing declining wages and poor work conditions, many have argued that NAFTA has been harmful to workers on both sides of the border.

Both pro and anti-immigrant advocates are able to cite research to proclaim the economic benefits or costs of undocumented workers to the social-political system (see the Pew Research Center, 2006 for analysis of public opinion). Generally, federal tax coffers are more likely to benefit from legal and illegal immigration while states are more likely to face unbudgeted costs (Paral, 1996; Tichenor, 2002; Zolberg, 2006). As for federal entitlements, immigrants with residency and citizen status are no more likely to use welfare benefits (AFDC, TANF, Food Stamps, Medicaid) than other U.S. citizens. However, the burden of providing for education, health care, and other services to immigrants that falls largely to the states and local municipalities exacerbates their balanced budget priorities. Illegal immigration into southern U.S.-border states has significantly altered their demographics and increased their budgetary obligations. Over a thirty-year period, the foreign-born population of California increased from 9 to 22% while the white population continued a gradual flight to other states (Zolberg, 2006). The changing demographics and budgetary demands compounded by a porous southern border led exasperated Californians in 1994 to approve Proposition 187. This public referendum sought to deny public education and numerous state benefits to undocumented immigrants and their children. Ellingwood (2004) characterized the shift in public sentiment: "In a state that had been only too happy to let undocumented immigrants pick its grapes, tend its children, mop its floors and clip its bougainvilleas, many residents now saw a crisis demanding action" (p. 30). Led by Governor Pete Wilson who as a U.S. Senator voted for the 1986 IRCA legislation, 59% of voters—mostly Republican, white, less educated and lower class—sided with the "save our state" proposition (Zolberg, 2006). Four years later, California voters also passed Proposition 227 which eliminated bilingual education, required that all public schools teach English only and refrain from providing instruction in students' native language.

Responses to the California measures were legally direct and politically enduring. The courts declared unconstitutional most of Proposition 187's provisions, leaving unresolved the state's immigration and public policy concerns.

INTRODUCTION

In due course, California (and later the nation) saw a dramatic increase in Latino/Mexican voting, the eventual election of several new Latino/Mexican state and U.S. legislators, and the demise of its Republican Party. However, these changes in the political complexion of California were not immediately appreciated in Washington, D.C. where President Clinton and the Newt Gingrich-led Congress interpreted a growing national enthusiasm for ant-immigrant policies. On the heels of the California movement, Clinton established substantially heightened southern border enforcement under Operation Gatekeeper. Through the welfare reforms of 1996, Clinton and the Congress targeted approximately 45% of its benefit reductions at the 5% of recently arrived legal residents and citizens who used them (National Immigration Forum, 2000; Zolberg, 2006). At the same time he signed the welfare bill into law Clinton denounced several of the immigrant provisions and vowed to redress them in the future. To succeed in the November election, though, Clinton acquiesced to the anti-immigrant lobby. This policy proved acceptable to most of the voting population as he won the election. Concurrent with the welfare reform, new immigration reform legislation sought to reduce legal immigration, tighten asylum procedures, increase sponsors' financial requirements, and establish more rigid preference categories. In sum these new policies represented the elimination of constitutionally guaranteed protections for legal and undocumented immigrants, the retrenchment of entitlements for legal immigrants, and the sustenance of free-market expansionist priorities. A number of examples below serve to illustrate the impact of the new agenda on immigrants and suggest, in part, why a pro-immigrant movement accelerated in the new millennium.

Operation Gatekeeper's policy of building walls south of San Diego and across the West and increasing the numbers of agents in other population centers forced border crossers into the deserts and mountainous regions where they risked their lives. As a result, by the year 2000 annual deaths at the border reached more than 300 (Ellingwood, 2004). While some asserted that the new border policy violated international human rights, the U.S. denied any culpability. Ellingwood quotes a border patrol official on the matter: "Death on the border is unfortunate, but it's nothing new.... It's not caused by the Border Patrol. It's not caused by Gatekeeper" (p. 69). The increasing number of deaths at the border had come to be viewed as the price paid by border crossers in a game of cat and mouse. Indeed this most dangerous game was escalated by a vigilante border patrol movement that took it upon itself to patrol the southern border and push illegal crossers into further peril.

In the wake of immigration reforms, undocumented workers were frequently removed from factories and detained in federal and state prisons alongside convicted felons for indeterminate amounts of time—more than three years for some—while the Immigration and Naturalization Service worked through its backlog of cases (Lynch, 2000). Middle-aged, gainfully-employed, tax-paying, family-supporting, community-participating, legal residents were arrested, detained and threatened with deportation for misdemeanor crimes committed decades prior to the time in which they gained legal status (Lewis, 2001).

Under the new welfare reform (with few exemptions), current legal residents who had followed the former law of the land, earned residency status and paid taxes, would lose their previous entitlement to social security benefits and food stamps until they maintained legal residence for five years. Future legal residents would also be barred from these benefits for their first five years. Individual states were granted permission to deny Medicaid, Temporary Assistance for Needy Families (TANF—the new welfare program), Title I and Title XX programs to legal residents who had contributed their tax dollars to these entitlement programs. Undocumented immigrants were barred from access to any supportive services that might enable them to sustain their ambitions for eventual legal residence and citizenship, again regardless of sales tax and payroll tax contributions. Under the reforms, public schools and non-profit organizations were required to screen the legal status of potential clients and report suspected undocumented adults and children to the Immigration and Naturalization Service. Among the most widely reported reform provisions debated but not passed in the Congress were the denial of public school lunches, food and benefits offered through the Women with Infants and Children (WIC) program, and other nutrition programs to the children of undocumented adult immigrants. A public outcry on behalf of these children was heard in the media. The children, of course, were innocent. It was their parents who broke the law when they came to the United States to work and raise their families.

As a result of the reforms, legally residing parents who used food stamps to purchase food for their children risked legal sanction if it was even suspected that the parents themselves consumed any of the food (Peterson, 2000). A child born of legal residents in the United States was able to receive health care services through Medicaid, but that child's sibling, born outside of the United States, was not eligible to receive such care (National Immigration Forum, 2000). The undocumented spouse or parent of legal residents or citizens were required to return to his/her country of origin to apply for residency in the United States yet have to wait a minimum of three years to be reunited with family in the U.S. (McDonnell, 2000).

These and other stories were told sparingly in the press during the late 1990s. To the extent that Americans were familiar with the outcomes of the anti-immigrant policies, as described above, there might have been another period of liberalization that reinstated rights and some entitlements. In fact, the courts did throw out many of the 1996 welfare and immigration provisions. But following the September 11, 2001 terrorist attacks, the American public's fear of unknown outsiders increased. It did not matter that there were no reports of terrorists crossing the Mexican border with the United States. President George W. Bush, who in the week prior to the terrorist attacks had met with Mexican President Vicente Fox and declared that the U.S. had "no more important relationship in the world than the one we have with Mexico" (Ellingwood, 2004, p. 231) was forced to postpone his plans for a guest worker program and pathways to legal status for undocumented immigrants. Instead, the anti-immigrant forces redoubled their efforts to curtail immigration by preying on post-September 11th fears among some

INTRODUCTION

Americans of Mexicans swarming over the border, taking low-paying jobs, cheating the health care system, flooding emergency wards, and speaking Spanish in our communities and children's schools.

But the pro-immigrant, Latino rights movement also grew stronger in response to the public angst and policies of the 1990s. Tichenor (2002) explains: "The unintended consequences of those restrictive laws is a new generation of foreign-born voters, who, like European newcomers more than a century before, have created fresh electoral incentives for national politicians to guard expansive immigration polices" (p. 288). In fact, both Zolberg (2006) and Tichenor (2002) argue that, despite the restrictive policies, the debate over immigration in the 1990s was won by pro-immigration forces who wielded enough political and legislative influence to subdue the anti-immigrant wave that had taken hold. The latter half of the mid-1990s saw unprecedented growth in naturalization rates and voter registration among Latinos largely in response to public condemnation of immigrants and legislative threats. With new voters at the polls, many anti-immigrant advocates paid high political prices for their earlier positions. President George W. Bush's proposal for an improved relationship with Mexico and his proposal for a guest worker program stemmed from his years as Governor of Texas where the growing political influence of Latinos/Mexicans was manifest. Bush had strategically and publicly denounced California and Arizona anti-immigrant policies and distanced himself from the restrictive polices of Congress. In fact, until the anti-immigrant forces once again gained momentum in the next decade, Bush, his political advisor Carl Rove, and the Republican Party adopted a Latino strategy, recognizing it as the fastest growing voting bloc with a population that was forecasted to grow to 25% of the population by the year 2050. Of course, by 2006 this strategy was abandoned as a broad-based anti-immigrant fervor escalated once again.

ERIE NEIGHBORHOOD HOUSE AND WEST TOWN

In recent years, Erie Neighborhood House has expanded its operations to multiple locations throughout the West Town community of Chicago. During the two years that I taught inside of Erie's original building, I would frequently peer out the third floor classroom windows to take in the neighborhood that Erie has served for more than 135 years. The courtyard at the entrance to Erie bustled with the comings and goings of Erie's many constituents. Erie Neighborhood House was most active at night when double-parked cars lined up and down Erie Street leaving barely enough room to pass between them. At night Erie served adult education students who worked during the day, children who received childcare while their parents attended classes, high school students who received homework help through a tutoring program, youth participating in recreation activities, and neighborhood residents meeting to discuss affordable housing or economic development initiatives. While Erie was not as busy during the day, the daytime activities included additional adult education classes, daycare for toddlers and preschool kids, after-school care for elementary-age children, Meals On Wheels for the elderly and disabled, and community meetings for a variety of purposes.

Erie Neighborhood House was originally a Presbyterian Church founded in 1870. In 1915, during the progressive era of Jane Addams' Hull House, it became a settlement house. One hundred twenty-five years later, the year I started teaching there, Erie's 1995 Annual Report highlighted the continuing mission.

> *Erie House has enabled West Town's immigrants and low-income residents to take control of their lives while becoming productive and responsible citizens. Since its inception Erie House has provided a helping hand to immigrant groups including Scandinavians, Germans, Poles, Italians, African Americans and most recently, Latinos.* (p. 1)

In the 1990s, Erie served a mixed though rapidly changing community—a fact made clear through observations of the housing stock. Interspersed throughout the neighborhood could be found public housing, older multi-unit dwellings, and new single family homes. Scattered throughout the neighborhood tired and worn frame houses with front stoops in disrepair and multiple mailboxes hung vertically along side entrances, signaled the division of two and three flats into four, five and six unit rentals. At one end of the street, across from a public elementary school was a high-rise public housing building, recently renovated after several years in disrepair. Out of view from the classroom window, one block away, were handsome, well-manicured, low-rise public housing units. Scattered two or three per block throughout the neighborhood were freshly constructed cinder block and red brick three and four story residential structures—consuming the vacant lots where old wood-frame houses once stood—casting shadows on neighboring two flat structures. Around the corner from Erie, adjacent to a Catholic Church and school and across the street from the corner *mercado*, a ten-foot high electronic fence surrounded the parking lot of a renovated warehouse—transformed in the early 1990's into residential lofts.

Throughout the 1980's and first half of the 1990's, Erie served a mixed neighborhood. Recently arrived Mexicans occupied many of the rental units. The older single-family homes and two flats were owned, most notably, by second and third generation Italians. African Americans and Puerto Ricans inhabited the majority of the public housing units. The newly constructed homes and renovated lofts attracted younger professionals, mostly whites. A few Erie students confided that one positive impact of recent investment in the housing stock—of professionals moving into the neighborhood—was a greater sense of safety on the streets; gangbangers congregated less frequently on the corners. Still, the students were anxious about the day when their buildings would be sold, gutted and renovated, or even razed. They despaired and were resentful of the fast approaching day when they could no longer afford to rent in the mixed community.

From our third floor classroom window, the John Hancock Building, one of Chicago's tallest skyscrapers, could be seen illuminating the eastern sky at night. Erie is located in a residential neighborhood in the southeast corner of West Town, just a few minutes from Chicago's business district known as the Loop. Between

INTRODUCTION

the Loop and Erie lie two of the most expensive commercial and residential areas in the city: River North and River West. Milwaukee Avenue passes Erie one-quarter mile to the north and continues through the neighborhoods of West Town, Wicher Park and Bucktown. It is one of several diagonal streets that fans out from the Loop to the suburbs and bisects Chicago's near perfect north-south and east-west grid, a grid that historically maintained clear racial and ethnic boundaries. In the 1980s cheap rent for vast living and workspaces in Wicker Park and Bucktown attracted artists who were followed by mostly white professionals in their thirties and forties. As rent and property taxes increased, many working class Eastern European and Latino residents were forced out of the community. Many of these residents moved further west to Humboldt Park or to adjacent suburbs. By the mid 1990s artists were priced out of Wicker Park and Bucktown real estate markets as well. Real Estate speculators' eyes then turned down Milwaukee Avenue toward the Loop to the port of entry community that Erie Neighborhood House had served for 125 years.

Chicago is often identified as a city of ethnic neighborhoods. Many of these are transformed through the aspirations of successive immigrant groups who inhabit them. Commercial strips marked by ethnic restaurants are often remnants of a previous generation that moved to the suburbs. While investment capital long ago abandoned some African American communities and real estate practices isolated other African American neighborhoods from full economic integration, Chicago has for the most part been a city of thriving neighborhoods. Small enterprise springs forth from abandoned warehouses; restaurants rotate in and out of once forgotten storefronts and tire-repair shops constantly change hands. During the first half of the 1990s, West Town was just such a community. The commercial sector was as diverse as the population. Immigrant-owned bodegas struggled to survive next door to hip, nouveau restaurants—symbols of impending gentrification. At the time, Latinos comprised 61% of the West Town population. The majority of the Latinos were of Mexican origin. Mexicans comprised 32% of the population of West Town and 52% of the total Latino population in Chicago. Puerto Ricans represented the next largest group (25% of West Town and 41% of Latinos). There were also significant populations of Guatemalans, Cubans, Dominicans, Salvadorans, Hondurans and Ecuadorians (Latino Institute, 1995). While other Chicago communities had larger immigrant populations, West Town reflected Chicago's Latino population, which mirrored the national Latino demographic more closely than any other city in the United States (Latino Institute, 1993). By the late 1990s, however, the complexion of West Town had begun to change under the pressure of gentrification.

On a sweltering, late spring evening in 1996, four hundred neighborhood residents, mostly Latino (most of these Mexican), a few dozen African Americans, and a smattering of whites, overflowed Erie's old gymnasium. They were there to hear the latest installment in the saga of the Erie Housing Coop, a project of Erie's Economic Development Department to maintain affordable housing and lay a foundation that would preserve a mixed-income, mixed-race, and mixed-ethnic West Town community. During five years of planning with a neighborhood steering committee, an experienced developer and the City of Chicago, the Erie Housing Cooperative obtained financial backing and tax breaks to build thirty-seven units in seven buildings scattered throughout an almost three-square-mile area. The occupants would come from a pool of existing, longtime neighborhood residents who would pay between $355.00 and $495.00 per month, serve on an oversight board, and assume full ownership of Coop units at the end of fifteen years. It was understood by the four hundred who crowded into the gymnasium that the thirty-seven units, too few for most of the people present, stood for something larger—the opportunity to secure stable, affordable housing and to continue living in the neighborhood for many years to come. At the forum, the long-standing neighborhood resident, State Senator Miguel del Valle, bellowing in Spanish and English, captured the attitude and frenzied applause of many assembled.

> We have a mood here tonight. Full. Full! My heart is warm by what I see here tonight because we have a room full of honest, conscientious community residents who are responsible individuals who want what is best for this neighborhood. And how dare! HOW DARE a small group of individuals try to dictate to us! If we can't get support for a private housing development, PRIVATE! Underline PRIVATE. . . . Then what the hell will they support?

Del Valle's reference to "they" was specifically targeted at the local city alderman Jesse Granato and the real estate developers who supported him. Two years earlier, seeking his first aldermanic term in order to represent most of West Town, Jesse Granato promised to support the Coop if the ward passed a referendum in its favor. The referendum passed. Granato's stance helped to usher him into office. However, within six months a small group of homeowners and developers surfaced and lobbied against the Coop, casting aspersions on the project developer and obfuscating the financing and ownership plan, labeling it "section eight" (government guaranteed and subsidized rent for poor people) and "public" housing. Alderman Granato rescinded his pledge and, siding with the developers' interests, withdrew his support in the City Council. This story, part of an exposé on Granato's ongoing receipt of campaign contributions tied to each of his zoning sponsorships on behalf of developers, was detailed in *Streetwise* (Frago, 1997), a biweekly newspaper published for Chicago's homeless community. Meanwhile, the city's mainstream dailies ignored the story.

While Granato and his aides stood on the sidewalk outside Erie Neighborhood House observing the comings and goings of local residents and showing little inclination to engage them, the crowd in the gymnasium grew more vocal. Senator del Valle continued his oratory, praising Erie Neighborhood House, distinguishing it from other agencies that had, as he described, "gone hiding and running with their tails between their legs for fear of losing funding." The pitch of the Senator's voice rose repeatedly with each crescendo of applause and response. After a time, with a more quiet voice, the Senator made his vision plain:

INTRODUCTION

> We believe there is room for everyone. We believe that the developers can build their homes. We believe that the upper income person is welcome in this community. We believe that in this community all races, all nationalities can live. We believe that in this community there should never be tolerated any form of discrimination based on race and based on income. Because that is not what a neighborhood in Chicago is supposed to be all about. That is not what a neighborhood in Chicago is all about!

CRITICAL, RESPONSIVE LITERACY INSTRUCTION FOR ADULT IMMIGRANTS

In the midst of dramatic community changes and the tumultuous immigration debates and policy changes of the 1990s, I met with my students at Erie Neighborhood House to help them improve their English. With greater command of English the students envisioned the opportunity to obtain better jobs, attend college, attain citizenship status and, for a significant number of them, work on community empowerment issues and combat the anti-immigrant forces that posed a direct challenge to their aspirations. Erie Neighborhood House staff members were leaders in the community and in the local immigrant rights movement at the time. They made it their business to inform the students and the entire Erie community of the welfare and immigration reforms and invited them to participate in the political process. Many of my students understood that forces of oppression were aligned firmly against them. If they were not sure about how to engage their opponents when I met them in our first classes, they knew they ought not sit back and watch their families and communities come under assault. It remained to be seen how curriculum would address this emerging sense of the world closing in. I decided to proceed by greeting the students' understandable defensive postures, their hopes for a better future, and their resolve to stand firm. I responded through various literacy activities and remained open to their responses.

This book captures my effort as a teacher researcher to work through a critical perspective and deliver responsive language and literacy instruction. In the Freirian tradition, the students and I collaborated in identifying the oppressive circumstances of their lives, problematizing the gentrification and anti-immigrant agendas, and raising our consciousness in order to further raise our voices. For several months, we met two evenings per week in order to interact with reading, writing, the English language and each other. In the safe space that we established in our classroom we deliberated over our places in the U.S. and the roles we should take in shaping its future. In addition to our collective meetings, I also tutored students before classes and occasionally in Erie's technology center. My teacher research agenda included the exploration of students' individual lives as well as their classroom personas. It included community forums hosted by Erie staff and, as mentioned, political events in the local and national arenas.

The book is divided into six parts. Part I will introduce the educational setting, students, and critical literacy contexts. Parts II through V each has an introduction and ethnographic narrative chapters that present individual students and classroom events.

The introductory chapters in Parts I through V of the book will address the *Critical Perspectives, Responsive Literacy Instruction, and Teacher Research* agendas that frame the teacher research narratives in each part. The many characteristics of critical pedagogy that are addressed include: social justice, equality, resistance, generative curriculum, dialogue, interracial and interethnic tolerance, gender liberation, language empowerment, direct political action, recognition and challenge of oppression. These characteristics will be explained to clarify possible critical opportunities and agendas for any educational context but will be directly related to the narrative chapters within each part of the book. These chapters will further examine the *Responsive Literacy Instruction* that is employed in concert with the established critical agenda and that is guided by a sociocultural theory of literacy learning. The instructional approach that is presented throughout the book prioritizes literacy engagement and response. Through a response-centered approach, we explored the many issues in students' lives, identified individual student plans for literacy growth and, I contend, were able to promote students' comprehensive language development. Finally, the introduction of each part will discuss ways in which *Teacher Research* methodology is used to capture and represent classroom phenomena. It will further identify how, as a teacher researcher, one can be better positioned to meet students' needs through critically responsive literacy instruction.

Following the introductory chapters of each part, narrative chapters will examine the students and their teacher evolving and learning together as their interests are explored through teacher research. Through portraits of individual students, extensive use of classroom dialogue, and rich descriptions of community events, the text will offer a unique perspective on immigrant, second language learners and the potential for critical, responsive literacy instruction to expand the horizons of immigrant students and the worlds they create. The narratives reveal how our participation in several community and national political events informed the ongoing effort to negotiate a curriculum that would situate students' interests at the intersection of social, cultural, and political contexts. This negotiation became the road map for our journey together as the need to serve a wider assortment of students' interests within the critically grounded classroom became clear. These chapters show how my students and I stood side by side to fight against the injustices leveled against immigrants in the 1990s. The primary focus of each narrative chapter will be the words and thoughts of individual students as they struggle to understand and confront this hostile environment while preparing for their future lives in American society.

Finally, Part VI will provide reflection upon and analysis of the critical, responsive literacy instruction that is described throughout the book.

PART I

GETTING STARTED IN A CRITICAL, RESPONSIVE LITERACY CLASSROOM

CHAPTER 1

CRITICAL, RESPONSIVE TEACHING AND GENERATIVE GROUNDWORK

CRITICAL PERSPECTIVES

When embarking on the challenge to create curriculum, Schubert suggests that we begin by asking "What knowledge is most worthwhile? Why is it worthwhile? How is it acquired or created?" (1986, p. 1). The answers to these questions lead to identification of appropriate instructional content and methods. Throughout my teaching career—in adolescent and adult literacy education, as the creator of a literacy program for freshmen in an open-admissions college, as a professor of graduate literacy studies—I have often returned to Schubert's questions when creating a new program or teaching a new class. But Schubert also offers us a complementary philosophical question to help guide the construction of curriculum: "What does it mean to live a good and fulfilling life?" (p. viii). Until I met the students at Erie Neighborhood House this second question hovered somewhere on the horizon in my teaching life. I had seldom appreciated the opportunity to act on this philosophical question. But it was exactly the pursuit of a better life that brought my Erie students to the United States in the first place. When I met them in the late 1990s their aim was to continue their pursuits in the face of the harsh political climate that is described in the Introduction.

Many of my intermediate and advanced English for Speakers of Other Language (ESOL) students had joined the Community Leadership program at Erie. Through their participation in the program the students sought the knowledge required to confront their political opponents. They also determined a need to improve their English in order to enhance their community organizing activities. It was thus critical to link the Erie classroom to the community in order to meet the challenges to their opportunities to live a good and fulfilling life.

Among the driving forces for critical pedagogy, Kincheloe (2005) identifies a commitment to social justice and equity, a belief that education is inherently political, and dedication to the alleviation of human suffering. In the tradition of Paulo Freire, critical educators proceed by first seeking out generative themes in order to more fully explicate students' perceptions of their circumstances. Identifying these themes helps the teacher to learn what students know and how they perceive their roles in the community. From there, teachers initiate instruction and, through dialogue with students, further clarify the agenda for collaborative learning experiences. In Freire's most famous book, *Pedagogy of the Oppressed* (1970) and in other works (1973, 1985, 1987) he describes his pedagogy and the use of culture circles, dialogue, and codification systems—all components of

CHAPTER 1

libratory literacy instruction. He proposes that interdisciplinary teams of anthropologist-educators visit local communities to examine economic productivity and labor systems, family and community structures, spiritual beliefs and cultural patterns. These researchers then engage potential students in dialogue, seeking their perceptions of the world around them and learning of their aspirations and the barriers to the realization of their dreams. Teachers then re-present these cultural practices and aspirations through carefully selected drawings and complementary written alphabetic and syllabic symbols, from which simple consonant-vowel word-family clusters are extracted. Through these re-presentations students learn to crack the written form of the linguistic code, but, just as significant, through attention to the meaning of the words and through the suspension of their significance, ongoing dialogue is cultivated. The dialogue proceeds as problem-posing: questioning the existing order; identifying the structure of social, economic and political relationships; challenging conditions of oppression; naming the oppressed and the oppressor; and seeking transformation of shared worlds. From this consciousness raising, curriculum and instruction becomes praxis, an ongoing dialectical process of critical reflection and action. Freire's pedagogy embodied a hope for a world with greater humanity and freedom, a world with resolution of the oppressor-oppressed conundrum, and a world with more love.

Freire's literacy work throughout the 1950s, 60s and 70s took place in Brazil, Chile, Angola and other third world countries. Purcell-Gates and Waterman (2000) have published accounts of a literacy program offered more recently in El Salvador in which Waterman brings together Frierian ideas of critical pedagogy with sociocultural forms of literacy instruction—a program of instruction similar to the one I present in this text. In the United States we have several examples of critical educators working in adult literacy education who have contributed their knowledge and shared their experience. Myles Horton's Highlander School in Tennessee supported teachers, civil rights workers, labor leaders and community organizers through progressive education. At Highlander, principles of generative curriculum and dialogic problem-posing were at the heart of efforts to preserve Appalachian culture and provide literacy instruction to southern blacks and whites in the struggle for enfranchisement and greater access to political power (Horton, Freire, Bell & Gaventa, 1990). Freire's work is further clarified in the American adult ESOL context by Wallerstein (1987) who identifies a four step process to critical teaching: 1) beginning with students' cultural capital; 2) posing problems that require reflection on oppressive conditions; 3) promoting dialogue to raise critical consciousness; 4) soliciting students' solutions to problems and fostering their inclinations for activism. Community-based programs like Erie Neighborhood House have long been seen as sites where there is a greater potential for conceiving of literacy education as a practice of critical reflection and political action (Fingeret, 1992; Jurmo, 1987). In her popular adult ESOL books (Auerbach & Wallerstein, 1987; Auerbach, 1992; Auerbach, et. al., 1996) Elsa Auerbach and colleagues provide explicit guidance to community organizers and ESOL instructors in the application of critical pedagogy with adult ESOL students in community education centers. They outline problem-posing procedures and instructional activities that can be readily adapted to different contexts (Auerbach, et al., 1996). Ira Shor (1987, 1997) offers descriptive accounts of learning to hear and yield to the voices of city-college students. He describes his methods for investigating simple objects and social situations, and moving students from description to local situating to global, historical, and future analysis. Caroline Heller (1997) describes a community-based women's writing group—one without a traditional teacher—in which the writers themselves both challenged and cared for one-another as they shared critical offerings and reflections on each other's writings. Heller's work exemplifies how dialogue serves to diminish distances and establish trust among students. It provides the foundation for learning.

Through open dialogue students reveal themselves. By cultivating that dialogue, teachers learn to hear students' voices and clarify how best to respond through curriculum and instruction. Critical teachers may possess greater understanding of those political, economic, and social contexts that restrict students' liberties and aspirations. But most critical educators believe that despite the knowledge they possess, they should refrain from adopting a highly authoritative stance toward students as such a stance can be alienating (Edelsky, 1999; Freire & Macedo, 1987; Giroux, 1981; Heller, 1997; Kincheloe, 2005). Freire and Macedo (1987) describe the process as a delicate dance that critical teachers perform as they establish an active presence in students' lives but do not allow that presence to "transform learners' presences into shadows of the educator's presence" (p. 140). Critical teachers face the challenge of remaining open to students' input while pursuing learning objectives that extend the students' zones of proximal development (Vygotsky, 1986). Though they may possess a clear idea of the best language and literacy instruction that will meet students' needs at given developmental levels, critical teachers often negotiate the curriculum with students in order to meet agreed-upon objectives. Still, the dialogic process may yield unanticipated outcomes. Despite the careful cultivation of generative themes, students' unfolding perceptions, the conclusions they reach and the actions they choose may differ from those envisioned. The critical teacher then reflects and responds. The dialogue continues and critical inquiry advances.

RESPONSIVE LITERACY INSTRUCTION

In 1991, U.S. governors convened to establish common educational goals for the year 2000, including the following: "Every adult American will be literate and will possess the knowledge and skills necessary to compete in a global economy and exercise the rights and responsibilities of citizenship" (U.S. Department of Education, 1993, ¶ 6). In establishing this goal, they clearly failed to appreciate the adult literacy and adult ESOL education system's vulnerability to periodic swings in public sentiment and political will. As attention to an "adult illiteracy crisis" waned amidst the sustained economic upswing of the late 1990s, during which the unemployment rate dropped to historic low numbers, the resulting lack of commitment of resources to achieving the goal of full adult literacy belied the governors' rhetoric.

CHAPTER 1

Such contradictions are not new to the field. The system has suffered years of neglect, political weakness, and fragmented funding. Support for adult literacy education has periodically surged and declined throughout the last century in response to one perceived crisis after another (Fingeret, 1992; Sticht, 1988-89). Sticht identifies the mass immigration during the early 1900s, the manpower mobilizations during World War I and II, the civil unrests of the 1960s, and the recurrent concern about international competitiveness dating back to the 1950s, as a series of "social crises" that sporadically stimulated policy makers to reinvest in adult literacy education. The Economic Opportunity Act of 1964, a component of the War on Poverty, marked the first sustained funding cycle (Sticht, 1988-89) and ushered in the era in which government would "define, curtail and govern" (Quigley, 1997, p. 89) adult literacy education. In Chicago, Illinois the City Colleges of Chicago emerged to assume control over the vast majority of funds and services. Fingeret (1992) identifies the changing slogans that have accompanied adult literacy efforts in recent decades. In the 1960s, the country set out to "eradicate poverty." In the 1970s, everyone had a "Right to Read." In the 1980s, the Presidential Literacy Initiative was going to be "the last gasp for illiteracy" (Fingeret, 1992, p. 1).

Throughout the twentieth century, changes in immigration policy impacted the demand for literacy education among adult immigrants. The first English language requirements for citizenship—that English be spoken and understood—were instituted in 1906. In 1917, Congress instituted a literacy requirement: the ability to read forty words in *some* language (Crawford, 1994). Kaestle (1988) explains that rates of immigrant illiteracy "declined rapidly" following restrictions imposed in 1921. There were simply fewer low literacy adults admitted to the country so illiteracy declined. In 1952 the law was changed to require reading and writing in English (Crawford, 1994). By the 1990s, students at Erie Neighborhood House and across the nation were required to pass a written English citizenship test as part of their naturalization process.

Revolving periods of immigration liberalization and restriction created recurring waves of immigrant participation in adult literacy and adult ESOL education. In Chicago, Jane Addams's Hull House was the most notable settlement house to provide services. Hull House, collaborating with the Chicago Public Library (which ended direct instructional services in the 1990s), provided language and literacy education, as well as vocational education, to immigrants. Erie Neighborhood House, which began as a Presbyterian Church in 1870, became a settlement house and community literacy education provider in 1915. Sixty-five years later, after decades of successive policy changes, the Immigration Reform and Control Act of 1986 granted amnesty to several hundred thousand immigrants with the provision that they develop English literacy, enroll in citizenship classes, and obtain residency status and citizenship. In 1996, as described in the introduction to this text, the Congress imposed greater restrictions on residency and citizenship. In response, Erie and other programs saw enrollment increase as immigrants sought to comply with the new INS policies so that they might continue to work and provide for themselves and their families.

Fingeret (1992) explains that approaches to adult literacy and adult ESOL education have generally fallen into four categories: 1) literacy as skills, 2) literacy as tasks, 3) literacy as social and cultural practices, and 4) literacy as critical reflection and action. Analyses of curriculum actually implemented in adult literacy and adult ESOL education settings have revealed the dominance of the first two models (Fingeret, 1992; Grubb, Kalman & Castellano, 1991; Guth & Wrigley, 1992; Purcell-Gates, Degener & Jacobson, 2001; Worthman, 2006). Hull (1991) contends that the focus on skills and tasks serves to reproduce the status quo for adult literacy students. The basic skills focus devalues the potential of adult learners and, as Ilsley and Stahl (1994) lament, often presents them as victims or enemies in the war on illiteracy or as patients suffering from an illness that must be eradicated. More critically, Hull (1991) claims that this ideological approach to instruction "mischaracterizes literacy as a curative for problems that literacy alone cannot solve" (p. 9). Many adult literacy teachers profess a belief in critical pedagogy, but research still reveals that most teach with the published materials that emphasize basic skills alone and have little to do with students' lives, cultures, and ambitions (Fingeret, 1992; Guth & Wrigley, 1992; Purcell-Gates, Degener & Jacobson, 2002; Worthman, 2006).

The critical, responsive literacy instruction that is described in this book is grounded in the lives of students. Their aspirations frame the agenda for curriculum choices. As discussed previously, this book demonstrates how teachers and students can problematize and respond to oppression. A critical stance is taken throughout. But critical pedagogy, in the absence of a fully developed theory of language and literacy learning is apt to yield the type of inconsistency described above in which teachers perceive injustice and inequity but deliver instruction that fails to link literacy learning with identified cultural and political contexts. The effort thus fails to be libratory. The instructional practices presented in this text reflect a sociocultural constructivist theory of learning that prioritizes literacy engagement—reading and writing—and, more specifically, students' responses to carefully selected reading materials. Through responsive literacy instruction the students develop their oral and literate uses of English. This response-centered approach de-centers the students as the objects of instruction. It focuses attention on students' responses to text, to each other, and to the cultural context. It moves participants to the frontiers of knowledge construction (Kincheloe & Steinberg, 1996) where together teachers and students develop a greater understanding of social, economic, and political systems and begin the work of changing those systems.

The responsive literacy instruction described throughout this text brings together complementary theories of literacy learning for intermediate and advanced English language learners. These theoretical perspectives include: Vygotskian sociocultural theory (Moll, 1990; Vygotsky, 1978, 1986), Gee's (1989, 1992) discourse acquisition and learning theory, Krashen's (1981, 1983, 2003) second language acquisition and learning theory, and Rosenblatt's (1978, 1995) reader response theory. Guided by these theories, I constructed a curriculum that situates thought and language in a social context. I guided literacy interactions to facilitate enhanced participation in those academic and political discourses that exert power and authority over the students' lives. By participating more fully in those discourses and responding dialogically to the texts and each other the students locate themselves and establish their roles in the discourse. It is through their responses that I am able to clarify the ongoing critical inquiry.

Vygotsky (1986) helps us to understand that the dynamic relationship between thought and language is a primary human communication function that develops in the early years of life. The written word is a secondary symbol system that represents but differs from oral language. Second language learners, whether attending to orality or literacy, also learn and work through a secondary symbol system. Similarly, Gee (1989, 1992) refers to literacy as a secondary discourse in which we participate more or less successfully with others who have established membership in that discourse community. Literacy in a second language then requires that students learn a secondary discourse in a secondary symbol system. It is commonly assumed that students need to establish second language oral proficiency prior to adding the second language literacy as a secondary discourse. However, there is evidence to support the approach of introducing literacy at the same time that oral language instruction is introduced with second language learners (Collier, 1995; Lesaux, Geva, Koda, Siegel & Shanahan, 2008; Pang & Kamil, 2004). This is particularly true when working with learners who have had several years of schooling and developed literacy proficiency in their first language (Cummins, 1984; Thomas & Collier, 1997; Genesee, Geva, Dressler & Kamil, 2008). In such cases, second language learners draw on their existing familiarity with literacy as a secondary discourse. Through metacognitive engagement they access thoughts and ideas across languages and begin learning second language literacy (Bialystock, 1997; August & Hakuta, 1997, Thomas and Collier, 1997). Krashen's (2003) well known comprehensible input hypothesis informs us that second language learning and production requires, first, that students have interesting, relevant topics that encourage the expression of ideas and opinions in order for language to develop. Several studies (Cho & Krashen, 1994; Chang & Krashen, 1997; Krashen, 1989, 1995, 1997; Pilgren & Krashen, 1993), have demonstrated that both teacher guided and independent reading provides that input and supports comprehensive second language development.

Based upon an assessment tool that examined oral language proficiency, my students were identified by Erie Neighborhood House as intermediate to advanced English language learners (Boyd-Batstone, 2006). Many possessed high levels of literacy in their first language. While teaching at Erie it was my intention to have students read and write in order to stimulate their language development. I also wanted to learn from their responses to the critical readings about many issues they confronted in their lives. In cultivating their responses to reading, I intended to challenge the dominant discourse by helping them gain access to and participate in it. Through their participation, I sought to help them explicitly and directly challenge the forces that had arisen to thwart their ambitions.

Literary and education scholars identify readers' interactions or transactions with texts as taking place on a continuum. Louise Rosenblatt's aesthetic—efferent continuum is the most well known (James Britton's spectator—participant continuum and Jerome Bruner's narrative—paradigmatic continuum share similar characteristics with Rosenblatt's). When reading through an aesthetic (spectator or narrative) stance "language users engage in a lived through experience" (Langer, 1992, p. 36). Lived-through experiences attend to emotional and inspirational sensations readers feel while immersed in the text. Readers envision (Langer, 1995) themselves in the story. They experience wonder, pleasure, anguish, and longing. Rosenblatt explains that in many cases engaging text through the aesthetic stance is a precondition for being able to take something away from the text. The reader moves to the efferent end of the continuum in order to make utilitarian sense of the text. When reading through an efferent stance we "hold meanings apart in quest of a more rational or logical understanding" (Langer, 1992, p. 36). Readers distance themselves from the immediate encounter and hold meanings and interpretations apart for analysis. They identify how they might go about living their lives and participate in worlds' affairs (Britton, 1993b) in response to the reading experience.

As a responsive literacy teacher my role was to facilitate students' transactions (Rosenblatt, 1978) with the texts and with each other. Response-centered teachers (Livdahl, Smart, Wallman, Herbert, Geiger & Anderson, 1995) locate students on the response continuum, stimulate and support their initial encounters with reading, and guide meaningful and productive interpretations and analysis. Through the cultivation of personal response students engage in cultural conversations that are socially, historically, and politically grounded (Lewis, 1999). In my class at Erie, I typically sought to guide my ESOL students' transactions with various readings by encouraging their lived-through encounters first. I cultivated their emotional responses and helped them to develop deeper understandings of word meanings, so they could employ the words and their new language with greater purpose in their personal and social lives. When planning for these transactions and when reflecting on students' responses, I considered different frames of analysis identified by Beach (1993): knowledge of textual conventions; cognitive and subconscious processes; cultural roles, attitudes and contexts; roles adopted in the social classroom context; readers' sensational and experiential engagements. As a response-centered teacher, I used these frames to evaluate students' transactions with texts in order to make ongoing instructional decisions.

In our Erie classroom, I sought to construct a transitional or hybrid discourse community to mediate language and literacy practices, cultural differences, and community expectations. We spent ample time reading, writing, talking, reflecting, critiquing, and challenging the intolerant attitude toward immigrants, and envisioning possibilities for greater participation in the community. I attempted to be a response-centered teacher, positioning myself in this milieu as an interpreter of individual interests, of students' responses to reading and each other, and of the world surrounding our classroom. In the late 1990s, that world included the efforts of many to curtail my students' ambitions and liberties. Thus, the responsive language and literacy teaching at Erie Neighborhood House took place

CHAPTER 1

in a political context that was so pronounced in its hostility toward immigrants that my role as a critical educator needed to be pronounced as well.

TEACHER RESEARCH

"What is it all about?" asks Purcell-Gates (2007), regarding the most appropriate role of literacy research:

> Literacy research is ultimately about providing the information needed for schools and communities to develop and provide [sic] fully informed citizens who are capable of using the literacy skills, including the thinking skills, necessary to contribute to the well-being of the world. (p. 1)

Purcell-Gates continues by arguing for a life span perspective of literacy that extends through adulthood. The goal, which is highly compatible with the desire to help students to live a good and fulfilling life, is to create "fully informed citizens who can and will participate actively in their civic duties for the good of society and humankind" (p. 1).

Kincheloe (2005) identifies teacher research as an essential dimension of critical pedagogy. Freire (1970, 1973) proposed that teachers begin their work as ethnographers taking time to learn the history, culture, and perceptions of students. They continue their inquiry through dialogic engagement in which students and teachers learn from each other. Through dialogue teachers continually reflect on students' knowledge constructions and evolving consciousness of the world and those words that facilitate expression in the wider community (Freire & Macedo, 1987). Similarly, the responsive literacy instructor, as I have described, strategically positions herself as an observer and interpreter of students' transactions with the texts and contexts. Those interpretations serve as the basis for ongoing observations about the knowledge and experiences most worthwhile for the promotion of students' interests. Critical, responsive literacy instruction thus requires that a teacher be a researcher.

Despite the rhetoric of many community literacy educators, the type of literacy instruction I propose is seldom documented in adult literacy and adult ESOL classrooms where the professional qualifications of teachers has long been a concern (Carlson, 1977; Crandall, 1993; Cranney, 1983; Diekhoff, 1988; Foster, 1988; Kazemek, 1988; Purcell-Gates, Degener & Jacobson, 2002; Shanahan, Meehan & Mogge, 1994). Teacher research has been identified as a model for professional development in adult literacy (Lytle, Belzer & Reumann, 1992; Padak & Nixon-Ponder, 1995; Rachor, 1995). Teacher research grants authority to classroom teachers to critically examine their teaching, engage theory and practice as dialectical processes, and share their experiences with others (Lytle et. al., 1992). Teacher research has the potential to fill the gaping void that currently exists between theory and method in adult literacy and adult ESOL settings. It challenges tidy assertions of what effective participatory and libratory adult literacy and adult ESOL classrooms might look like.

As a teacher researcher at Erie Neighborhood House, I recognized the need to be critical of not just the social and political environment. I also needed to challenge my own beliefs and remain open to the types of questions that confront any teacher. Among such questions are those previously identified by Schubert regarding "a good and fulfilling life" and the knowledge and experiences most worthwhile to provide for students. But teachers' questions also include: What do I need to know in order to enrich the lives of my students and my life with them? How will I know if I have enriched our lives? What will I do with that information? What will I do when my lessons fall apart, when students' response is flat, when my best theoretical insights are not panning out before me with the students? Such questions persist in the life of any teacher and presented themselves during my teacher research at Erie.

Teachers' inquiry agendas and unique insights should be given more space in educational scholarship. Teachers' thinking and knowing has long been the focus of educational research (Dewey, 1938; Hansen, 1995; Jackson, 1968). But most research on teaching—as sound and helpful as it is—still objectifies teachers who, at the outset of the twentieth century, find themselves more than ever treated as cogs in the accountability machine of public schooling. Cochran-Smith and Lytle (1993) move beyond an agenda that focuses on teachers' thinking and knowing. They identify teachers' active decision-making processes and the knowledge they generate as valuable contributions. Teachers' intentions and their response to students' feedback can be fostered through understanding of their participation in inquiry projects. Through systematic inquiry, Cochran-Smith and Lytle assert, teachers better understand how to negotiate the curriculum with students. They redefine relationships and problematize issues of culture, learning, language, literacy, and power. As teacher researchers, teachers probe, question, and look for insight into those issues they value most and then move forward to better guide students' learning and eventual achievement.

In this book, I describe the classroom community that my immigrant students and I created at Erie Neighborhood House in the late 1990s. Our efforts sought to unite language and literacy education with the struggle for acceptance and opportunity, though I believe we were not alone in this effort. Rich, never-before-heard stories are abundant in community literacy programs. Stories of adults returning to the classroom, where they exhibit their vulnerabilities to teachers and classmates, are often inspiring and, just as often, wrenching. Few of these stories are recorded yet so many are calling out to be heard. Adult immigrant students and their ambitions should not be overlooked in the educational literature. We must not allow these students to be neglected, shunted aside, and demoralized by the anti-immigrant rhetoric of recent years. But if we fail, and the students are thrust aside, we must tell that story as well. As a teacher researcher employing disciplined, systematic fieldwork, data analysis, and interpretation methods, my aim is to draw attention to the many stories that surfaced in my Erie classroom. I entered my Erie classroom as a researcher interested in learning about effective literacy instruction for adult immigrants. Like others (Delgado-Gaitan, 1993; Moll

& Diaz, 1987), I very quickly became an activist exploring how critical, responsive literacy instruction could serve my students' efforts to pursue their dreams in the face of intolerance.

CHAPTER 2

"IN ENGLISH MY NAME MEANS HOPE"

It is through the openness of dialogue that people come to know, particularly dialogue where distances are diminished, where trust is established, and where inclusion forms the foundation of learning. (Caroline Heller, 1992, p.37)

WRITING BEYOND OUR NAMES, COUNTRIES, AND YEARS

"Hello, my name is Luis. I am from Mexico. I have lived here for three years." Luis turned to Cyntia on his left.

Cyntia scanned the several faces in the room. Leaning back in her chair, she pulled her waist-long, thick, jet-black hair back over her shoulder and announced: "Hello, I am Cyntia. I have four years in the United States. I am from Guatemala."

Around the table in our small classroom the students continued their introductions. From previous experiences in ESOL classes they knew this procedure well. With a warm smile beneath his pencil thin mustache, Timoteo offered a soft, gentle greeting: "*Buenas tardes*. Hello, everyone. I am Timoteo. I come from Mexico."

Maya looked anxious. Among the group of young adults she appeared their senior by at least ten years. But in comparison to her classmates, her command of English did not reflect the number of years she had lived in the United States. In a barely audible voice, she announced, "I am Maya. Me come from Mexico. I have, oh, I think twenty years maybe." Twenty years earlier, we later learned, Maya joined her Mexican boyfriend—her future husband—in Chicago where they had raised their family.

Jacinta, like the four others, had performed this introductory ritual in prior ESOL classes, though when she was in my class the year before we observed few such customs. With a singsong cadence and her head bobbing, she exhibited little regard for the tradition: "Hello, my name is Jacinta, I am from Mexico. I have lived in Chicago four years." She sighed and rolled her eyes before casting them in my direction.

Certainly, one's name, country of origin, and the number of years spent in the United States were critical components of the students' self-identities. These identifying elements formed the soil from which new relationships could be cultivated. I had suggested that the students introduce themselves but offered no criteria for their presentations. As it turned out, all of these students knew each other before their introductions. Most were members of a Community Leadership class that had met twice a week during the previous six months to discuss political and economic issues that affected the immigrant community in their neighborhood

CHAPTER 2

of West Town. I had already met most of them when visiting their Leadership class to discuss the possibility of an English language complement to their Spanish language Leadership meetings. Tim, the Director of the Adult Education Program at Erie Neighborhood House, conceived the idea to offer the class and asked me to teach this group of highly motivated students. They had been studying local issues like affordable housing, national events like recent Immigration and Naturalization Service raids on factories in search of undocumented workers, and international matters like the increase in Mexican deaths at the U.S./Mexican border. Tim believed that if these budding community activists were to be successful when participating in widening their spheres of influence they would need to improve their English. Most of them had already completed at least three levels of ESOL instruction. Still, many attended the first session of my class with trepidation. Somehow, word had spread that I would be offering an Advanced ESOL class. Therefore, it had attracted a few additional students who were acquainted with the Leadership members but not necessarily interested in the activist agenda that interested Luis, Cyntia, Maya, Timoteo and Jacinta.

As the introductions continued, we met Sergio, Lucía and Victoria from Mexico and Justine from Haiti. Before class Sergio informed me that he was an unofficial but acknowledged leader among the Leadership students. With a scar across his neck and cheek, the sides of his head shaved to a stubble, and his mohawk pulled back into a three inch tail, he had an imposing look about him. He peered at me. "I am Sergio. Everyone here knows me."

Dutifully, as I would come to expect of all her actions during her year in my class, Lucía introduced herself: "Hello, my name is Lucía. I am from Mexico and I have almost three years here."

"Hello, my name is Justine. I am from Haiti." Justine shot a glance my way and giggled. She was not a Leadership student but was well known at Erie. "When Steve leaves the room, please don't go speaking in Spanish all the time. I speak French. I speak Kreyól. I speak English. So don't be speaking Spanish all the time." She punctuated her demand by pointing at a few students who already knew her well. "Oooh, I don't like it when people do that. No, I don't like it!" Justine had been in Chicago for over three years and during her time at Erie, she had, in fact, picked up a lot of Spanish. She finished her demand still smiling and giggling. She was well aware that she violated the ESOL rules of introduction.

The formal, systematic introductions surprised me. But I, in turn, surprised the students, telling them that we weren't finished with our introductions. I asked them to pull out paper in preparation to write. A few lacked paper or a writing instrument, which revealed their expectations that this would be an oral language class only and suggested the role that writing played in their previous ESOL courses. I announced my interest in learning more about their personal interests and community concerns and asked them to write about either or both. Also, in preparation for a short reading that I planned for our first class, I asked the students to write about their names. Possibilities included whether or not they liked their names and why, how they might change their names if they could, or possibly how they had already changed them upon arriving in the United States. I set them to writing—in Spanish if they felt more comfortable—with notice that they would read aloud or talk about their pieces afterward.

While most began writing, Maya looked at me rather helplessly. I squeezed past several students seated around the table in our cramped classroom to claim a seat next to Maya and present options for this and future assignments: I could do my best to translate her oral Spanish into English. She could speak Spanish and the class would translate for her during our discussions. She could speak English and we would guide her usage. She could speak English to the best of her ability and I would take notes of her usage for ongoing tutorial sessions with me. But I also assured Maya that I would not require her participation. She could listen and contribute when she felt inspired and comfortable. I would think no less of her though I was sure she would eventually feel more confident. I then procured a book from our classroom library, *Organizing for Our Lives: New Voices from Rural Communities* (Street & Orozco, 1992, p. 87), to show a black and white photograph of a Mexican boy and Mexican girl peering into the camera lens, their chins resting on their arms crossed atop a table. A cartoon-like caption painted on the wall above the children reads: *I'm not shy. I'm thinking.* Maya smiled at the children. "OK, I try," she said.

I then shared the photograph with the other students who recognized immediately how it played both with and against the stereotype of the quiet, timid immigrant. Still, they appreciated the need to overcome the barriers to English language proficiency in order to successfully traverse the landscape of their adopted country. As I had done with Maya, I explained that I did not want them to be intimidated by the literacy-based instruction I had planned nor by a strict requirement that they speak in class. Thereafter, and throughout the year, the students would declare, "I'm not shy. I'm thinking," in order to claim a momentary preference for listening, for thinking, rather than speaking. I was to learn throughout our year spent reading, writing, listening and speaking together that these students were indeed far from shy—and they were definitely thinking.

Upon completion of their writing, most of the students looked curiously around the room unsure as to how they would present themselves to one another. But Jacinta, a student of mine the year before, volunteered immediately. She presented her personal goal of improving her English to help her to succeed as a leader in the community. Among several concerns for the community, she placed "safety for the kids" at the top of her list. She professed to like her name because it was the name of a Mexican flower. Moreover, it pleased her that few people in Mexico or Chicago shared her name. Despite their friendships with her, few students knew the origin of Jacinta's name. The audible sighs heard around the table revealed that Jacinta's name—as exposed through her writing—had been an intriguing curiosity for many, including me.

Timoteo was among the most active and well known of the Leadership students. Timoteo's classmates knew he was from Mexico, was religious, and worked in a factory. He had little to say about his name but in class we learned that his factory made painters' drop cloths, a product that required Spanish language descriptors for most of the students to comprehend. Justine folded her arms across her chest and stared at me with an "I told you so" expression on her face while Timoteo offered his Spanish translation. Timoteo also worked through English and Spanish descriptions of in-line roller blading, an emerging passion of his recently acquired after spending the summer watching the daredevils on the Chicago lakefront. As we pondered the image of a tall, thin Timoteo lurching across the crowded beach sidewalk, he began telling us of his concerns regarding the proliferation of gangs in the neighborhood. The gangbangers needed guidance and direction, but Timoteo felt too close to their age to provide it. Through his Community Leadership class he had also become interested in educating Mexican immigrant neighbors about their rights. To that end, he sought to improve his English in order to understand the discussions taking place at Erie and at other community events.

Cyntia launched into her presentation by first announcing her reluctance to speak in English. Pulling her hair back over her shoulder, she explained that she worked in a factory where Spanish was spoken throughout. With hopes of finding a new job, she participated in Erie classes, including Spanish GED (certificate of General Educational Development, a high school equivalence award) and Community Leadership. She believed that more Latinos in the community needed to continue their education. A single parent herself, she also expressed concern for the children of single-parent and two-parent working families where adult supervision may be lacking. As for her name, Cyntia informed us that it came from Greek Mythology. She was indifferent about it, except when people, particularly English speakers, pronounced it with a "th" sound. "They think I don't know my name because I don't know English very well," she complained. Then she repeated her fear of speaking English in public. "I'm afraid they're gonna make fun of me," she explained.

Hoping to establish some common ground and make a pedagogical point, I responded to Cyntia by describing my fear of speaking Spanish in public, a fear that people would then assume my listening comprehension to be on par with my speaking ability. Given my exposure to the language in mostly academic settings, my listening comprehension in Spanish lagged behind my speaking ability in Spanish. I suggested that some of the students might share comparable difficulties with their English.

My pedagogical incursion was lost among the students, however, as Luis expounded upon Cyntia's fear. "We get scared and that's why we try to go someplace where the people they speak Spanish.

Jacinta weighed in on the issue, saying: "That's related to discrimination in the language."

Before she could be asked what she meant by this, Luis said, "They just making fun of you but I don't think they gonna say 'you can't speak English, you can't stay here.' They just make fun of you. That's not discrimination."

Jacinta went on, complaining about "Hispanic" people who knew English and refrained from spending time with other Hispanics, even denying that they, too, spoke Spanish. This was another form of discrimination, she claimed.

Luis countered Jacinta's interpretation, noting, for instance, times on the street when he simply did not want to be bothered by other people. So he pretended not to know Spanish when approached by other Latinos.

A little confused by Jacinta's initial declaration of "discrimination in the language," but wanting to understand more, I asked: "So, what is discrimination?"

Jacinta replied: "For me it's when somebody is making fun of us. They try to be like racist. That's discrimination."

Sergio entered the discussion by suggesting that discrimination can occur with words, not always through action: "It's when you, someone hurt you with the language. It doesn't matter how. When you feel hurt, it's when you feel discrimination." He continued, describing how discrimination can be nonverbal and subtle as well: "You feel like some people hurt your feelings and in that moment you feel like you being discriminated in that moment. . . . Somebody can be on the other side of the window and he's not doing anything but because of the way he's looking at you, or not paying attention to you, you can feel discriminated."

Cyntia returned to the discussion that she had initiated by agreeing with Sergio and then adding: "For me, it's something the blacks and brown people have that is making them afraid. It's the way the person feel."

Cyntia had the last word on the issue, at least for that evening, as the students decided it was time to move forward with our introductions. However, the students' comments lingered in my mind over the next few months as I learned more about their feelings and more specifically how they felt as targets of discrimination. As they struggled with English the students experienced emotions that did not always find release through language. Over time I learned to cultivate the students' emotional responses to events in their lives, to political and legislative maneuverings against immigrants, and to the readings we selected so that I could be a better guide of language and literacy experiences in the classroom.

Continuing our introductions, we met Victoria from Mexico. Victoria spent her mornings studying child development at Harold Washington City College and her afternoons as a child care worker at Erie. Ted, the director of Erie's adult education program, told her she might benefit from our English class because it would address concerns about immigrant rights. In our class, Victoria voiced her worries about gangs, but she was more troubled by teenagers who disrespected their immigrant parents. She wanted to reach out to teens, to convince young girls not to get pregnant and drop out of school. "They should go to the park and participate in recreation. They should have a chance to be kids," she insisted. In terms of her name, Victoria informed us that family and friends in Mexico called her Monica. When she arrived in the United States a few years earlier, she decided to use her middle name, Victoria. She preferred the sound of a dreamy, elongated second syllable rolling into the last two. Swaying her head from one shoulder to the other while presenting her new name, she emphasized the journey that was required for "Victoria" to emerge. She chuckled and explained that her family still called her Monica, but the rest of the world—coworkers, fellow students, politically active friends—was to call her Victoria.

CHAPTER 2

    Lucía was next. Lucía informed us that she lived with her mother and was a babysitter for her niece, not by choice, but because she felt obligated to do so by her family. Because she had presented a politically-charged reading at a public forum the year before, I assumed Lucía to be a Leadership student. However, she was not. Lucía explained that her goal was to study medicine and computers and go to college to become a doctor or nurse. Thus, after three years in Chicago and after receiving her GED in Spanish she was determined to improve her English. Among her community concerns were violence and crime. But she was most troubled by discrimination, which "begins in the home," she argued. "The fathers [parents], they teach their children about the color of the skin and what to think. Children's thoughts start with the fathers." Lucía told us that she liked her name, but if she could change it she would choose "Gaviota" because, she said, "it means freedom." She then let us in on a secret. Lucía was named, by her father, after a "beautiful girlfriend whom he loved when he was a young man." But she was not Lucía's mother. When Timoteo asked how Lucía's mother felt about the naming, Lucía told us that her mother was unaware of this secret tale. After several jaws dropped, smiles began to emerge as it was understood that Lucía had bestowed a treasured confidence.

    Given Sergio's bold introduction earlier in the class, I was not sure what more to expect. Upon receiving my assignment, he began writing feverishly, filling almost two pages before we resumed our introductions. Still smiling over Lucía's story, he raised his hand. He did not have much to say about his name. "Like I said, everyone already knows me, but I have some things to say." He turned to his paper and began reading, occasionally lifting his eyes to offer clarification where he thought necessary.

> *I don't like to say this but we brought the problem to this country. I feel bad for people that came from other countries. They can't take care of their families because they feel the pressure of this country. They feel like they have to do something. They are not in their country [where] they can say: "I'm free." Even if you have your green card or whatever, that just doesn't matter, you know. Here you feel like you got to do something for yourself and to be in this country you have to work.*

> *We belong to this blood and our blood can't just stay and sit. Our blood have to keep moving and working to live. Spanish people is like that. We can't sit and just look at people working. We not like that. . . . You see most of the people that is Spanish or Latin people is working in the field, is working in hands jobs, as handymans. Not working in offices, not taking the jobs that American people have right now because we don't have the skills and we don't have the education. We not taking your jobs. We are helping you with your jobs. That's my thoughts.*

Sergio closed his notebook and studied the faces at the table before continuing:

So because of that I feel like we are doing something for this country but our education is going down because we got to work. Because we don't have time to go to school and because most of the people that we're living in this country we came from different communities in Mexico that we didn't have the education that we should have. We just have the education that our relatives or parents give us, education in the family. And that's the only education that we have.

The classroom was silent. The students weren't shy. They were thinking. Through his writing, Sergio found release for his angst and revealed himself to his peers. After a time, Timoteo responded: "Sergio, I agree with you. But first you said almost everybody knows you. But I did not know you. I just know you personally but I did not know what you are thinking or know your voice. Now I do. I'm learning more about you." Later that evening, Sergio informed me that he was trying to encourage the other students to pursue the new educational option that our class offered. Unfortunately, Sergio was only to attend a few more classes. His employer, a defense contractor, demanded that he work overtime hours in the factory for the next several months in order to meet a new government order.

READING BEYOND OUR NAMES

Sandra Cisneros, in *The House on Mango Street* (1989), describes a Chicago neighborhood that seems less transitory and culturally diverse than Erie's, but with its Mexican working class residents and front stoop culture, it is very similar to Erie's West Town neighborhood in the 1990s. The narrator of Cisneros's story is a young adolescent Mexican girl who reveals herself, her family, her neighborhood, and its residents through a series of vignettes. Through the eyes of the young girl, the neighborhood and the surrounding world appear inscrutable. She is bewildered by the actions of older girls and the woman next door, by her mother and aunt, and by her membership among such people. She even puzzles over the name given to her: "Esperanza."

In English my name means hope. In Spanish it means too many letters. It means sadness, it means waiting. It is just like the number nine. (p. 10)

At the second meeting of our class, I shared the chapter of *The House on Mango Street* titled "My Name." I presented copies of the chapter along with composition notebooks to the students. Though Cisneros and *The House on Mango Street* had become mainstays of the multicultural literature canon, only Luis and Victoria had heard of the author or the book. I identified the notebooks as Reading Response Journals, and told the students they should be used exclusively for reactions to our readings. Other notebooks would be used for other writing.

Luis, who had recently graduated from a local high school, volunteered to read the chapter aloud. His reading was fluent with few miscues or mispronunciations. When he finished reading the short chapter I asked for student responses. Cyntia responded first, explaining that Esperanza's name came "from her mother's mother" and that Esperanza did not like the name. It was too long.

CHAPTER 2

Victoria countered that on one hand Esperanza did like the name because it meant "hope" and was "strong." On the other hand, Victoria, chuckling, paraphrased Cisneros: "Mexican people, they don't like strong women. And English people," she added, "make [Esperanza's] name sound funny with the syllables."

Justine asked: "Why the Mexican people don't like strong woman?"

Victoria, Jacinta, Lucía and Cyntia all laughed aloud, demonstrating some shared understanding of gender roles in their culture. Victoria explained: "Because the Mexican men—before, not now—they want the women to submit and they like the women to do everything for them."

"Why?" Justine asked, still not satisfied.

"Why? I don't know. That's the way they grew up. But now it's changing. It's not like fifty years ago," said Victoria.

As if providing a rationale that was beyond challenge, Timoteo responded to Justine: "That was the culture."

I found it interesting that these young, fairly recent immigrants considered the cultural norm described by Cisneros to be outdated. Just as the norm puzzled Esperanza, it did not match the students' perceptions either, though it was familiar. I asked for more responses to the chapter. Following a long silence, I split the class into three groups, asking each to focus on three different sections of the assigned chapter, and to consider: 1) What is the author's meaning in the paragraphs? and 2) What do the paragraphs mean to you?

In their groups, the students read their assigned paragraphs, discussed the two questions, and wrote entries in their journals. When we reassembled, I reread the beginning of the chapter and asked for students' responses.

Cyntia reiterated that Esperanza did not like her name—what it meant or how it sounded.

Jacinta explained that she, personally, liked Esperanza's name, but felt bad for her: "She's not feeling good. It makes me feel sad about her thoughts."

I suggested that if we had experienced sadness in our own lives then we could more readily perceive Esperanza's sadness. The students agreed this was part of the process for understanding Esperanza and her story.

Cyntia voiced her appreciation of Esperanza's feelings: "I think that when we are young and when we are not happy, we find something that we don't like it. I think that in our country we used to have names after some of our parents, grandparents, fathers, friends."

I reread aloud the next set of paragraphs in which Esperanza describes her grandmother as fiercely independent and strong, until she is taken away and forced into marriage.

Luis promptly offered an explanation: "[Esperanza] wants to be like her grandmother but after her grandmother got married she change her mind. Now she doesn't want to be like her . . . [The grandmother] was living a nightmare and [Esperanza] didn't want to be like her. She wasn't able to do the things she wanted to do. She didn't have no feeling, and she was always walking around her house with no feeling."

I asked, "How does that make you feel?"

Justine responded for her group: "We feel that the women at that time were not able to do what they wanted to do. They were not free. She was not free. When you not able to do what you want to do, you not free."

I asked about Esperanza's feelings toward her grandmother, for whom she was named.

Justine explained: "She don't want to be like that. I feel bad about that too. Sitting in the house all the time, that's baaad. I don't like that. You got to do something."

"I have a question," Timoteo announced. "What does she mean when she say, *She looked out the window her whole life*? I don't understand."

Justine shared a similar curiosity regarding Esperanza's description of her grandmother. I reread the sentence and the one before and after it ending with . . . *she sits her sadness on an elbow.*

Cyntia then responded: "Her husband makes her feel crazy."

Timoteo asked: "So she was frustrated or something?"

"He made her feel like she was in jail," Justine decided.

"Yeah!" Victoria proclaimed, finding herself swept up in the discussion.

Encouraged by Victoria, Justine repeated: "Yeah, she feel like she was in jail. She didn't want to be like her grandmother."

Timoteo's question made other students feel free to ask about other lines that were unclear to them. We discussed these lines, at times delving into their symbolic meaning, at other times finding that Spanish translations would suffice. We then turned to the final paragraphs in which Esperanza explores alternative names for herself: "Lisandra," "Maritza," "Zeze the X."

Justine was first to respond: "What does she mean: 'Zeze the X'?"

"She wants to be called another name, like she really is, like she is strong, happy. I don't know, like funny," Victoria, who had chosen her new name with the elongated second syllable, observed.

"Tell me more. What kind of person is that, 'ZeZe the X'?" I asked.

Jacinta said, "A child."

"Something like wild, a wild person," Timoteo said.

"She's racy," Luis added.

Timoteo jumped in again: "It sounds like she's in a movie."

Justine, visualizing the name on a marquee or billboard, waved her hand across an imagined sky and exclaimed, "Zeze the X!" All of the students laughed aloud, including Maya who had barely spoken throughout the first two classes.

Reflecting on some of the stories the students shared about their names in the previous class, I proclaimed, "So that's the secret Esperanza that nobody knows."

The students were in agreement. There was more to meeting Esperanza than just learning her name, her ethnicity, or how many years she had spent in the United States. Still, Cyntia insisted that Esperanza's thoughts and feelings were those of a child. As we grow older, stronger and more comfortable with ourselves, she maintained, we become more secure about our identities and, indeed, our

CHAPTER 2

names. Cyntia explained that as adults we can look back on our younger years with better understanding of the anxiety and turmoil we once faced. We then move on.

During the year, I learned that the students were interested in reflecting on their lives in Mexico and elsewhere. But they were more interested in moving beyond their pasts. They were hopeful about charting new identities and telling new stories. Before ending our introductions to one another, I suggested that students reflect on Cisneros's writing, this time with an adult's sensibility, revisit their earlier discussion of names, and then compose a new story, essay, or reflection. They might consider Esperanza's musings, our comments and analysis, and Cyntia's assertions of the differences between adolescents and adults. Lucía, however, was the only student who rewrote her earlier draft, choosing to compose a reflective essay (see chapter 7). Over time I learned that the students considered writing and other assignments optional. Given their many work and family demands outside the classroom, they chose which assignments were worth their time and effort.

NEGOTIATING THE CURRICULUM

As we neared the end of our second meeting, I presented a plan for future classes. I noted that the students hoped to improve their English, including reading, writing, speaking and listening, in order to improve their community through political activism, higher education, or better employment. The students acknowledged this as a common goal. I described how much we had learned about each other in two class sessions. I noted that following our formal introductions on the first evening, we were able to use writing to expand on those presentations, to describe ourselves as individuals and social participants, and in some cases, to reveal ourselves in ways we perhaps never had outside of class. The students nodded their heads in agreement.

I then revisited the response to the Cisneros chapter. I noted the students' willingness to identify with the feelings of a young girl and to embrace her bewilderment. I noted Cyntia's insight into the divergent lives of adolescents and adults and suggested that, not only did such an observation seem relevant and important, but it also gave us a framework to explore similar themes together using the English language. Again, the students agreed. The story stimulated a language-rich experience for them to meaningfully engage each other.

With these points made, I proposed a very simple plan for how to spend our time during our twice weekly, three-hour class meetings. I proposed that we begin each session with reading. Reading would be followed by response and discussion. Following the discussion, we would turn to writing. Our writing would be mediated by discussion in response to the reading and further expand on it. We would end each session by reading our writings aloud and, once again, share our reactions to each other's contributions. I assumed that the students would be self-conscious about developing their speaking and listening skills. I assured them that two periods set aside for responding to the readings and our writings would provide ample opportunity for listening as well as speaking. I also promised that I would help them with their grammar through direct instruction in group and individualized formats. However, given the dominance of oral language grammar instruction in their previous ESOL classes, the students felt insecure about my literacy-focused and response-centered approach. Thus we renegotiated the schedule to reflect an hour in each session for what we identified as Talk, Reading (and response), and Writing (and response).

By the end of our second class session, it became clear that more than just the Community Leadership students wanted to participate in the class. As mentioned, word of an advanced level English class had spread and many students wanted to take part. As a group, the students displayed a great diversity of educational backgrounds, literacy needs, and personal motivations for taking the class. I saw a need to provide accommodations to the non-Leadership students and monitor ongoing responses to what I offered. Creating critically responsive curricula for all who took part in the class required constant negotiation among the students' needs and interests.

Table 2.1 Class Members' Interests and Concerns

Personal Interests	Community Concerns
1. Going to college	1. Safety for children
2. Getting better jobs	2. Gangs
3. Computers	3. Violence and crime
4. Children	4. Discrimination
5. Roller blading	5. Education for people in the community
6. Moving back to Mexico	6. Immigrant rights
7. Parents who want me to work, not go to school	7. Relations between Mexicans and Puerto Ricans
8. Does our class meet your needs? What is a good class? (teacher's addition to list)	8. Respect for older people
	9. Teenagers and pregnancy
	10. Schooling for teenagers
	11. Changing negative/wrong attitudes about Latinos in the U.S.
	12. What schools should be like (teacher's addition to list)

I proposed to the group that in our next class we begin reading the autobiography of Jesse Lopez de la Cruz who was a United Farm Worker activist in the 1950s, 60s and 70s. I informed the students that Lopez de la Cruz's story portrayed the symbiotic personal and social relationships of a community leader, and could serve as a model for those interested in becoming leaders themselves. I also told the students that studying this text would provide a way for us to engage with the English language through our talking, reading and writing. For future topics, I suggested we wait and see where our interests led. The students agreed to the plan. For Talk, I suggested that we could refer to a posted list of students' personal interests and community concerns (Table 2.1) identified during our first

CHAPTER 2

meeting if no other topics were advanced. We could refer to our list to remind ourselves of what we once considered important. I posted the list on our classroom wall with one additional item of "personal interest" and "community concern" listed by me. I wanted to engage the students in regular critique of our class, leaving open the possibility for them to make recommendations regarding method and content.

In order to assist the reader as the book unfolds, background information about the students is provided in the tables below. Table 2.2 identifies students who came from the Leadership class. Table 2.3 identifies other students who joined the class for advanced ESOL instruction.

Table 2.2 Community Leadership Students

Student/ Age	Home Country	Class Entry and Exit	Highest Education & Work / Family
Luis/ 19-20	Mexico	Entered September Completed December	H.S. graduate Catering
Timoteo/ Early 20s	Mexico	Entered September Completed November	*Secundaria* Factory worker
Sergio/ Mid 20s	Mexico	Entered September Exit September	*Secundaria* Factory worker
Maya/ Late 30s	Mexico	Entered September Exit late October	ESOL student Mother of 3
Cyntia/ Early 20s	Guatemala	Entered September Exit mid October	Pursuing Spanish GED Working, Mother of 1
Jacinta/ 19-20	Mexico	Entered September Completed December	H.S. graduate Worked at *Taqueria*
Victoria/ Mid 20s	Mexico	Entered September Completed December	*Preparatoria*/college student Child care worker

Table 2.3. Non-Leadership/Advanced ESOL Students

Student/ Age	Home Country	Class Entry and Exit	Highest Education & Work / Family
Justine 19-20	Haiti	Entered September Completed December	GED Student Occasional work
Lucía/ Early 20s	Mexico	Entered September Completed December	GED graduate Babysitter for niece
Amalia/ 18-19	Ecuador	Entered October Completed December	H.S. graduate McDonald's
Brisa Mid 30s	Honduras	Entered October Exit November	ESOL Student Day care provider Mother
Olivia/ Late 30s	Brazil	Entered October Completed December	Music conservatory Prior Secretary Tourist
Pablo/ Early 40s	Mexico	Entered October Exit November	*Secundaria*/ESOL Student Temp. Labor Father of 3

Secundaria is the Mexican equivalent of approximately eighth grade.
Preparatoria is the Mexican equivalent of approximately eleventh or twelfth grade.

PART II

NAMING INJUSTICE

CHAPTER 3

RACE, CLASS, GENDER, AND LITERARY CONVERSATIONS

CRITICAL PERSPECTIVES

When I joined the dedicated staff and students at Erie Neighborhood House, I became more conscious of the many overlapping barriers that denied the adult students the opportunity for full civic and economic participation. Immigration, trade, labor, and social welfare policies severely impacted the students' residency status, work opportunities, and ability to sustain their families. Gentrification of the West Town community and deceptive aldermanic maneuvers denied affordable housing for the students. Educational policy (which I will further explore in Part V) limited access to improved work opportunities. I witnessed Erie staff and students' efforts to prevail against those forces that circumscribed the lives of the immigrant population, and saw that with each turn they faced new barriers. These barriers were erected upon a foundation of intersecting social, cultural, economic and political factors that are not easy to disentangle for individual analysis. As mentioned previously, immigration policy leads liberal and conservative partisans motivated by economic, national, international, family, gender, racial and even environmentalist interests to forge unexpected alliances. Likewise, different immigrant constituencies with little in common beyond their immigrant status have at times competed for favorable treatment and at other times united for common goals. We cannot reduce the immigrant experience or immigration policy to isolated discussions of border enforcement, labor demands, ethnic fairness, or immigrant rights without considering the wider and complex context in which each of these discussions takes place.

In 2007, President Bush and the Congress attempted to acknowledge the complexities of immigration and craft a comprehensive policy that addressed multiple concerns. When the effort failed, federal policy makers took a more simplified approach. The Department of Homeland Security launched an effort to crack down on employers who hired undocumented workers by requiring verification of employees' social security identification. They set out to fine employers and seize undocumented workers in order to deport them. Federal courts have halted some of these efforts, however, since it was found that the verification system was slow and replete with errors, leading to the unjustified dismissal of many employees and the potential incarceration and deportation of legal U.S. residents and citizens. In the mid-1990s, the Immigration and Naturalization Service (INS) had implemented similar policies. Lohrentz (1995) reported that as a result of INS's "Operation Jobs," in which manufacturing plants were raided, workers seized, and some deported, eighteen companies in the Chicago area suffered losses of $2.4 million in a single year. Chicago lost $1 million in tax revenues and 920 workers lost their jobs. Consequently, access to employment became more difficult for Latino legal residents. Lohrentz (1995) explains:

> In the aftermath of the INS raids, many employers admitted that they now ask Latino applicants to produce specific documentation beyond the requirements of the law. . . . This discrimination affects the overall labor market for Latinos by potentially shutting them out of certain jobs because they look or sound foreign, hurting their ability to negotiate fair wages. (p. 8)

As many economists point out, seizing upon undocumented workers and their employers—what many consider to be a simple matter of law enforcement—inevitably impacts the economic well-being of an employer, a region, and the nation. But the policy has also led to civil rights violations. The policy promotes discrimination because it frames Latinos, regardless of their legal status, as crime suspects. Hard line anti-immigrant advocates, who unequivocally denounce illegal border crossing and the employment of undocumented workers, choose to ignore the collateral impact of these policies. They choose to disregard human rights violations and the global economy's impact on immigrants seeking employment wherever they can find it.

But Justine and the students in my class could not ignore the anti-immigrant vitriol that was directed toward them. As will be shown in chapter 5, they weighed multiple factors in order to understand why people were challenging their opportunities to work. As members of an economic class, various constituencies of workers, racial and ethnic groups, gender groups, and families, the students examined circumstances of their lives from multiple perspectives. They concluded that race was a motivating force behind many employment discrimination practices and immigration enforcement policies. But race did not define them and their opportunities. As will be shown in chapter 4, when contemplating Justine's life and the limited educational progress she made, we see a complicated story of adolescent conflict and identity formation. Each of the students, of course, wrestled with personal issues in trying to achieve their goals. They brought these to the classroom and exhibited them as they responded to readings and each other. In chapter 5, when reading about a United Farm Workers activist, they were able to draw from multiple experiences and share unique perspectives in order to better understand their own working lives.

The critical pedagogy that Paulo Freire practiced and that became influential in early U.S. adult literacy efforts most often provided support for poor and oppressed people by situating literacy learning in economic contexts. But several scholars have challenged the exclusive focus on labor and economic participation that typified early expressions of critical pedagogy. Hull (1991, 1997) and Gowen (1992) have critically examined relationships among adult literacy instruction, workforce participation, and economic opportunity and found interwoven issues of gender, class, and race to be factors in the workplace. Feminist and postmodern critics have challenged what they consider to be universal assumptions of early efforts at explaining critical pedagogy. While Rockhill (1993) identifies the mere act of naming oppression to be a romantic notion espoused by critical pedagogues, Ellsworth (1989) maintains that too much of critical pedagogy has been a manifestation of male, white, Christian, middle class values that dichotomizes one aspect of identity formation from another and is consequently repressive itself. hooks (1990, 1994) offers provocative criticism of critical pedagogy as well as the feminist movement which has been comprised largely of white, middle and upper class women. Both, she maintains, have failed to be relevant to women of color. Still, hooks expresses her admiration for Freirian pedagogy as a radical way to engage multiple forms of oppression as they exist in the lives of students. Weiler (1992) contends that much of critical theory has failed to address the overlapping and contradictory influences of gender, race, class and sexuality on the formation of identity, interactions, and perspectives. While not an education scholar, the lesbian-feminist Chicana writer Gloria Anzaldúa (1987) offers poetic autobiographical accounts that describe her experience of being caught between and alienated by two cultures (Mexican and Americans) though she offers hope for diverse cultures to come together in the future. Finally, Lather (Lather & Smithies, 1997) demonstrates how researchers may identify multiple meanings and subjectivities in the interpretation of educational phenomena and student participation, thereby rendering spurious any definitive claims of oppression and prospects for emancipation. Long-term critical pedagogy scholars (Giroux, McLaren, Darden and others) and Friere, too, have accepted these critiques and have pushed for a broader critical agenda that recognizes distinctive and overlapping dimensions of oppression related to race, gender, sexual orientation, religion, language and other matters. As critical educators, we are called upon to include these in our conversations and inquiries.

In his list of central characteristics of critical pedagogy, Kincheloe (2005) includes dedication to the alleviation of human suffering, a commitment to understanding complexity, and a willingness of teachers to act as researchers of their students. Edelsky (1999) adds consideration of democratic participation, wealth disparity, resource allocation, and health care as topics for critical inquiry. These are all topics that are addressed by students in the chapters that follow. A Latino Institute report titled *Chicago's Working Latinas* suggests that Latinas in Chicago have struggled against numerous obstacles and the "triple oppression" of race, class and gender (Latino Institute, 1987, p. 1). Since the majority of students who participated in my class at Erie were Latina, I witnessed this "triple oppression" and sought to facilitate some supportive networking. I endeavored to construct a critically responsive curriculum that would meet their needs to sustain family and social networks, but also help them to attain measures of independence through continuing education. These students hoped to preserve their language and culture and those values that represented strength at home and in the community. But they also wanted to know the "American" culture and system, to participate, contribute and gain from its bounty, to declare their membership in it, add their voices, and contest the challenges facing them.

CHAPTER 3

RESPONSIVE LITERACY INSTRUCTION

Louise Rosenblatt (1995) calls for literary and, hence, literacy experiences that support readers in developing more sensitive, rational, and humane outlooks on the world. In the tradition of John Dewey, Rosenblatt further suggests that "literary experiences might be made the very core of the kind of educational process needed in a democracy" (1995, p. 261). Through the study of literature, students are able to engage each other in critical examination of society and move toward heightened participation (Kraver, 2007; Raines, 2005; Whitmore, 2005). In the two chapters that follow this introduction, I describe Justine and other students' transactions with literature selected to match their reading levels and interests, and that would, hopefully, prove to be "a potent force in the growth of [these] critically minded, emotionally liberated individuals" (Rosenblatt, 1995, p. 262).

Many adult literacy educators who adhere to functional and critical perspectives might claim that literature (narrative, dramatic text, poetry) is irrelevant to students' interests and is inappropriate in adult literacy and adult ESOL classrooms. Functional literacy education situates students' language and literacy learning within a purposeful or activity-based (Lave, 1993; Sticht, 1987) context. In the workplace, family or other locations where literacy is essential for performance of tasks and accomplishing particular objectives, functional and activity-based instruction supports students' literacy learning and cognitive development in directly relevant and tangible situations. While sharing the focus on contextualized learning, critical literacy education departs from functional literacy by further problematizing the context with consideration of students' (including workers') rights and opportunities. Students and teachers proceed, as Freire and Macedo (1987) suggest, by first "reading the world" (the critical context) in order to then "read the word" (the text that represents the world and that can be rewritten). Despite the logic of both functional and critical perspectives in adult literacy such curriculum is not commonly found. The need for contextualized literacy instruction that supports students' immediate interests and ambitions is widely recognized but unfortunately this type of instruction is seldom delivered in adult literacy education (Purcell-Gates, Degener & Jacobson, 2001; Worthman, 2006). I attempt to meet this need through critically responsive attention to immigrant experiences and students' lives.

Purcell-Gates and Waterman (2000) argue that sociopsycholinguistic developments of the last forty years have not been fully understood by critical pedagogues and adult literacy educators. Consequently, they fail to promote higher levels of reading and writing engagement. Edelsky (1999) asserts that the whole language movement attempted to bring the sociopsycholinguistic perspective of literacy instruction to full bloom in classrooms but too often neglected its original mission to foreground social justice in curriculum development. The movement also came to be associated with the white, middle and upper classes, was located more often in wealthy suburban elementary schools, and was thus viewed with suspicion by some African Americans and Latinos who feared that under this curricular philosophy their children would not learn the skills needed to participate successfully in society. My goal in uniting critical and sociopsycholinguistic perspectives is to bring a social justice agenda and effective literacy instruction to adult immigrant students. The critical responsive stance I take includes careful literature study as a way of engaging students; my hope is that as the Erie students identify with the struggles of characters in the texts they read, they might be able to better envision the positions they take in their life struggles.

Lewis (1999) explains that careful questioning practices support students' movements from personal to critical stances when they engage with literature. She guides her students' journey through text worlds in order to support them in examination of their lives. In connecting their personal experiences with culturally, historically, and politically constituted texts, they position themselves critically and engage in "cultural conversations." Langer (1992) suggests that readers' interpretation of texts in a community of readers opens the community to "difference, empathy, awareness, and change," and in such an environment, students "enrich their personal development, critical thought, thinking abilities, and understandings of social differences and connectedness" (p. 54). Such illumination, many argue, is most readily found through transaction with narrative. Coles describes the influence, enticement, and challenge of stories.

> The whole point of stories is not "solutions" or even "resolutions" but a broadening and even heightening of our struggles—with new protagonists and antagonists introduced, with new sources of concern or apprehension or hope, as one's mental life accommodates itself to a series of arrivals: guests who have a way of staying, but not necessarily staying put. (1989, p. 129)

As readers engage with the struggles of the protagonists and antagonists, they engage with the conflicts and motivations that drive them. Readers live through the experiences of characters who are often situated in opposition to the culture. Readers, for a time, incorporate the intellectual and emotional spirit of the characters into their own beings, and they sense, feel, and even understand what it means to also stand in opposition to cultural forces.

A prerequisite for the type of experience described here is, of course, authentic reading material. But real books are rarely found amidst the workbooks that have been dominant in the field of adult literacy and ESOL for decades. Adult literacy and ESOL teachers hoping to facilitate student response to engaging reading material must create a library with appropriate materials. As explained in chapter 1, Krashen has provided considerable evidence in support of promoting extensive, independent reading among second language learners, but such reading has been given too little attention in the adult literacy and adult ESOL fields. Teachers need to be resourceful in collecting materials that are relevant to students. Rosenblatt (1995) explains that the choices should meet students' experiences and levels of emotional maturity. Special attention should be given to the dynamic transaction between the book selection and the personality of the reader. With careful construction of the environment and transactional experiences, students' critical reflection on stories and culture can become habitual. ESOL and adult literacy teachers need not be overly concerned that they lack preparation and training in literature instruction. Probst (1992) in fact suggests that the dynamic transactions

CHAPTER 3

between readers and texts might be just as well facilitated when teachers use materials that they have never seen before. Hynds (1992) echoes that idea, suggesting that teachers should "stop, listen and learn," adopt a "deliberate, appreciative silence," and forego traditional questioning practices in favor of an emphasis on students' questions and emergent ideas.

Kazemek (1991) argues that by neglecting literature in adult literacy classrooms we wage a "relentless war" against the imagination. He calls for a conception of "adult literacy as storytelling," a way to free the imaginative power of teachers and students. In my classroom I presented more literature and original source texts than adult ESOL programs typically provide. I carefully selected and recommended reading material that would engage students' social and cultural worlds. When I presented reading material to my students, I promoted and guided their use of reading strategies and conducted vocabulary previews. But I also looked to students' transactions with the material, the significance they made of it by their "talking back" (Enciso, 1997) to the characters, the story, and the author. I cultivated the students' personal stories and promoted their responses to literature as a way to share and expand on the meanings of personal stories. Adopting a responsive teaching stance through the use of reader response inquiry with second language learners has only recently received scholarly treatment (Bauer, 2001; Boyd-Batstone, 2003, Martinez-Roldan, 2003; Mohr and Mohr, 2007). It has come in the wake of increased recognition of the need for second language literacy learning. Because adult ESOL instruction has been devoted almost entirely to oral language instruction (Gajdusek, 1988; McKay & Weinstein-Shr, 1993), the profession has failed to realize that relevant, accessible literature has the potential to spur imaginative encounters that are not only language rich but that also present possibilities for voice and agency. Wells and Chang-Wells (1992) argue that exclusive emphasis on oral language use is misguided. They add that the dichotomy between orality and literacy is of little importance if we can enhance both by attending to interactions with reading. Evidence synthesized by The National Literacy Panel on Language-Minority Children and Youth (August & Shanahan, 2008) confirms that literacy learning should be part of the second language program and can even lead to overall language development. While I acknowledge calls for adult literacy instruction to be functional and am mindful that many students do not want or desire academic literacy (Farr, 1994a), I believe that my advanced second language and bilingual students could benefit from literary experiences as a means of envisioning new opportunities and contributing their stories to the culture.

TEACHER RESEARCH

In his examination of literacy research that has made a difference in education, Richard Allington (1997) identified studies that "gather information broadly, deeply, and systematically in order to construct better understandings of some of the major issues confronting us" (p. 7). Allington's challenge is one which I attempt to meet in my teacher research. As described previously, my quest as teacher and researcher at Erie Neighborhood House was to find connections between language, literacy, work, immigration, immigration reform, aspirations, opportunities, and teaching. To make sense of all of these and to create curricular experiences that encompass them is more naturally a teacher's task. But as a teacher researcher, these tasks were also part of my research agenda. To show the reader how the research data and stories presented in this text were obtained, in this section I explain the fieldwork, data collection, analysis and interpretive procedures that were used.

As presented in the Introduction, this teacher research is an ethnographic study that encompasses the cultural milieu of Erie and its West Town neighborhood, the political climate of the mid 1990's, the students' interests and ambitions, and my own agenda as a teacher and researcher. I determined that a qualitative research agenda served my role as a sociocultural mediator and supported my effort to learn more about critical, responsive pedagogy. As a teacher at Erie, I sought to explore and understand the culture of the agency and interactions among students and staff there. In the classroom, my inquiry focused on the constructive dynamic with and among my students. Qualitative research and ethnography in particular encourage fluid integration of these multiple variables. They attempt to account for the disparate realities of teachers' and students' lives, and for the hopes and ambitions of teachers and students that are sometimes in conflict. I wanted to account for these variables, our lives in transition, and our emerging hopes. My inquiry also involves ongoing action, response, reflection and reconceptualizing of the phenomena I experienced—captured most genuinely through the thick description (Geertz, 1973) of qualitative research. My presentation of classroom life with students includes the success stories, the unexpected moments, and the disappointments that characterize my experiences as a teacher.

Wolcott (1988) describes various levels of participation in qualitative research. He indicates that one might be an "active participant," "privileged observer," or "limited observer." In some contexts I was a limited observer. For instance, when I attended the public forum in Erie's gymnasium for the Erie Housing Coop, or when I traveled to Washington, D.C. for *La Marcha* (described in chapter 8), a demonstration for Latino and immigrant rights, my observations were limited to what I saw, recorded and perceived. I had limited access to those who organized these events. Their motivations, other than those displayed for public consumption, were not confided to me. In other cases, I was a privileged observer. For example, through my professional relationship with Tim, the Director of Adult Education at Erie, I was privy to information regarding students, other teachers, adult education policy, and funding. Tim's knowledge of immigration policy and history helped me not only to understand the policies, but also to know how activists were strategizing and organizing to combat the new policies.

For the most part, my role was as an "active participant." As a teacher researcher, I was actively involved in the events that are presented here. But the classroom walls do not mark the boundaries of my inquiry. As described earlier, my response-centered teaching stance positioned me as an interpreter of many overlapping contexts. As an ethnographer, I interpreted the cultural environment, including the many outside influences on the students and evolving curriculum. While most of the book focuses on interactions in the classroom, it should be clear that class discussions drew from a variety of contexts. As will be shown, the many activities of Erie Neighborhood House were welcome components of our curriculum. The gentrification outside of Erie was an occasional topic of our discussions. The immigration reforms were also brought into the classroom, not necessarily through reading the legislation and responding to it directly, but through consideration of the cultural, racial, and political environments that fostered the reforms. My work as an interpreter of the overlapping contexts of our classroom makes my responsive pedagogy not just a teaching approach but also a research method.

Cochran-Smith and Lytle (1993) describe teacher research as "systematic and intentional inquiry." It is systematic in that there are "ordered ways of gathering and recording information," and of "recollecting, rethinking and analyzing information." Cochran-Smith and Lytle refer to activity that is most often "planned rather than spontaneous." Teacher research is inquiry when it "stems from or generates questions and reflects teachers' desires to make sense of their experiences" (p. 24). Throughout my two years at Erie, I conducted research. I archived my lesson plans for future analysis and comparison with field notes and transcripts. I created files for each of my students so that I could collect their reading response journals, drafts of their writing, conferencing records, test data, and other information. Following each class session, I typed up field notes including summaries of the class, observations and concerns about particular students, knowledge and speculation about students' lives and interests, thoughts on students' response to the curriculum, my assessment of the instruction, plans for future instruction, information about Erie and the community, and news of the world outside Erie. As mentioned earlier, I also recorded all of my classes and tutoring sessions on audiotape and transcribed the discussions that took place.

Eisner (1991) believes that the formulation of themes is essential in the educational critique. Since I was asked to teach a group of Leadership students, many themes were already set forth. My lesson plans and students' response to instruction reflected many of these themes. Over time I found that my field notes, with reflections on daily events and future plans, emerged as a more useful identifier of significant themes. The field notes helped me to be a more reflective teacher and to develop my talent as a response-centered teacher and researcher. But I also learned not to fully trust my field notes. They contained only my initial interpretation of events and those interpretations were not always found to be accurate. My understanding of students' comments and intended meanings (often complicated by their second language usage) reflected in my field notes were clarified upon listening to audiotapes. The tapes allowed me to revisit classroom discussion over and over again to better interpret students' contributions. Indeed, while my audio notes were very detailed, I also found when transcribing dialogue that there were still newer interpretations to be made.

To analyze the data, I read and reread the field notes to further identify provisional themes. I analyzed my audio notes in search of alternative or disconfirming evidence, but also to more clearly appreciate the context of each class session and what that context suggested for the meanings of particular classroom discussions. I looked to the transcripts in order to see more vividly how a given chapter would take shape. When I set out to draft a chapter, I turned first to the transcripts. The transcript dialogue formed the core for construction of each chapter and allowed me to establish the centrality of student voices for each theme. I then looked back to the audio notes, field notes, lesson plans, and archived student work for triangulation of data and support in framing the dialogue and constructing the narrative with reference to the many themes. In shaping initial drafts and making revisions, I referred to all of these sources in an ongoing dialectical, analytical process.

As a whole, the chapters in each part of the book follow a narrative arc beginning with a group of community leaders and transitioning to a group of students who were initially more interested in advanced ESOL instruction alone. This latter group emerges by the end as having been influenced by the first group. The plot thickens as I continue my effort to look "broadly, deeply, and systematically" (Allington, 1997) at the students' lives and responses. The weaving of many themes into the story represents my emerging consciousness of immigration policies. But the weaving of critical themes also represents my response to students' commentaries on various issues. These issues include race, power, politics, ethnic tolerance, Latino family culture, and educational perspectives. When such issues surfaced they entered my consciousness as a teacher, researcher and writer.

CHAPTER 4

JUSTINE: SEARCHING FOR THE GOOD FIGHT

We need to teach in such a way as to arouse passion now and then; we need a new camaraderie, a new en-masse. These are the dark and shadowed times, and we need to live them, standing before one another open to the world. (Maxine Greene, 1996, p. 29)

THE VISION OF A BICULTURAL ADOLESCENT

"Come on, Steve. You know I can't read that," Justine complained.

Justine and I stared at a placard alongside the "Flag for Danbalah" in the Sacred Arts of Haitian Vodou exhibit at the Chicago Field Museum of Natural History. The flag depicts a dark-skinned black man dressed in gold, red, green, and blue. He sports an orange and gold miter and holds a staff in one hand and a chicken in the other while a serpent rising from a skeleton is poised to strike. A border of orange silk ribbon and strips of maroon and black sequins surround the mosaic image. Like most of the sequined, beaded, and stitched flags in the exhibit, this one represents a blending of Catholic and Vodou themes in Haitian culture. The "Flag for Danbhalah," the placard informed us, represents the Rada Serpent Deity and St. Patrick with miter, staff and ason. Justine claimed to be unfamiliar with the image, so I suggested that she try to read the placard though I knew it would be difficult for her without her glasses.

I had been teaching and tutoring Justine, or at least trying to, for about eighteen months. From the start, I observed that her vision was poor. She squinted to see the board. She passed on opportunities to read aloud in class. She requested that I enlarge her dictated and typed stories. After months of my gentle inquiries and offers to find affordable vision treatment, she finally confessed that a pair of glasses awaited her at an optometrist's office. Her father, who paid for the exam and glasses, was furious that she refused to even pick them up. Though she selected the frames, she ultimately determined that they made her look like Urkel, a nerdy television character, and she was not about to let any adolescents at Erie, particularly the GED students, see her wearing those glasses.

Like her father, her ESOL teachers before me, and her GED teacher, I was yet another adult who grew occasionally exasperated with Justine. During the two years I spent at Erie, and after I left, she floated from one class to another in no particular order. She attended GED class one week, introductory ESOL another

CHAPTER 4

week, and occasionally attended my evening class with the Leadership students. Since she refused to wear her glasses, her development as a reader was limited. As she struggled to overcome traumatic childhood experiences and establish her identity among other adolescents she sabotaged most of the efforts we provided to help her achieve her stated goals of passing the GED, attending college, and becoming a health care professional.

Erie House offered more than educational opportunities to Justine. Erie was her home away from the home of her father and stepmother in Chicago, away from her mother's home in Haiti. Justine played basketball, went to dances, learned about jobs, and found friends at Erie. Justine was accepted as an honorary, albeit loud and irresponsible, Mexican immigrant by the ESOL students, and as just another teenager by the GED students. Erie was a place where Justine could pass the second half of her suspended adolescence as she waited for the English language to root and blossom and for an education to hopefully accrue. While she waited, however, it seemed that she remained a fifteen year-old even as she turned eighteen, nineteen, and then twenty.

By touring the Sacred Arts of Haitian Vodou exhibit with Justine, I hoped to learn how the honorary Mexican immigrant, dressed in a Michael Jordan jersey, felt about her home country and culture. At each display Justine told me what she knew about the work of art and I then read the placard aloud. We compared her understanding and conjecture to the curator's notes and then moved along, with the significance of the blended Christian and Vodou images in our minds for continued musing. She beamed whenever we came to a representation of Sen Jak, the patron saint of Haiti. "Ah, Sen Jak," she proclaimed warmly. When Justine's GED class arrived an hour into our tour, she immediately joined them and, while she responded to many of their sincere queries with adequate explanation, she refrained from demonstrable exhibitions of pride or leadership. She followed the others about, moved from one collection to the next, and occasionally joined in ridiculing depictions of a culture that, compared to theirs on the near northwest side of Chicago, appeared more primitive.

OUR READING PLAN

I taught Justine using a variety of language experience activities and required her to read English language stories for the first time in her life. Many of these were high interest-low readability texts with simpler syntax and vocabulary. We read original and abridged novels from adult literacy publishers. Justine claimed that in previous ESOL classes she had not read more than sentences and paragraphs and that teachers or tutors never read stories aloud to her. Despite her vision problems, under my guidance she read a dozen, low-readability novels, often taking them home to read in bed at night with her younger sister. She employed many of the comprehension strategies that I taught to the students, most who had sufficient English word recognition abilities to be able to develop their fluency and expand their word recognition repertoires through extended, strategic engagement with readings. But Justine still struggled with some letter-sound and syllable combinations.

For our tutoring sessions Justine stated her interest in learning about black history, not Haitian black history, but black history in the United States. From our classroom library, we selected two high interest-low readability historical fiction slave narratives: *The Freedom Side* (1990) and *Last Chance for Freedom* (1990), both by Marcie Miller Stadelhofen. *The Freedom Side* tells the story of Becky who leaves her fiancé, Gregory, to escape slavery, venture across the Ohio River via the Underground Railroad, and finally join her father in Canada. *Last Chance for Freedom*, in turn, tells the story of Gregory who was initially too frightened to leave with Becky. Gregory eventually summons the nerve and cunning to escape the South, but finds his path to freedom fraught with ethical dilemmas when he meets up with John Brown who is planning an assault on Harper's Ferry.

Each tutoring session began with my reading aloud the *Narrative of the Life of Frederick Douglass* (Douglass, 1963), which had proven too frustrating for Justine to read alone or with guided assistance. I then led her in repeated readings, echo reading, and choral reading with *Becky* and *Gregory* (we took to referring to the books as *Frederick, Becky,* and *Gregory*); and word-recognition instruction (vocabulary, syllabication and phonics) with words often taken from the *Becky* and *Gregory* stories. Justine was responsible for reading or rereading *Becky* and *Gregory* chapters between tutoring sessions and "making a journal," as she referred to it, where she recorded her thoughts prior to, during, and after each chapter.

Though she was a second language literacy learner who needed glasses, I still administered an informal reading inventory, the QRI II (Qualitative Reading Inventory II, Leslie, 1995), to learn more about Justine's reading behaviors in her target language. Below, I highlight the results:

Reading Word Lists
- Independent with first grade level list
- Frustrated with second and third grade level lists (no instructional level)

Reading Words in Context
- Instructional support required with first and second grade level narrative and expository text (Independent at first grade level when accounting for acceptable semantic substitutions)
- 28% of miscues in initial position of words and 70% of miscues in final positions of words

Comprehension
- Instructional support required with first and second grade level text.
- Frustrated by third grade level text

CHAPTER 4

For readers who are unfamiliar with reading inventory diagnosis, the information suggests that Justine could succeed with primer level text by herself but would need guidance with first grade level materials and above. Of course, I still had to account for the influence of Kreyol and French on her English language literacy development, but the QRI II data supported my instructional approaches with *Becky, Gregory,* and *Frederick.* It also offered clarification of the appropriate word recognition skills and second language vocabulary to teach through our immersion in the three novels. During the summer between my first and second year at Erie, Justine and I met several times and established a regimen and working relationship that, along with corrected vision and continued tutoring, I was confident would lead to her improvement of reading in English.

READING AND RESPONDING

For a few years Justine awoke early each morning to orchestrate breakfast for her younger cousin and sister and send them off to school. Then she marched east with her stepmother or other students who lived en route to English classes at Erie Neighborhood House. When she joined my evening class with the Leadership students, she also started attending a morning English GED class where she encountered English-speaking Puerto Rican, African American, and Mexican high school dropouts, adolescents who were ever conscious of their social status and their representations of urban, adolescent cool. Many, male and female, were gangbangers. These students were not the same as the Mexican immigrants with whom Justine had attended classes the previous three years. While most of the GED kids left inappropriate behaviors at the classroom door, they maintained dispositions toward learning that, in part, had led to their previous school failures. Having attended local high schools that were far from welcoming, academically engaging sites where kids might recognize themselves as a priority, these kids attended school without ever learning how and why they might seek an education. To avoid being ostracized by these peers, Justine adopted attitudes similar to these students.

Justine informed me that in the GED class she refused to read anything but the very end of practice GED passages so that she could answer key questions and appear smart to her classmates. The teacher reported that Justine's strategies did not help her succeed with the GED practice tests. Meanwhile, she attended my evening class for a few weeks in September, but then her attendance ebbed through the next three months. She stopped attending tutoring sessions until her GED teacher, former ESOL teacher, and I compared notes, ganged up on her, and cajoled her into starting over with me.

When we resumed, she wanted to continue reading *Gregory* and *Frederick* (she had finished *Becky* on her own during the summer). She stated, "I want to read black history and slavery." She hadn't read any *Gregory* or *Frederick* chapters since the summer, nor had she reviewed the word study materials I provided, though she did visit the library periodically to read Haitian newspapers and had checked out a book about Michael Jordan. She toted this book around without ever reading it. She still had not started wearing her glasses.

Justine proclaimed, during our first session in January, "You read out loud to me. I make the journal. It's my job to make the journal." We looked through her previous journal entries and discussed the chapters of *Frederick* that we had read three months earlier. She recalled the passages in which Frederick learned to read. "He did a good job. He did a good job," she repeated before adding, "He was learning to read." We recalled the section in which Douglass received advice from a white Baltimore merchant mariner to escape to the north. "That's just like Becky," Justine mentioned. We recalled how Gregory was adamant about not trusting a white man, though Becky decided to do so and escaped north. But Frederick Douglass decided he could not trust the white sailor and was eventually sold to a Maryland plantation where daily life was more cruel and brutal. During that same session, we also began reading *Gregory*, using various assisted reading methods, identifying words for further study, and discussing Gregory's impending decision to escape. I did not discern any improvement in Justine's reading since our tutoring had stopped three months earlier.

In a subsequent session, we began a new chapter of *Frederick* titled, "The Valuation." I asked Justine to predict the chapter's content. First, she suggested that maybe Douglass would become free, but then quickly withdrew the suggestion. It was too soon given the number of pages left in the book. She did not know what "valuation" might mean. I explained the term, offered examples, and again asked for a prediction, but still she had none. Even after we read the passages in which Douglass was appraised and sold, she was unable to link the chapter title to the story developments. She knew that Douglass would be free by the story's end and that was all that she considered important. Of course it was also difficult to fathom the valuation and selling of another human being. During our study of the chapter, Justine learned more about the brutal existence that Douglass endured on the plantation: his suffering there was far more severe than what he experienced as a slave in Baltimore. She learned about the forced labor, the living conditions and the whippings, details that were mostly absent from *Becky* and *Gregory*. She read about Douglass's grandmother, who, too old to work on the plantation, was sent out to die in the forest. "It's because she's a slave, that's why they do that. But they gonna die too," Justine said. "The people who do that to a slave they think they never gonna die. They do that to a slave, they gonna be paid back. When you do something wrong you always gonna be paid back. My grandma says when you do something wrong you gonna pay for that when the day comes."

In "The Valuation," Douglass laments his decision not to escape when he lived in Baltimore. He fears he might never escape the plantation. But Justine was more confident of Douglass's cunning, reflecting on how he tricked the Baltimore kids into teaching him to read: "Frederick, he always be thinking to everything. Maybe he might do something someday, but not now." I asked if she was still confident of his escape. She nodded assuredly: "Yep. Even if he don't have no papers. It happened to Becky." Later, she explained: "So, he's still fighting for his freedom.

CHAPTER 4

One day he be like Becky. Becky tell them to say 'Gregory good-bye'. Even though it's not a true story, it's good. And Mr. Rombey [the white man who helped Becky] was there." Justine understood that *Becky* and *Gregory* were works of fiction, while *Frederick* was a true story. But in her mind they were all stories and with each she had already peeked at the ending to learn of the outcomes. As with her own educational narrative, she knew how the stories were supposed to end, but carrying through the unfolding plot proved more uncertain.

The next chapter of *Frederick*, titled "Slave Breaker," focused on Douglass's increased suffering. Justine asked why he was being whipped so often. I explained that he was as an awkward field worker and therefore, from the master's perspective, his punishment was warranted. As we read further, we learned that his condition grew more desperate. I asked Justine if things were getting better or worse. Despite her recognition of Douglass's decline, she responded: "It's getting better."

"Even though he's being whipped more?" I was puzzled.

"It's not gonna stay like that all the time," she felt sure.

I continued reading. Douglass described how he was broken, crushed, and experiencing the worst time of his life. Justine responded, "Oh, he never said that before. He got a whipping a few times but he never talk about it a lot." Douglass continued describing the depths to which he was sinking. He contemplated suicide. He wrote: "I no longer cared to read."

"Damn!" Justine exclaimed. "That's bad!"

But Douglass maintained some hope. He worked along the banks of the Chesapeake Bay, watched the ships pass, and dreamed of escape. "There is a better day coming," he wrote.

"I think so," Justine interjected. "He wanna kill himself but he gonna change. I know one day a better day will come. It's not gonna stay like that every time." I asked if that was her hope or something of which she felt sure. She responded: "One day he'll be free. He's gonna fight for his freedom. Even though he's a slave. . . . One day he's gonna see that he's not working in the fields again . . . . He gonna find his freedom someday just like Becky. Even though *Becky*'s not a true story, he's gonna be just like Becky because he keeps on praying to God." I asked if Becky prayed to God. "No, there's a white man come to get her," she said. "Frederick don't have a white man come to get him so God is gonna help him. Becky had a white man but he don't have a white man. The white man—Gregory didn't believe him."

As we finished the chapter, Justine felt sure that in the next we would see Douglass gaining his freedom. She turned to the end of the book to show me a picture of an older Frederick Douglass holding his index finger just above his forehead while making a point amidst his oratory. Justine said that when alone she had occasionally turned to this picture. She looked to me, raised her index finger next to her forehead and smiled. "He's gonna be free," she guaranteed.

During our next session before reading the chapter "The Turning Point," Justine again predicted that maybe Douglass would be free. I asked about the title and the word "turn." "Maybe it's gonna be better. Maybe it's gonna turn better," she responded, but was unwilling to offer any detailed conjecture. I began reading the chapter: *You have seen how a man was made a slave. Now you will see how a slave was made a man.* "Something good gonna happen," Justine announced. But as we waded through the chapter, the treatment became more brutal, with more whippings. Justine frequently sighed or exclaimed "Damn!" At one point, Douglass escapes to the forest for a brief respite, knowing that his most severe punishment yet would await him upon his return. Douglass returned to the plantation, but as he waited for his punishment, a new resolve came over him. *I decided to fight*, he explained.

"That's good!" Justine exclaimed.

Frederick fought the master, Covey, and won, explaining, *He had drawn no blood from me but I had from him.*

"That's good!" Justine repeated.

The battle with Covey was a turning point in my life as a slave, Douglass wrote. I asked Justine what she thought a "turning point" was, repeating the line twice, but she still wasn't sure. "I think now he's trying to be free. He don't want to be a slave anymore," she said. I asked again and she came a little closer: "Now he fight back with [Covey]. He wants freedom. He don't want to do all the work anymore. He's tired." I explained that a turning point is a particular moment of truth when significant change is going to take place. The old ways would no longer continue. She seemed to understand. I could not resist asking Justine if she had come to any turning points in her life recently. Justine did not respond.

Consistent with our usual approach, we then moved on to *Gregory*, employing echo reading and repeated reading procedures, identifying vocabulary words and miscues, and focusing in this session on 'ai' vowel clusters (e.g., rain, railing, repair, faith). She read during this session at a faster pace and with more expression. In the story, Gregory reached his turning point and was preparing to escape. "The Quaker guy's gonna help him to run away," Justine explained. "Because he don't have no white man to help him. Becky had a white man help her. But he have to find a place before he run away." It didn't occur to me that the author of *Becky* and *Gregory* characterized the white men, Mr. Rombey in *Becky* and the Quaker in *Gregory*, as particularly heroic figures worthy of Justine's constant attention, though they were pivotal characters essential to the escapes. In Douglass's nonfiction narrative the white men offered no such help. Justine characterized them as evildoers whose places in hell were secure.

After five successful sessions we took a break for the winter holidays and planned to resume in January. During the break Justine would be responsible for reading three more *Gregory* chapters on her own. In preparation, we previewed the chapters and identified possible response journal topics. Justine balked, however, at reading one of the chapters. "I don't know who John Brown is. I don't know John Brown," she complained, suggesting that it was unfair to have to encounter a new character on her own. I explained that she hadn't known Becky, Gregory, or Frederick before we began. She agreed. I looked forward to learning of her response to the character and deeds of John Brown.

CHAPTER 4

TURNING POINTS

Unfortunately, I didn't tutor Justine again for three months, and then only for four more sessions. She still attended her GED class and participated in numerous Erie activities. We marched together with an Erie consortium at the local alderman's office in support of local affordable housing initiatives. We sat next to each other at a neighborhood hearing on the implementation of welfare reform. I frequently encountered her in the gymnasium playing volleyball and basketball. On one such occasion, I broke up a fight between her and another young man. Tim, the Director of the program, informed me of a number of shouting matches and physical altercations she had initiated.

After numerous missed appointments, Justine telephoned one afternoon to inquire about resuming tutoring. She had celebrated her nineteenth birthday, and had had a long talk with her father about her future. She told me, in so many words, that she had reached a turning point and wanted to work on her reading. I insisted that she also begin wearing her glasses. During a brief visit to discuss tutoring, I asked about the recent events in her life. She knew she was getting into trouble at Erie and could lose the sanctuary it provided. She described an incident in which she was peripherally caught up in a gang fight while accompanying a new girlfriend home from GED class. Justine claimed that she still wanted to read *Frederick* and *Gregory*. She had read a few chapters of the latter and wanted to tell me about them. I told her about the Sacred Arts of Haitian Vodou exhibit and we decided to attend. I insisted she bring her glasses.

Justine was full of news but without her glasses when we met again for tutoring. Through Erie and a city employment program, she was getting a summer job at nearby Pulaski Park. She would get paid for participating in a theater program and would spend the summer dancing, singing, acting, and writing. She had another altercation with a receptionist at Erie, who had discovered Justine playing with water in the bathroom. She had a fight on her Sunday church bus and drew blood from her opponent. She was unrepentant.

Justine told me about several fights with her stepmother and revealed more of her family's convoluted history. It was painful to hear about her childhood though she spoke with little emotion. I learned that her father was in love with Justine's mother and they had had one child before Justine was born. However, the stepmother's family used one of his sweat-stained shirts to "work vodou on him" and trapped him into marrying the stepmother. Still, he remained in love with Justine's mother and fathered a third child with her. He angered his wife (Justine's stepmother) by bringing fifteen year-old Justine and her younger sister to Chicago before sending for her. When Justine's stepmother came to Chicago, she cloistered herself in their apartment until being coaxed out to attend an introductory ESOL class at Erie. She attended classes for two years but learned little English. Meanwhile, she watched as Justine made friends and attended the GED level class (though that level required much higher literacy ability than she possessed).

Growing up in Haiti, Justine witnessed pivotal incidents of violence. She saw a man get his throat slashed in a dispute over rent. She understood that her uncle was killed or "disappeared by vodou people." Once, while Justine was playing with some other children at her father and stepmother's home in Haiti, a young boy beat her up. Days later, she returned to beat the boy to a bloody pulp. She explained to me that she earned respect from the other children for this and since then she always fought until she saw blood.

We continued reading *Frederick* and *Gregory*. Reviewing Douglass's turning point before continuing with the next chapters, Justine explained that it was necessary for him to confront the slave master, to fight back and, in fact, draw blood. I asked about the recent violence in her life, if it was as justified as Douglass's fighting. With a tone that reflected a sense of shame and embarrassment, she replied: "Oh, come on Steve. I don't want to talk about it." She then described Gregory's choices, which she had read about on her own: to continue on to Canada where he would join Becky, or to stay and fight with John Brown. "He decided he had to fight with John Brown," she said. "He wrote a letter to Becky. He had to fight for the freedom of the other people, of all the black people." I again asked Justine if her recent fighting was as justified as Gregory's. She responded that she was ready to put her fighting behind her. Among other reasons, she feared banishment from Erie House.

SOMETHING WORTH FIGHTING FOR

In what would be our final tutoring session, Justine and I were reading another chapter of *Frederick*. He had been sold to a new master, this time a minister who was even crueler than the previous owners. The minister whipped the slaves simply to demonstrate his cruelty and the certain punishment that awaited any transgression. Justine railed against the minister, declaring that he was "not a man of God." He was a "man of the devil." She was delighted that Douglass did not succumb to the more severe treatment. He established a secret Sunday school literacy class for slaves of local plantations. Justine was proud of him. She explained that he first learned to read and that was his first step to freedom. "And now he is teaching the other slaves how to read. Maybe they can have freedom someday. All the slaves and Frederick." I agreed with Justine that reading was important to their attaining their freedom, but reminded her that Douglass's turning point came when he decided to physically fight back against the master. I was not convinced that literacy alone was sufficient. Justine nodded, considering the two: reading and fighting, fighting and reading.

Suddenly, Tim barged into our classroom. He had received bad news and needed to vent his frustration. The local city college, Malcolm X College, which supplied teachers for many of the adult literacy and ESOL classes at Erie, had decided to cancel four classes at Erie because of state budget cuts. "Don't they know that I can have four hundred people demonstrating in front of their building tomorrow morning?" Tim exclaimed with anger and discouragement before leaving.

Upon Tim's departure, Justine unleashed a more passionate tirade than I had ever heard from her: "So, what is my stepmother gonna do? She been here for two years and she still trying to learn English. . . . It's so hard when you don't know

CHAPTER 4

any English. You walking in the streets. You walking in the stores. You can't talk to nobody. What are all these people gonna do? What are they gonna do?" She was almost crying by this point, but continued, "My step-mother, she answer the phone and she hang up when it is somebody who speak English. . . . Two years ago I cannot speak any English. I go to class. It takes time. What are all these people gonna do? They have to have English classes . . . at Erie."

Justine then described a visit to Cook County Hospital, generally considered the poor people's hospital, during which she had observed a nurse verbally abusing a recent immigrant, telling the immigrant that, among other things, she should take English classes somewhere. Justine recalled her anger at the nurse, telling me, "What if she lose her job, if she could not keep her job anymore and she was homeless? What would she do if there was no one to help her anymore and when she asked people for help they would just ignore her? And no-one would help her?"

Justine's passionate outpouring of emotion marked a turning point in my appreciation of her sense of compassion and justice, which, because of her irresponsible behavior, surprised me. Listening to Justine, I was sure that if Tim were to organize a demonstration Justine would be there. I remembered that she had joined the Erie Neighborhood House caravan of Mexican immigrants when they marched on Washington, D.C. eight months earlier. I thought she had gone primarily for a weekend of socializing. But I now appreciated that, though she did not make the best use of her educational opportunities, she did value them as her right. Though only an adolescent, she appreciated that one might have to fight for the right to language and literacy.

Still, we never finished *Frederick* and *Gregory*. We left off with Gregory fighting at Harper's Ferry and Douglass teaching other slaves to read and write. Of course, Justine already knew how Frederick Douglass's autobiography ended. She had peeked at the ending and seen the picture of Douglass on the last page with his finger raised. She had no doubt that Gregory would eventually meet up with Becky.

Weeks after what would be our final session I was touring Harper's Ferry, West Virginia and learned of a connection between Douglass and Gregory. Frederick Douglass, I learned, had counseled John Brown against the raid on Harper's Ferry. I looked forward to informing Justine of the connection between the two stories, to motivate her to finish reading the two books. Then we would read about John Brown. I envisioned a potential turning point in our tutoring sessions, but also in Justine's attitude regarding the role of fighting in pursuit of justice. I sent a postcard—a photograph of John Brown—to Justine and suggested that we continue reading together. I hoped that eventually we might even read about the slave revolts that led to Haitian independence long before the United States Civil War.

However, we did not meet again for tutoring. We never finished the two books. Last I heard, Justine had not worn her glasses and had not completed her GED.

CHAPTER 5

PERSONAL AND POLITICAL NARRATIVES

In order to participate in a non-marginal way in the U.S. economy, you must become an American by giving up your loyalty to your home country and language, and you must learn the language of the American elite. In order to become an American you must meet certain standards. . . . If you aren't allowed to become an American, there's still plenty of room for you in this country—at the bottom. (David Spener, 1996, p. 74)

THE SHADOW OF HATE

"If you read this book, you gonna cry if you read it. Every time I read I got to ask: 'Oh man, How come he don't do this?' If you read this book, oh man, your heart is gonna break, I tell you." Justine looked around the table to make sure everyone was listening before continuing to talk about *The Narrative of the Life of Frederick Douglass*. "If you read it, your heart is gonna break. They kill like this thirteen-year-old boy, right. He just put his feet and stomping on his head and the blood come out of his nose. God, I think I don't let nobody do that to me."

As explained in chapter 2, our class decided to divide each meeting into three segments: Talk, Reading, and Writing. By the second week of class, I had also introduced the students to our classroom library and guided each in selecting a book for personal reading outside of class. As we assembled for Talk in the third week, I asked questions that students would come to expect from me: "So, what are you reading?" "Are you liking your book?" "What's up with [that character] now?" Do you want to tell us about the story?" But this was only our third week together and their second week with their books. It was too soon, perhaps, to expect the students to feel comfortable talking about their selections. So, I had turned to Justine with hopes that she would be a model of enthusiasm for the others.

Justine enjoyed the attention she received from telling Frederick Douglass's story to her new classmates. She pressed forward reviewing several events of Douglass's life:

Frederick was a little boy and he's a slave. He don't have no freedom like we have today, right now. He had to do a job and he can't go nowhere. And he got whipping. Oh man! And his mother died, his mother died when he was a little boy. And he don't know how to read, he don't know how to write. He

CHAPTER 5

moved to Baltimore. . . . The wife [of Frederick's master] taught him how to read and write, like the ABC's. And then he [the husband] said to her: "Why you gonna teach the slave to read and write?" And after that [Frederick] begin to read the letters and after he begin to tell you if he had the letters, and he could even make the words with the letters.

Justine's enthusiasm led her into details of the story that the others could not possibly grasp without more context. When she began comparing Douglass to Becky and Gregory, I helped her to sketch broader outlines of each story, clarifying the settings, the respective characters, and general arc of each plot.

When Justine finished, I again asked others to talk about their books. But no one was prepared or willing to share much beyond titles. They weren't as far along with their books and, as mentioned, they weren't used to talking about their reading. So we turned to our chart of personal and community concerns (see Table 2.1) for a discussion topic.

Victoria nominated "Discrimination" from the list and, attempting to draw other students into a conversation, she identified problems between blacks and whites, between males and females, and a history of discrimination against Native Americans. Looking around the table to see who might be willing to engage with her in discussion, she added employment discrimination as yet another form of discrimination for us to discuss.

I asked if anyone had ever experienced any of these. Luis mentioned an instance of job discrimination. He also recalled a time when a group of Puerto Ricans playing basketball in the park refused to allow him, a Mexican, to play. Then, lowering his eyes, he explained that even some Mexicans born in the United States don't like Mexican immigrants. Nodding her head, Lucía explained that such discrimination is sometimes linked to the struggles between Spanish (whom the students identified as white) descendents and indigenous peoples of Mexico. Victoria agreed, but added that treatment of Native Americans in the United States, where so many were massacred and where survivors were placed on reservations, was worse.

Justine returned to the theme of Puerto Rican's discrimination against Mexicans with a story about her cousin being severely beaten by a Puerto Rican teenager in the neighborhood. The cousin spent several days recuperating in the hospital. Justine proclaimed, "That's why I don't like [Puerto Ricans]."

Justine's comment touched off a plethora of responses, most consisting of pleas for her to reconsider her position.

Victoria offered: "Last month, I'm sure that Italians break into my building, into the apartment downstairs. But I cannot say all the Italians are like that. There are good and bad people. We cannot judge all the people for one."

Lucía added, "I think that [Justine] cannot generalize for somebody that she know. She cannot blame all the people. Like me, I don't know a lot of black people, but I'm not going to say that all the black people are bad. I'm not going to see somebody that is black and say they are bad people."

Justine responded by professing a belief that skin and blood did not matter to her, and that she understood sweeping statements were not fair. In fact, she cited none other than Jerry Springer, who had recently corrected someone on his television program for making stereotypical remarks about black people. She adopted an alternative perspective: "I am black, but some [blacks] are bad."

"But not all of the Puerto Ricans are bad," Lucía insisted, refusing to let Justine off the hook.

Reluctant to completely abandon her disposition toward Puerto Ricans, Justine replied, "Yeah, that's true. But some are bad," Justine replied. "I think everywhere you go, if you on the street all the people are speaking to me. I see you, I'm gonna say 'hi' to you. If I have something and you ask me, I give it to you. If God give it to me and you don't have it, I have to share it with somebody who don't have it. But with the Puerto Ricans, I don't want to. I will help the Mexican people."

Addressing a class comprised of Mexicans, one Guatemalan, and an Anglo-American person, Justine may have thought she had avoided offending us. When Luis proposed the possibility of my being Puerto Rican, Justine said that if I was a good teacher she would not say anything bad about me. But Lucía was not satisfied. She challenged Justine to explain how she could claim that skin and blood do not matter but still dislike all Puerto Ricans. Shifting back and forth in her chair, Justine repeated her admission that skin does not matter, but reframed her position. She had enough anger welling up inside of her that she was reluctant to concede that her views about Puerto Ricans were irrational. She sat up straight in her chair. "I feel that the man who do this to my cousin, I feel that I hate him. But I don't feel that I hate all the Puerto Ricans."

Recognizing that an inroad had been made, Lucía, Luis, Victoria, and even quiet Maya continued chipping away at Justine's attitudes, voicing ideals with which few could disagree: We must yearn for a world without discrimination, they asserted, a world where it is more possible to love and accept one another.

But equal rights and justice must play a role in such an idealized world, and Justine was learning more and more through her reading that these had long been absent in the African American experience. Justine held her ground against the barrage of opposing opinions and countered by noting the history of white people's treatment of blacks. Her Haitian uncle, living in the United States for several years, had told her stories of his poor treatment. Most significant, she felt her positions were bolstered by her personal experience and feelings she had as a black Haitian living in a Mexican and Puerto Rican neighborhood. Justine's immediate, tangible experience was more salient to her than an idealistic hope for a more tolerant community. Recovering her uncompromising point of view, Justine asserted: "You know, I go like this: If you like me, I like you. If you don't like me, I don't like you. If you talk to me, I talk to you."

Some of the students tired of the debate with Justine. Still others seemed to admire Justine's persistence if not her beliefs. The discussion reverted to the centuries-long conflict between white people and indigenous people in Mexico.

Toward the end of our discussion time, I asked the class if we should at least strive for a world without discrimination. Justine responded: "You should try, but if somebody do something to you, if they gonna hate you, you know, how you gonna like some people who hate you?"

CHAPTER 5

The room fell silent. The students were not shy; they were thinking. The looks on some faces reflected recognition of Justine's dilemma. Others looked solemn, perhaps searching for an answer, believing that one ought to exist.

THE PERSONAL EMERGING AS SOMETHING MORE

Her name is Annabella. She's from Durango's Ranch. She's twenty years old and in her family are nine members. They are three sisters and four brothers.

She came to Ciudad Juarez with her uncle and aunt. The reason she came was because her family was very poor and somebody needed to go out and make money. Her first job was at a factory when she was fourteen years old. She was too young and it was very difficult to find a job. Then she changed her name and age. She started sending money to her mother but she was unhappy because she missed her family. When she began to work she felt that she lost her young life, like playing and entertainment with the same age friends. But she felt better because she continued helping her mom and family. You know, she cared about her young life but her family was first even if she did not enjoy life.

These are the first paragraphs of a story Jacinta wrote in response to one we read in class, "The Battle for Farm Workers Rights" (Lopez de la Cruz, 1991). Jacinta's goal was to tell the story of someone she admired, someone who showed courage and perseverance, and ultimately succeeded in the United States. She audiotaped an interview with her friend, Annabella, transcribed the interview, translated it from Spanish to English and, through conferences with me, wrote, revised and edited the story. Jacinta contributed her story to a collection of student writings of immigrant and workers' experiences.

I selected "The Battle for Farm Workers Rights" in part because the protagonist, Jesse Lopez de la Cruz, dictated her story to a writer who then transcribed and published the story. The writer preserved much of the narrator's speech, presenting direct quotations throughout, and a rough, unpolished syntax that reflects spoken rather than written discourse. In choosing the "Battle for Farm Workers Rights," I speculated that the familiarity of the spoken word in Lopez de la Cruz's story might help Jacinta and the other students to appreciate and construct similar narratives. Of course, I also selected the story for its content. It is a story of a Mexican immigrant who's personal and family tribulations led to her involvement in community organizing and to leadership in the United Farm Workers Movement.

More specifically, the story is the autobiography of Jesse Lopez de la Cruz. As a young girl in the 1930s, Lopez de la Cruz emigrated from Mexico to Southern California with her family. When prolonged unemployment and other tragedies became unbearable, her family began working as migrant farm workers throughout California. Lopez de la Cruz met her future husband in a migrant camp and eventually started a family while residing in a camp. After several years enduring poor working and living conditions, and after disease, poverty and violence decimated the family, Lopez de la Cruz joined César Chávez and Dolores Huerta as an activist in the United Farm Workers Movement. Again, Lopez de la Cruz's story provides an example of how personal and family problems can be resolved, in part, through social activism.

I introduced the story to the students, writing its title at the center of newsprint hung on the wall, and then asked for predictions, "What do you think this story will be about?" My request was met with silent stares. I knew my students weren't shy or uninformed. But as I awaited their responses, I imagined them thinking, "Why doesn't he just give us the story so we can read it and get it over with?"

Eventually, Victoria volunteered, "They don't have rights? Maybe they are discriminated?"

I responded, "Who doesn't have rights? What kind of rights? Where are they?"

The students gradually understood my intentions and offered suggestions, "human rights," "farmers' rights," "workers' rights." I probed further and it was determined that the story might be set in Mexico, or possibly the United States—California perhaps. Luis decided the farmers must be fighting for something and we listed the following possibilities on our concept map: *basic needs, better rates per hour, better work conditions, better life conditions, minimum salary, medical insurance, safety on the job, rights against landowners*. The students were clearly aware of labor issues. Moreover, I observed that their comments conveyed partiality toward the farm workers' cause. None proposed any consideration of an employer's side of labor-management disputes, nor awareness that undocumented immigrant farm workers were often pitted against legal farm workers in the labor disputes of the 1950s and 60s.[1]

I followed the discussion by asking the students to write predictions in their Reading Response Journals. Justine understood it was time to "make a journal." She and Jacinta started writing while I explained to the students that ideas from our discussion could be fashioned into a story prediction and they should not be concerned about whether or not their prediction might be borne out by the reading. We would use their predictions throughout the reading of "The Battle for Farm Workers Rights" to consider possibilities for personal and political activism. Most of the journal entries were repetitions of the list we generated as a concept map. Lucía and Victoria, however, conveyed a more advanced appreciation of narrative genre through their hopes and expectations that the farm workers might resolve their problems and win their battles. Few of the predictions were confirmed or proven inaccurate immediately, leaving a few to wonder about the value of the prereading effort. Clearly many were more concerned about reading with minimal oral mistakes or miscues. Because they were second language literacy learners, I discriminated between English language mispronunciations and graphophonic, morphemic, syntactic, and semantic miscues when offering focused group and individual instruction on skills and strategies.

I followed up on our initial foray into the story by introducing and listing story grammar elements, characters, place, and time. I explained that these elements would help us to keep track of important parts of the story. We could regularly

CHAPTER 5

update our list with the introduction of new characters and changes of place, and we would track events as they unfolded over time. Justine and Jacinta were familiar with story structure analysis from their time spent with me the year before, but for the other students, the story grammar proved to be more of a puzzle. Throughout our time reading about Lopez de la Cruz, the students scanned the story grammar list to recall details and propose new developments in the story. They learned to employ this analytical tool in order to make more extensive and focused journal entries.

Prediction activities like the Directed Reading Thinking Activity (DRTA), response journals, and story grammars have been standard tools in reading instruction for at least a few decades. It did not surprise me, however, that the students were unfamiliar with them. I had previously spent several years teaching reading to adolescents in a second-chance school where I discovered few, if any, who had previous exposure to such practices. Once tracked into remedial reading in elementary and middle school, they suffered through the same "basic skills" pedagogy year after year until most recognized the futility of their schooling and dropped out.

Similarly, the adult ESOL instruction that my Erie students had experienced was dominated by a very structured sequencing of grammar skills; it offered few if any extended engagements with reading and, therefore, no strategic processing of narrative texts. Prior to joining my class the students were seldom, if ever, given opportunities to read extended text. Even those who obtained the GED through a Spanish language exam had much less appreciation for narrative, as the GED test and most GED preparatory programs, both English and Spanish, focus on basic comprehension of brief, abridged passages. My introduction of reading strategies was the first exposure to this type of instruction for most of the Erie students.

To be clear, learning reading methods and strategies was not my primary goal for the students. Nor did I believe that mastery of these processes alone was the key to students' success. These were just preliminary steps in the promotion of engaging reading experiences. I selected "The Battle for Farm Workers Rights" for a reason: to meet and inform my students' interests in community leadership. It was the unfolding of the plot of Lopez de la Cruz's life as an activist with its numerous problems and resolutions—story grammar elements—that proved most interesting in Lopez de la Cruz's story. The students learned that Lopez de la Cruz's activism began with recognition of problems at home. Midway through the story, the students began to talk about Lopez de la Cruz's home life.

"The situation was bad for everybody, not just for them. It says that everybody was suffering the same situation," Sergio said, having joined us for what would be his last class. "But for Jesse, she didn't want to stay there with her mother-in-law and her nine kids. She had to make the tortillas, do the dishes, and all the jobs that she not supposed to do because they were not her kids. . . . She moved from there and started her own way by herself. Then she learned to drive. Then she start going out with people."

Jacinta, Luis and Timoteo agreed with Sergio that Lopez de la Cruz's life started to change when she decided to stop helping her mother-in-law make tortillas.

Jacinta explained Lopez de la Cruz's interests, "She was not with her own family. If some people in your own family that's OK. But she doesn't want to feel that anymore.... I think that her thought was to improve her life for her [future] kids."

In the story, Lopez de la Cruz forced her husband to move them into their own home where she sets out to establish her own way of life. Given these changes and knowing the direction of the story, I asked if Lopez de la Cruz was portrayed as a helpless person or a fighter. Was she a strong or a weak woman?

"A fighter!" Timoteo declared without hesitation. "She wanted to learn driving. And her husband didn't teach her, and she asked her sister. Now she goes to the store and buys groceries."

"And she makes her husband take her out," said Sergio. Recalling that Jesse's husband used to go out all night without her, Sergio asserted, "She wanted to go out. She didn't want to go out with somebody else besides her husband. She can't stay at home until he realized that she was right, that she was suffering."

Timoteo added, "I think she was very intelligent, the way she convinced her husband to take care of her."

The students agreed that Lopez de la Cruz first established her strength in the home. She set up a new home, learned to drive, and worked in the fields before her children were born. Once this was confirmed, Sergio speculated, "I don't know how it will end but it says that she was speaking out because the troubles coming and I think something's gonna happen to her kids. But why does she go back to working in the fields? There's something there, too."

"Maybe she wants her own money," Cyntia responded. "She doesn't want to depend on her husband. She wants to feel if my husband is not there, I want to have money."

I agreed with the students that Lopez de la Cruz was a fighter at home. But her family was still poor. Standing up to her husband might only be the beginning of her fight. I turned to the last paragraph we had read together to prompt more discussion:

> It was like that for all of us. I would see babies who died. It was claimed that if you lifted a young baby up fast, the soft spot would cave in and it would get diarrhea and become dehydrated and die. After all these years, I know it wasn't that that killed them. It was hunger, malnutrition, no money to pay the doctors. When the union came this was one of the things we fought against.

"So maybe when the union comes it gets better for everybody," Timoteo said when I had finished reading.

"She was strong not only at her house, but even outside, fighting for the rights of everybody," Luis concluded.

Cyntia, in response to my request for a prediction, assured us that we would see a happy ending. "All these stories have happy endings," she stated derisively.

Jacinta's story of her friend Annabella, continued below, resembles Lopez de la Cruz's early life.

CHAPTER 5

While her father drank he was very irresponsible. He didn't care about his family even though he earned money here at Chicago. Annabella's mom decided to go to Ciudad Juárez even though her father wasn't there. Her older sister was married. Everybody found jobs and studied. She said to God: "Thanks God for getting all my family together." They were living in their Grandfather's house but they had problems because there were a lot of people. Then they found a little room where they moved. Later they bought a house. Right now her little brothers and sisters are working and studying.

The reason they moved to Ciudad Juárez was because they were very poor. Her father needed to cultivate a lot of beans and corn. Later those products had to be sold and then they had money. Annabella didn't go to school everyday because she needed to help at labor land. Her mother bought shoes and clothes for them while her father was in the bar.

THE PERSONAL EMERGING AS POLITICAL

Following our initial venture into "The Battle for Farm Worker's Rights," Sergio announced that he had attended his last class. His factory employer demanded that he begin working twelve-hour days to meet a new order. Sergio was paid well but lamented his personal circumstance, "Years are coming and they passing by, and you getting no respect. You working in a factory and going nowhere. I want to do something. If I go to school and get a degree in something, I'll be somebody later. It doesn't matter when." Sergio was bitter but also aware of the broader context: "It piss me off when you're trying to get something from them, you're trying to help somebody and you talk to them and they kick your ass. They treat you bad. They just use you. That's the way it is here in this country. You're like a machine. You're new, they're happy with you. You're old, they kick your ass and bring in new workers."

Sergio's departure left the class with one fewer male voice. Like most adult education classes, my class consisted mostly of women. Victoria, Justine, and Jacinta were outspoken while Cyntia, Lucía, and Maya were initially reserved, however by the third week a sense of trust was emerging. The students shared opinions and stories that in more public, less familiar surroundings, especially where English is spoken, would have remained concealed.

In our fourth week, Luis decided to stir things up a little. He nominated "Abortion" as a topic for discussion at the beginning of class, announcing that it was controversial and might get everyone talking.

Everyone agreed to discuss the topic but the room fell silent for what, to a teacher, was an excruciating amount of time. Still, this was the students' requested Talk time. I needed to wait.

Finally, Luis volunteered, "I'm not shy, I'm thinking." The class erupted in laughter.

With the laughter subsiding, Lucía stated matter-of-factly, "It is the body of the woman and she has the right to decide."

Cyntia, a single mother, was equally firm in her opinion. "I think men should say nothing because they never know how it is to be pregnant or have a baby. They don't know. They should say nothing about it. It is the woman's right. If the woman want to have an abortion, she can have it."

Jacinta stated that there are other choices for women. "Abortion is not the solution. Maybe she wants to have an adoption to give the baby an opportunity in the future."

"She can give it to the father," Luis agreed.

Jacinta asked whether or not abortion was legal in the United States. Luis was not clear about the difference between pro-life and pro-choice. The students gave various explanations, some inaccurate, of the two positions and I stepped in to clarify the positions as well as the laws in the U.S.

Cyntia expounded upon her belief in the pro-choice position. "I think that the woman has the right to do what she wants to do. Nobody has the right to criticize her because they are not in her situation." Cyntia paused and with a hint of anger in her eyes continued, "When the babys come nobody's gonna help you. Nobody's gonna give you money for the Pampers. Nobody's gonna give you for the milk. Nobody's gonna give a bed for the baby. People can say, 'No, [abortion] is bad.' But they not gonna help you."

Luis reiterated his concern, "What if the father wants responsibility for the child?"

For Cyntia, the father was of no consequence, "If the woman doesn't love the man, if she don't want to get married then it doesn't matter. . . . Maybe he's not a good man." Cyntia paused again, but this time smiled, "Maybe he doesn't have any money."

Amidst some laughter at Cyntia's comment, Luis exclaimed, "What? So, do I have to be rich?"

"You have to be rich, handsome, and tall, "Victoria explained to Luis.

Luis, a handsome young man, though short and employed as a caterer, responded, "So how many abortions do you think we are going to have then?" More laughter gripped the students.

With the exception of Jacinta and Maya, who remained quiet and did not reveal their opinions, the women in class declared their pro-choice position with certainty. They acknowledged their departure from the stereotype of devout, Catholic, Mexican pro-lifers. They declared that they were young and in the United States. Besides, Victoria and Lucía explained, abortion was common in Mexico, despite it being illegal. Both had known of young women who had illegal abortions and suffered the consequences of inadequate and non-hygienic health care in Mexico. They knew others who crossed the border illegally to have abortions in the United States. Most of the women agreed that the government should not dictate a woman's choice in the matter. Yet the right to that personal decision, Lucía asserted and the other women agreed, needed to be protected by the government. Even the most personal decisions, they seemed to be saying were political.

On many evenings our Talk topics were less focused. With new students frequently joining our class and students straggling in late from work, the students

CHAPTER 5

often used the time to introduce themselves and describe their lives to one another, getting to know each other a little better. During our fourth week, we met Amalia, a middle class, eighteen-year-old from Quito Ecuador who had graduated from a local suburban high school, was working at a downtown McDonald's and now attended our class while waiting to start college. The same evening, Lucía shared the ups and downs of babysitting a three year old niece ten hours per day, six days per week.

A few others shared personal anecdotes before all eyes turned to Maya. After the first couple of nights with Jesse Lopez de la Cruz, Maya informed me that she was able to understand about "seventy-five per cent" of the story during our read-aloud. The class members agreed that it was acceptable for her and others to ask questions and receive clarification about details of the texts in Spanish during and after reading. So I assumed that Maya was succeeding in understanding the content of the story. I observed that she was listening and thinking but Maya still hadn't talked much. With everyone looking her way, Maya said: "My life is not too much." She then described her family routine, with a husband and four children. I asked if the house was hectic when she returned home from class in the evening.

"Sometimes, yes. There's so much noises. The TV, everybody's in the home. We have four rooms in the apartment." Maya screeched and squealed, mimicking the noises her children made. Then she sighed: "I think I want to tell a little bit of my life." She looked down at the story we were reading—Lopez de la Cruz's story—and began talking, "Me worked in the factory for eleven years. And then three years ago when I'm pregnant with my baby, me started sick. Rheumatoid arthritis." She mumbled the words, holding her hands out, tensing her fingers into crooked hooks and jags. Then taking each hand in the other and rubbing them back and forth, she massaged her knuckles. "Now, I feel more better. But then my joints, my ankles, my shoulders, knuckles. Three years, I think, is my hard time for everything in my life. But maybe I'm started adapting for the new life. Because before me working, me sick."

"When did you get sick?" Luis asked.

"Some days in the morning, my fingers were like this." She held them out again, revealing their arthritis. "I run them under warm water for fifteen minutes or twenty minutes, and then go out to work."

"Why this happening? Why did this come?" Luis wanted more.

"The arthritis comes and no can straighten the muscles. Now it's OK. Now, it's not too uncomfortable. Not very bad. More better than before."

Because she mentioned that she worked in a factory for eleven years, I asked: "Did it start because of your job?"

"Yeah, that's what I want to know," Luis added.

"Yeah, because my job is in the packing, in a packing factory with the meat and chicken," she explained.

"You working in cold and then hot weather," Luis said. This was not the first time he had heard of such problems.

"When I work in the summer, it's sometimes 35 degrees, but it's 100 outside," she said. "My doctor say my problem start maybe in the factory." Maya explained more about how she and the other workers would go outside in the summer heat for relief from the cold factory, and then return inside, repeating the cycle throughout the day. The company provided different types of gloves, but their hands would perspire and be affected by the constantly changing temperature. She also mentioned that she developed breathing problems.

Amalia joined Luis in probing further. Both wanted to know if other workers had the same problems, if she had a lawyer, if she was seeing company doctors or independent doctors.

Maya explained that other workers had breathing problems, but the company officials said it wasn't their problem, according to them; she became sick on her own. She turned to Luis, "But you right. When we went to the company to make the exam, the doctor said: 'You don't have nothing. Only, *you* think you have something.' I hold my hands out and they are swelling. But he say 'You don't have nothing. It's only you thinking.' They think it is psycol—" She stumbled over the word and I gave her assistance. "Psychological," she continued, quoting the company doctor. "'You don't have nothing,' he said."

"That's when you went to a different doctor?" I asked.

"Me go to a different doctor. He say, 'You are real sick. You are sick.' He gave me a letter to no have work for one year. Me feel better but the company only give one year for disability. Then you lose work." When she returned one year later, she was unable to get her job back. "Then me cry. Me cry a lot because my life was so different. Me like my work. Me like the money for my children."

"How much were you getting?" Luis asked.

"How much? $7.50 three years ago. For me it was good since me no have school in Mexico. My plan is to work maybe five years more and start studying something, and buy a house. A different life!" she exclaimed, before adding on a more somber note, "When my work finish we use the money in the bank. Now, no house, nothing."

Maya took solace in knowing that at least her children were achieving. The baby, with whom she was pregnant when the arthritis surfaced and wreaked its havoc, was healthy and thriving. The local Catholic church and schools had been good to the family during their difficult times by relaxing tuition obligations. Her oldest son was in his freshman year at Notre Dame University, having earned a scholarship through the support of the local Catholic high school.

Later that same evening, we returned to Lopez de la Cruz's story, first reviewing the list we had previously generated regarding the numerous problems Lopez de la Cruz endured in the migrant labor camps. The list included *no home to live in, too little food, poverty, living in tent houses and shacks, weather related sickness and disease, parents and children dying, large families, housing discrimination, job exploitation*. I wondered whether or not it was Lopez de la Cruz's story that finally prompted Maya to risk speaking in English and sharing her story with us.

Before we turned to the story, however, Luis reminded me that I needed to provide my regular grammar review after Talk time. He noted that Maya repeatedly used the wrong pronoun, "me" instead of "I". This was an occasion when I would have preferred to skip the review—Maya's story was too powerful to reduce it to an exercise in grammar skills—but the students insisted. I acknowledged Luis's point and taught a minilesson on subject and object pronouns. Maya took notes and expressed gratitude to Luis and to me.

A couple of weeks later when Jacinta had begun sharing her story of Annabella, the person she admired, Luis was still searching for a writing topic. I suggested that he collaborate with Maya to write her story. Luis liked the idea but he also felt awkward about working with her and eventually decided against that idea.

While Maya's and Lopez de la Cruz's stories exhibit the pressures and anxieties of middle age, immigrant mothers struggling to secure the well-being of their families, Jacinta's story of Annabella is testament of the hope that characterizes younger immigrants. Her story continues below.

> *One day her father arrived home [to Mexico]. He came from Chicago without money. Then Annabella had problems with her father because he still drank, but not too much. Her older sister came to Chicago. Later, Annabella came to make more money and to keep helping her family while her father tried to change his life. She likes to work at factories; she's thinking in the future for her brothers and sisters. Also she's learning English at Erie House, saying: "Those free classes could not be found in Mexico.*

THE POLITICAL MIRRORS THE PERSONAL

At the class meeting following Maya's story, we were floating from one topic to the next during our Talk time. Amid the discussion, Justine abruptly asked, "Who's going to Washington?" She was not one of the community organizers, but was going to *La Marcha* anyway. It was a big event at Erie, Justine's home away from home. It was also a chance for her to get away from her stepmother for a weekend.

Timoteo, Victoria, Cyntia, and Luis were going. Maya could not go—too many family obligations. Jacinta lamented that she could not attend because she had to work at the *taquería* located in the storefront below her family's apartment (though she ultimately did manage to make the trip). Amalia had no idea what Justine was talking about. Timoteo explained that thousands of people, Latinos, were going to be marching in Washington, to the White House, in support of Latino and immigrant rights. Erie had several vanloads making the trip. We would drive fifteen hours overnight, march and demonstrate all of the following day, spend the night at a local church, and then drive back to Chicago the next day. Lucía quietly stated she would not be going. Amalia looked at Timoteo as if he were crazy. This was the first of many of our conversations about the trip to Washington which will be a focus of chapter 8.

Moments later we returned to "The Battle for Farm Workers Rights." We had finished reading and, alongside our list of story problems, I intended for the students to generate a list of resolutions to the problems that were presented in Lopez de la Cruz's story. My goal was for the students to recognize that much of Lopez de la Cruz's social activism was rooted in her desire to resolve problems at home and in the local community of migrant workers. I wanted the students to link the two. To get the discussion started, I asked how Lopez de la Cruz's and the farm workers' dealt with their problems

Timoteo quickly responded, linking Lopez de la Cruz's story to contemporary issues, revealing further why he was marching in Washington. "By organizing," he said. "I think what is happening [in the story] is the same right now. She was fighting with the Congress or something. She was telling them they created this problem. It was then, because before, New Mexico, California and Texas belonged to Mexico. And then they forget. But they put the fence between the United States and Mexico. They brought the *braceros*.[2] They came here. There were families of three generations. Then there were people who tried to send them back to Mexico. And [Lopez de la Cruz] said, 'You crazy. The *braceros*, they are our blood, and remember that our grandparents, they were illegal once.' They were fighting to get back with one another. That's what they're doing right now with—if you citizen you have rights. If you resident you have almost rights. If you illegal you don't have any rights. It's almost the same thing in the story that is happening now."

Timoteo turned to a page in the story where Lopez de la Cruz voices her complaints to the growers and read, *Another thing the growers did was to bring the illegal aliens. . . . So it's a problem you created. They are our blood brothers and blood sisters, and you're using them against us.* Timoteo looked up from the page. "That's the part I most like it. They trying to do the same thing now."

Vigorously nodding his head, Luis interjected, "The illegals against the residents and the others."

"They're trying to separate all the Latinos from the Mexicans. I think they are afraid because there are many people from Latin America who are angry. And they don't want us to get the power," Timoteo explained.

Timoteo made the link between the story and contemporary issues that I hoped might come from the discussion, but I wanted to draw the story out more, get the students to examine the story more critically and then return to interpretation of its significance in the mid-1990s. I asked about Lopez de la Cruz's contention that the growers and politicians were pitting the two groups against one another, the legal Mexican workers against the undocumented Mexicans brought in as scabs to break a strike. The students recognized that Lopez de la Cruz and César Chávez refused to differentiate between documented and undocumented workers' rights.[3]

Victoria mentioned the posters, tee shirts, and bumper stickers that had been circulating at Erie since the Democratic National Convention in August and that had resurfaced in anticipation of the trip to Washington. One poster depicted the Statue of Liberty wrapped in barbed wire, with the caption, "No human is illegal." Victoria said, "It's human rights." Pointing at different students, she said: "You cannot say you are legal and you are not legal. That's a human. And no human is illegal."

I drew a circle on the board and divided it into a pie chart, representing the division of power between growers, politicians, and farm labor as described in Lopez de la Cruz's story. I showed how the growers tried to cut a smaller slice for the farm workers by dividing the documented and undocumented workers into two

CHAPTER 5

groups and setting them against one another. I then asked how that picture or chart might be drawn today.

Victoria explained that in the 1960s California had an agricultural economy, but now it was "more economic things.... In Chicago it's industrial," she said.

This led to a discussion of the reasons Mexicans and others migrated to Chicago in the first place. I offered my understanding of this history. At one point it was the railroad and heavy industry like steel that attracted Mexican labor. More recently, there were many factory and warehouse jobs available, particularly suited to Mexicans who had limited English but a strong willingness to work. And by the mid-1990s there were service jobs for everyone. I returned to the pie chart and asked where the power was concentrated. Timoteo claimed that the power was concentrated among the factory owners. Victoria offered the example of a grocery chain hiring people regardless of their legal status, but then releasing undocumented workers when the Immigration and Naturalization Service came. This led Luis and others to claim that, as far as they could tell, employers were willing to hire anyone. They were not dividing undocumented from the documented workers.

I then asked, "Is the struggle now the same as with Lopez de la Cruz? Is it against the factories, the employers, or someone else? If there is a division, who is trying to divide legal residents from illegal residents?"

"The government!" Luis stated emphatically.

"No, no. It's not the government. It's the people who have the money and the power. It's the people who have the, how you call it, the capital," Victoria retorted.

"I think it's the government because the government says the fault of the economic problems here is of the immigrants, the illegal," said Luis.

"OK, but who is the government? Is it the legal people?" Victoria asked.

"No, it's the Congress," Luis replied.

Amalia, who recently joined the class, decided to enter the discussion, "I hear that illegal people don't pay taxes." Amalia's comment touched off the same discussion that had been circulating through the media for a few years regarding immigrants and the taxes they did or did not pay, and the benefits they did or did not receive.[4] Ultimately, most of the students agreed that undocumented people used very few benefits compared to the taxes they paid.

"If that's the case," I asked, "what's the problem?"

Timoteo answered, "The reason this is happening is because of the election. This happens every four years to win the presidency. They have to focus on something."

"But this time they are putting more importance on the immigrants. Before, they choose another thing to get to be President of the United States. Now all of them are talking about the immigrants," Victoria added.

"Why? The employers are better off if they can hire illegal people. I don't understand why it's a problem. Who has a problem here?" I asked.

Victoria responded: "I think the people who have now the power they think that if there are more legal people Latino American, then the Anglo is going to change. Because they are going to be less in the future."

Timoteo and Lucía agreed. Victoria continued: "For example, Afro American people and Mexican American people is growing to be more in the population. The people are going to take the power."

"So do you think it's a matter of race or ethnicity?" I asked. "How many of you think it's a matter of race?"

Luis, Lucía, Victoria, Timoteo, Maya, and Amalia all thought so. I asked Justine, who had been silent through most of the discussion of the story, "Justine, is there a history of racism in this country?"

"I think so," she said.

"The black people were slaves," Amalia said. She knew some United States history.

"The black people doesn't have any rights before," Victoria said.

Justine volunteered more. "Even right now, they always say, 'Oh, the black people do it.' If something happens right now they say, 'Oh, the black people do it.'"

Hesitantly, Luis said, "I heard that many years ago the black people and the white people were separated in the buses. The white people were in the front of the bus and the black people in the back."

Victoria explained, "Then the black people start to fight for their rights. And then mostly the Mexican people who came to the United States they start coming and their population started growing. So the people start getting the power and I think that's the issue. They feel they let the people grow up [i.e., if their population increases], they gonna lose the power."

I asked what role culture and language might also play in this fear.

Victoria explained, "If Latino Americans grow up the people want to know the culture from their country and their language. Now, for example, the Mexican people have their kids in the elementary school. Some of them want to learn two languages, not just one. Spanish is expanding."

Again, we had drifted from the particulars of Lopez de la Cruz's story as the students took on more of a teaching role. I yearned to unearth the feelings and opinions the students expressed above. But I was still concerned that we identify the resolutions to Lopez de la Cruz's and the farm workers' problems before leaving the story behind. The students were clearly able to recognize and examine some of the larger issues that linked Lopez de la Cruz's struggle to their contemporary struggles: labor relations, economics, political and governmental expediency, race, language, power. But within this larger context, what specifically did Lopez de la Cruz fight for?

"She put for us the example that we have to fight for our rights," Victoria said.

"But, specifically, what did she accomplish?" I demanded.

"Better drinking water," Timoteo said

"Better pay," Lucía said.

"What about the pay?" I asked.

Lucía responded: "With a fifteen minute break they have to go and walk to pick up the check themselves. And come back all tired. Now [the owners] bring the check to them."

CHAPTER 5

"She got bathrooms," Justine continued.
"She fought for bilingual classes for the kids," Lucía said.
"The houses were too close to each other," Victoria said.
"They got bigger spaces between the houses," added Lucía.

We appended more to the list of resolutions, and then returned to our problems list. I asked the students to identify those problems and resolutions that were both personal to Lopez de la Cruz's life and also relevant to all of the farm workers. Moving through the list of each problem and resolution, checking them off with two different colored markers, we found that in most cases the personal was also social and political. The struggles of one were the struggles of all. Problematizing the personal helped to clarify the community agenda, and working on the community agenda led to alleviation of personal problems.

A ROLE FOR POLITICAL NARRATIVES

We finished our story of Jesse Lopez de la Cruz. After most of the students filed out of the room, Jacinta and Timoteo stayed behind to talk about the class. Timoteo expressed his initial surprise that we were not following the Community Leadership curriculum more closely. He thought we'd replicate the class in English. But as discussed, my intention was to place literacy experiences, more than the Leadership course or most other ESOL courses did, at the heart of the curriculum.

Jacinta observed that the two classes were indeed compatible, "You know, like talking about the community, like we are learning tonight. It is almost close with Jesse Lopez de la Cruz because she was organizing. She was a woman and she came out like an organizer or a leader. So we are almost close [to the other curriculum]."

I responded, attempting to clarify the purpose of biographical reading like Lopez de la Cruz's. "How does someone change their life to becoming a community organizer?" I asked. "How do you go from being someone who works at the local *taquería* and goes to school and lives in the local neighborhood and doesn't leave the neighborhood very often, and then go out to the world and organize people?" I was describing Jacinta. "This," I pointed to Lopez de la Cruz's story, "is a real life story that we can see and appreciate."

Jacinta understood that I was challenging her and responded explaining that the story we read brought the content of the Leadership class into greater focus. She could better understand through the character and struggles of Jesse Lopez de la Cruz how she might think about future organizing activity.

Timoteo added: "For learning English, I think this is a very fine way that we are learning. But it's kind of different than what we do [in the Leadership class]. I think its fine because we learn talking English and we learn reading and writing English. Then we can do in Spanish whatever we want."

Ultimately, the concern that Jacinta and Timoteo were driving at, a concern that I shared, was that many of the students in our class were joining in hopes of receiving advanced English instruction. These students were less likely to have the same level of interest in community organizing as the Leadership students had. I wasn't planning to change my emphasis on literacy, but content was a more delicate matter. I shared with Jacinta and Timoteo some of the short stories, public policy, and labor economics literature that I was considering for future units. I explained that it would require careful navigation of all of the students' evolving interests to find their confluence with reading materials and discussion topics and situate them within a critical consciousness. Jacinta and Timoteo agreed that engaging the new students in ongoing critical dialogue would be counted among their first community leadership challenges. We would jointly construct the future curriculum.

I also suggested that continuing to read and examine biographies of community leaders on their own would be a continuing source of inspiration to them and, of course, support students' English development. From our classroom library I selected a biography of Mother Jones, a turn-of-the-century labor leader, for Jacinta. For Timoteo, I chose a bilingual biography of Rudy Lozano, a Mexican community activist in Chicago who had been assassinated.

Likewise, I suggested to all of the students that Jesse Lopez de la Cruz could serve as both a model of activism and an inspiration for writing. I encouraged the students to write about people they knew and admired. Lucía wrote about a friend in Mexico who was blinded in an accident but went on to a have a successful personal and professional life. Cyntia wrote about her mother. As mentioned, Luis considered interviewing Maya and writing her story, but later rejected the idea and began writing his own story of immigrating to the United States as a sixteen-year-old. Timoteo wrote a story of a local parish priest, his mentor. Jacinta wrote about her friend Annabella. The final paragraph of Jacinta's story shows that some stories do have happy endings:

> *In her life in Chicago she has found a new family with us. Even though she had a big compromise* [i.e. obligation] *with her family, she always tries to be happy and friendly to her friends. Now, she's living in her friend's home and everybody respects her because she shows respect to them. Annabella is the friend I admire. She taught me how to receive respect from the people around me. And she shows me how to value myself.*

PART III

LANGUAGE, LITERACY, AND POWER

CHAPTER 6

AGENCY AND DISCOURSE

CRITICAL PERSPECTIVES

Purcell-Gates and Waterman (2000) explain that in most countries of the world, including the United States, people with low literacy are marginalized in the dominant culture and relegated to a low status. They are often viewed as linguistically, intellectually, morally and even ethnically inferior by the educated classes (p. 6). Confronting these characterizations and the social and cultural conditions that are associated with low literacy ability leads many teachers to adopt a political stance toward literacy education. Kincheloe (2005) calls on all educators to recognize that education is inherently political. Teachers must support students in resisting the ideological dispositions of the dominant culture and promote social change while simultaneously cultivating student intellect. Intelligence, Kincheloe explains, is "not simply socially influenced; it is politically inscribed and constructed in part by the nature of one's relationship to power" (p. 121). Instructional contexts are infused with ideologies that are internalized by students as they negotiate their acquisition of language and literacy and develop perspectives of the world and purposes for continued learning. A challenge for critical educators is to provide experiences that illuminate the social and political power structures yet remain open to students' responses and interpretations.

Critical educators might reconsider the adage "knowledge is power" and examine how those in power use knowledge and information to promote particular ideologies, which, if successful, prevail in the mindset of the masses. Frank (1993) identifies several ideologies that traditional critical theorists believe to be dominant in the United States: 1) a focus on the accumulation of wealth through a capitalist system that is supported through pervasive consumerism; 2) confidence in a rugged individualism that maintains that anyone can make it under capitalism, while those who fail can be blamed for their failure; 3) a belief in math and science as high status knowledge that creates technology and, therefore, progress; 4) a cult of efficiency that fragments knowledge and work, separating labor into two categories: intellectual and manual; 5) a belief in the Western canon, a Judeo-Christian nuclear family, patriarchy, heterosexuality, and a standard English. Critical theorists maintain that these ideologies should not be accepted as given; rather they simply reflect values reproduced through the dominant culture. Paulo Freire believed that a critical eye should be focused upon these ideologies, the values they promote, and their marginalizing impacts. But he also suggested a critical perspective as a way of being in the world.

CHAPTER 6

> Whether it be a raindrop, be it a bird that sings, a bus that runs, a violent person on the street, be it a sentence in the newspaper, a political speech, a lover's rejection, be it anything, we must adopt a critical view, that of a person who questions, who doubts, who investigates, and who wants to illuminate the life we live (Freire, 1985, p. 69).

Through critical lenses, many literacy researchers have revealed anti-democratic literacy practices in schools that support the reproduction of inequity in society. Countless critics of No Child Left Behind (NCLB) literacy polices in the United States condemn the hyper-vigilant national focus on school accountability through testing (Allington, 2002; Altwerger, 2005; Bracey, 2004; Kozol, 2007, to name just a few). Under NCLB, we find the standardization of assessment practices, the homogenization of curriculum, and an overall emphasis on reproducing the knowledge that is sanctioned by the dominant middle and upper class white culture. Students who are members of dominant cultures are more likely to succeed, but those outside the culture may be further marginalized and subordinated (Courts, 1991). Lewis and Simon (1996) argue that schooling has traditionally failed to recognize literacy as both personal and political, and therefore has silenced students and restricted their opportunity to develop new forms of expression. Shannon (1992, 2000) reveals how school reading materials typically reify a European heritage, but when given alternatives the majority of teachers (most of them white) still select commercial literacy materials that sustain that heritage. Oakes (1985) exposes ability grouping, based in part on the use of these reading materials, as a practice that condemns non-mainstream children to failure and perpetuates their *at-risk* status. Still, as Carlson (1996) notes, even those teachers who resist the "dehumanizing dirty work of social class reproduction" (p. 274) are bureaucratically constrained through prescribed curricula, a fact of educational life in the No Child Left Behind era (Allington, 2002; Altwerger, 2005; Evans & Walker, 2006; Land & Moustafa, 2005).

Acknowledging the education system's complicity in reproducing the social, cultural, and economic status quo may leave some feeling hopeless. This criticism of literacy instruction in the U.S. might suggest that second language literacy instruction for my students at Erie might accomplish no more than help them to secure a low-level status in society. My adolescent and adult students attended ESOL classes professing that improved English would lead to a job as a shift foreman or dock supervisor, or would open up the opportunity to attend college. However, the real prospects for success, the limitations of literacy education, and the complexity of navigating the social and political landscape are not necessarily lost on these students. Rockhill (1993) described seemingly contradictory assumptions expressed by Mexican immigrant women. These women considered "learning to read and write English as crucial to getting ahead *and* they said it was unnecessary, for one could get by all right without it, *and* one could never learn enough for it to make a real difference in their lives" (p.163). Nevertheless, Rockhill's subjects, like the students at Erie, chose to learn English. I believe it is ideologically arrogant to suggest that the hardships of migration, the danger of border crossing, sixty-hour work weeks and six to twelve hours per week in the classroom are all miscalculations made by immigrant students. The decision to accept low-status employment, to study English, and to seek advancement represents more than systematic displacement and social stagnation in the students' lives. Despite realistic appraisals of the benefits of English, as Rockhill's subjects expressed, most immigrants realize some benefit to learning English. In choosing to participate the students are agents in transforming their lives.

It is not enough for critical educators to merely guide students in naming injustice or identifying oppression. Promoting students' membership in the dominant culture is likewise not enough if students lose their cultural identity in the process. But it is also inadequate to pursue a multicultural inclusion agenda in which everyone is given a seat at the table only to observe unequal power relations. As will be discussed further in Part IV, multiculturalism without a critical stance is likely to be shallow and insipid (Nieto, 2000). Instead, critical literacy education calls upon teachers to adopt an activist agenda that interrupts the hierarchies of privilege and asserts difference as both worthy of celebration and as authoritative. Critical educators must cultivate students' pride and determination in order to help them recognize themselves as agents of social transformation. Together, they can then establish their ongoing agenda.

The curriculum we constructed in my class illuminated students' personal experiences and motivations. It also incorporated many of the political activities sponsored by Erie staff. Rather than identify students' language and literacy deficits to remediate, I prioritized students' participation and the agency they exhibited in order to establish the language and literacy agenda. In the following two chapters, Lucía and her classmates explore personal uses of language and literacy. Lucía, a gifted emerging writer, makes significant breakthroughs in her journey across two languages. Through rhetorical explorations and careful consideration of her communicative audience, she confronts the challenge of succeeding with the English language. In chapter 8, many of Lucía's classmates travel to Washington D.C. to participate in *La Marcha*, a national demonstration in support of Latino and immigrant rights. In preparation, we read and discussed a short story by Nicholasa Mohr (1993) that describes the experience of a young Puerto Rican woman coming to racial consciousness and summoning agency in her first visit to the United States. The chapter further explores our understanding of the political roles we inhabit in historical struggle for civil rights. Wrapped up in the spirit of *La Marcha* and Erie's promotion of cultural pride and political solidarity, Lucía challenges her classmates and the Erie community when she writes: *Maybe someday we immigrants are going to take off our blindfolds and are going to make a big group that is going to defend our own ideas and beliefs.*

RESPONSIVE LITERACY INSTRUCTION

In the critical tradition, Edelsky (1999) challenges literacy educators to promote critique, hope, and action. More specifically, she calls on teachers and researchers "to tie language to power, tie text interpretation to societal structures, or tie reading and writing to perpetuating or resisting" (p. 15). In this section, we will examine how language and power are intertwined and how literacy interactions can be

CHAPTER 6

understood as discourse practices that facilitate or restrain membership in various social contexts.

Vygotsky, well known for his theory of learning in the zone of proximal development (1978), explains that a defining quality of humans is their use of language to communicate. The words we use are signs that designate potential meanings as well as tools that assert meaning. Communication requires that we engage others in mediation of the sign and tool system. We perform a dance between thoughts that are intended and thoughts that are understood. Vygotsky (1986) further describes the relationship between thought and word:

> The relationship of thought to word is not a thing but a process, a continual movement back and forth from thought to word and from word to thought. In that process, the relation of thought to word undergoes changes that themselves may be regarded as development in the functional sense. Thought is not merely expression in words; it comes into existence through them. (p. 218)

Once words are written, Vygotsky (1978) explains, they undergo transformation from being first order symbols (representing direct speech) to second order symbols. In the process, speech serves as an intermediate link to the written form but eventually plays a subordinate role as the written word becomes the direct symbol for meaning-making activity. Through this transformation literacy comes to represent different practices from orality and has different requirements for participation. The "continual movement back and forth between thought and word" in written language still transforms the thought, the word, and the meaning. But the written word is not speech written down. Literacy serves different purposes from orality (Heath, 1983; Purcell-Gates, 2005) and is used to communicate across space and time (Kucer, 2005). That said, transactions with literacy often include oral communication as respondents engage one another and make new meanings. Literacy, like speech, is learned in expanding and overlapping sociocultural contexts.

Complementing Vygotsky's identification of the written word as a secondary symbol system, Gee (1992) defines literacy as a secondary *discourse*. A discourse, he explains, is "a socially accepted association among ways of using language, of thinking, and of acting that can be used to identify oneself as a member of a socially meaningful group or social network" (p. 21). Gee explains that discourses are defined by their membership, but also by their relationship to other opposing discourses. Some discourses inherently promote themselves at the expense of others. Gee suggests that literacy is a set of secondary discourses that we both acquire and learn. Like Krashen (2003) he differentiates between acquisition and learning. Acquisition is a subconscious process of trial and error in which learning takes place through immersion in language and literacy culture and events. Learning involves conscious, meta-linguistic knowledge that comes from formal instruction and analysis of language and literacy practice.

Acquisition enables us to perform with others while learning promotes higher level knowledge of acquisition and performance. Gee and Krashen agree that teachers frequently fail to promote one or the other, though both are necessary for success. Some instruction promotes learning without acquisition while other approaches fail to promote learning as participation in dominant and powerful discourses. Dominant and powerful discourses are not isolated phenomena of language, however. They are integrally connected to other forms of power that structure social relationships.

The language and literacy practices of schools in the U.S. typically reflect dominant middle and upper class white discourses and therefore promote easier access and membership for students of that background. Attempts to redesign language and literacy instruction to promote greater access for non-mainstream students has often resulted in the rich getting richer—students who enter schooling as members of the dominant discourse still achieve more than others (Newman, Griffin & Cole, 1989). Purcell-Gates (1995) asserts that academic writing is the "most written of written texts" and, therefore, the most impenetrable for students of any background.

Delpit (1993) cautions educators against being overly deterministic regarding discourse membership. She points to her work in Papua, New Guinea where two languages exist more harmoniously. She also refers to her work mentoring successful African American students in order to demonstrate that non-mainstream student can succeed in the academy. While Gee (1989) directs us to confront and reform the dominant social structures that govern powerful discourse memberships, Delpit seeks to alter the powerful discourses by expanding their membership.

For my Erie students I presented literacy as a tool for participation in political, economic, and cultural discourses. My aim was to help them recognize forms of resistance and contend with dominant discourse practices and the power that sustains them. Throughout the book I describe students' acquisition and learning of English literacy through contemplation of the powerful political structures that they confront and through the action they might take in response. As their teacher, I monitored their use of orality and literacy to discern their distinctive and complementary roles. I linked these to their motivations and interests, and made better use of the Talk, Reading, and Writing segments of the class. Lucía, in particular (chapter 7), takes on the English language by exploring rhetorical structures and devices and the role of audience as she employs language and the power it can yield with calculated effort. Lucía navigates her way through various texts, including informational essayist texts, in order to penetrate and participate in their discourse. I monitored her progress and offered strategic reading guidance and reading recommendations to support her journey. But it was her determination to break through and master different rhetorical conventions that is most significant to understanding her development.

One premise of bilingual education is the ability to use meta-linguistic knowledge acquired and learned through native language literacy for second language literacy contexts. Though literacy is a separate discourse from oral language, it is elastic. We are able to stretch our linguistic and cognitive faculties to transactions with texts in other languages. Biliteracy instruction promotes secondary discourse transcendence but the second language literacy learner still

CHAPTER 6

tends to be an outsider in school and in the political economy. Of course, those who do not possess any literacy have even more barriers to participation in a culture that presumes literacy and marginalizes those who cannot exhibit it in its sanctioned public form. Ruiz (1997) asserts that it is voice and agency, not language that leads to student empowerment. But we can unite language with agency. Cummins (1993) suggests that we should learn to construct the zone of proximal development so that students' voices can be "expressed, shared and amplified" (p. 20). He maintains that when we find large-scale failure of subordinate groups we should turn attention to those educational policies and practices that reinforce coercive power relations.

But we might also investigate the home and community life of students to discern the sociocultural capital upon which communities thrive outside of school (Weinstein-Shr, 1993). We can investigate the existing "funds of knowledge" (Moll & Greenberg, 1990) in order to return to the classroom and reconstruct a curriculum that is more inclusive of different ways of knowing. As we look closely at changing classroom practices, a critical discourse perspective informs us that we should dismantle divisions between bilingual and multicultural education (Nieto, 1993) and work toward a wider and more nuanced appreciation of difference. In biliteracy instruction we should move beyond a focus on cognates and reading strategies. We should share power in the classroom (Bartolome, 1993) and teach second language students an awareness of oral and literate discourse strategies, their distinctions, relationships, and compatibilities (Sperling, 1996). We can heed Jimenez (2003) call to construct second language literacy experiences that foster the voices of those who are the targets of anti-immigrant polices.

Rebeca Garcia-Gonzalez, a teacher at Cesar Chavez Elementary School in San Francisco, California, describes the excitement she and other teachers shared when learning that *La Marcha* would take place in Washington, D.C. (Garcia-Gonzalez, Mejía & Porter, 1999) While they were unable to travel across the country, they did take the opportunity presented by the event to construct relevant curriculum that would encourage agency and advocacy. Her elementary students studied the Mexican-American War and Chicano history and culture, and organized a local demonstration for kids to exhibit their ethnic pride and solidarity. The children read and wrote poetry in order to contribute their voices to the national event. Halfway across the country in our third floor Erie classroom, my students and I prepared for *La Marcha* through engagement with media and literacy and through continued contemplation of how language and literacy could serve the aim of confronting the powerful forces that were legislating against their interests. We then piled into the vans for the journey to the nation's capital where we would give voice to those interests.

TEACHER RESEARCH

In *The Call of Stories* (1989), Robert Coles describes an early professional experience in which his mentor, Dr. Ludwig, helped him to better account for patients' stories along with their clinical diagnoses and therapeutic agenda. Dr. Ludwig admonished: "The people who come to us bring us their stories. They hope they tell them well enough so that we understand the truth of their lives. They hope we know how to interpret their stories correctly. We have to remember that what we hear is their story" (p. 7).

After the final class of my two years teaching at Erie, while I was collecting my belongings and straightening chairs, one of my students returned to the classroom and requested that I use her real name when I set out to write about our experiences together. Gloria did not stand out among others in class and is not given much attention in this book. She enrolled in the class at Erie, in part, to escape the eleven- and twelve-year-old cousins she was visiting during a six-month vacation from Mexico City. She was seldom excited about the topics we studied. Immigration, labor markets and livable wages, and neighborhood gentrification did not interest her much. She often used our writing time to correspond with a friend in Mexico City, asking me to edit her English language letters.

But on the last evening of class, Gloria's participation was more significant than usual. We were finishing a unit on the history of intolerance in the United States, and she read aloud a report she had written about Charlie Howard, whose story is recorded within the book, *Us and Them: A History of Intolerance in America* (Carnes, 1995), a collection of stories that the class elected to read. Gloria informed us that Charlie was a young gay man who was thrown off of a bridge in New England, a place Gloria would likely never visit. The paper shook in Gloria's fingers as she read. She paused frequently, scanning the room to see if we were listening. The story and her commentary afterward prompted other students, most notably Lucía, to relate additional, devastating testimonies of discrimination and violence against gays and lesbians, their friends and family, in Mexico and Chicago. Despite our intention of celebrating after our last class, these stories proved a sobering way to end our time together.

Clearly, Dr. Ludwig's advice to Robert Coles, that he learn to listen to patients' stories in order better know and treat them, is relevant to teaching. The stories we read together in my Erie classroom were important to the students but they also wanted their personal stories to be known. They knew that as subjects of my research there was the prospect of being characters in still another story that might be told to the wider public. Gloria returned to the classroom that evening after everyone had left, I believe, with the hope that her contribution to our shared world would continue to be recognized. In some sense she believed that there might have been more than language and literacy instruction taking place during our time together. Upon her return to Mexico City, Gloria's voice—*her* story of Charlie Howard—might be heard beyond our classroom.

In preparation for our trip to Washington, D.C. for *La Marcha*, I showed a video of the famous oratory from Dr. Martin Luther King, Jr. at the Lincoln Memorial in 1963. When discussing the 1963 demonstration more than thirty years later, the students considered the role their upcoming march might play in history. Timoteo suggested a possibility, "Maybe later they are gonna be talking about rights and we are gonna be in a book or something." In describing her many years as an early childhood teacher and writer, Vivian Paley (1996) once explained, "Everyone who walks into the classroom is a potential character in [my] books." She stated that

CHAPTER 6

part of her motivation to enter the classroom, year after year for decades, came in part from asking herself: "Is there a book in it?" Paley explained that she became a better teacher when she envisioned the possibility of a story to tell. The prospects for teaching are intensified when a teacher stands before a classroom of unpredictable characters bursting with unique stories to share as the class narrative unfolds. In her books written over many years of teaching, Paley offers wonderful examples of teacher research, though she does not claim to be a researcher. Paley's stories go well beyond suggestions of methods that others might try. In fact, her methods are quite idiosyncratic, applied with love and respect for her unique four-, five- and six-year-old charges in order to help the children make sense of their social, intellectual, and emotional worlds. The children are Paley's characters and their growth and development are her ambitious plotlines.

I previously explained the research methods—fieldwork, data collection, analysis, interpretation—that made this teacher research effort and book possible. After poring over and coding the field notes and transcript data and identifying significant themes, the teacher researcher's challenge is to construct the narrative that best serves the experiences shared in the classroom. The social, intellectual, linguistic, and political worlds my students engaged in shaped their evolving characters and the plot of our story as a class. In presenting our story, I offer fairly traditional narratives, sewing the characters and their development into the quilt of immigration history.

Wolcott (2001) laments the proclivity of researchers, quantitative and qualitative, to desert their subjects, leaving them to fend for themselves, while the researcher moves on "untainted by human hands and most certainly untouched by human hearts" (p. 21). He notes that in order to avoid that predicament, qualitative researchers often turn to narrative in order to better portray the researcher and the researched as fully human subjects. The researcher, in writing his account, strives to display research participants' voices and evolving characters with due complexity. This is a central challenge of the writing of research. John Van Mannen (1988) believes that the writing of an ethnography is, at least, as important as the fieldwork and the data analysis. Certainly, if I were not to write this account, my research would have little significance.

Of course, as a teacher researcher I can look back and realize that I had an impact on my students and that we significantly changed our ways of interacting with the world. When discussing the research agenda with my students, I explained that at least one objective I had was to become a better teacher. Through this teacher research effort and by writing about it, I have become a better teacher and, I believe, a better citizen. Because there was, as Paley described, "a book in it," because my aim was to give testimony, my attention to students and their lives was heightened. Through my writing I hope to make a contribution to educational literature, in general, and to community-based adult literacy ESOL education, in particular. To accomplish this objective, I have chosen to guide readers through a critical narrative with biographical sketches, extensive dialogue, plot lines, themes, and an ending that offers little closure because it projects the ongoing story of immigrant struggles into the future. Analysis and interpretation are embedded in the narrative, leaving the reader with much to contemplate and the opportunity to reach his or her own conclusions. My hope is that the reader will approach the story through both aesthetic and efferent stances (Rosenblatt, 1978) so that new and unanticipated meanings may emerge. It is also my hope that this story inspires other teachers to share stories of their classrooms and their students' lives.

CHAPTER 7

LUCÍA: SAMPLING RHETORIC AND RAISING HER VOICE

Understanding a text isn't a gift from someone else. It requires patience and commitment from those who find it problematic. To study is not to consume ideas. Studying is a form of reinvention, re-creating, rewriting, and this is a subject's, not an object's task. (Paulo Freire, in Leistyna & Woodrum, 1996, p.11)

THOUGHT AND LANGUAGE

It is better because we have to think. I don't say that in grammar we don't have to think, but I think when we are writing we have to stop thinking in Spanish and start thinking in English. . . . In this class, the first paper I wrote, I wrote in Spanish, and when I try to translate I thought it was hard. So I threw it in the garbage and started writing in English. Then I was trying to think in Spanish and write in English but that was hard. But since I have been writing in English it is easier for me to think in English and write in English. (Lucía, Erie Neighborhood House student, 1996)

Lucía was a writer. But learning to write in English—learning to move between thinking and writing in English, as she describes above—was the challenge she pursued in my class. Lucía's previous teachers, notably Tim, encouraged her to write. I recognized her ability early on and encouraged her to experiment with her writing. Hoping to inspire both her writing and her interest in a medical career, I gave her a book of poetry by William Carlos Williams, a doctor and poet who served the poor through both of his vocations.

Tim and I were certainly not the first to recognize Lucía's prowess. Her mother taught her to read before she started school in Mexico. Lucía loved math and science during her elementary years but, despite her obvious ability, she did not enjoy reading. She recalled a particular dislike for *Don Quixote de la Mancha*, the Cervantes classic. On the other hand she recalled a fondness for a collection of poems by Neruda, *Veinte poemas de amor,* as well as a novel she read when she was ten, *Little Women* by Louisa May Alcott. Lucía completed the *secundaria* at age 14, and hoped to attend *preparatoria,* and then a university in Mexico City.

CHAPTER 7

However, Lucía's father sent her and her sister to cosmetology school instead of *preparatoria*, the route to university studies.

I learned about Lucía's life primarily through her writing and the discussions it prompted between the two of us or in small groups of students. Lucía was terribly shy. She recalled that her shyness kept her from raising her hand in elementary school classes, even when she knew answers and was aware that rewards came with recognition of her ability. Soon after moving to Chicago and visiting a couple of programs, she settled on Erie Neighborhood House as the place to study for her Spanish GED and learn English before going to college. She succeeded in earning her GED within months—it was much easier than she imagined—after which she focused on English. She was initially placed in a level three English class at Erie. Within six months her teacher recommended yet another advance to the next level. After a few months with Tim at level four, he told her once again that it was time to move ahead. Though apprehensive about what awaited her with each move, she acknowledged they were appropriate steps to take. She was ready for what I had to offer, telling me,

> Before this class, I haven't read many books in English because I couldn't understand them. When I chose the first book here [*The Call of the Wild,* 1990] it was difficult because there were many words I did not know. But I said [to myself], 'If I quit this book, I'm not going to read anymore.' I said 'No, I have to read and see if I understand.' And I understand and I feel good.

By December 1996, when she shared this account about her reading and writing habits, Lucía had become a reader of English. She attributed reading and talking in class and individual reading and writing in her response journal to her development. Our in-class reading and interactive response-oriented discussions offered more English immersion and exploration than she had ever experienced, in or out of school. Response journal writing with class reading and personal selections prompted more thinking in English than she had previously experienced. She explained, "It's more difficult because I have to think about things, but it is better. I have to use the language for thinking, not wait to use it for the future."

READING AND RESPONDING WITH PERSONALLY SELECTED TEXTS

"It is the best book I have ever read," Lucía confided to Olivia and me one evening as we waited for other students to arrive.

"It's a book about dogs?" Olivia was surprised at Lucía's taste. However, within a couple of weeks the two were exchanging literary recommendations. They shared summaries and critiques before class, during breaks, and sometimes during class when we would settle in for an hour of personal reading.

Having observed that the bookmark in Lucía's first personal selection moved no more than twenty pages in two weeks, I was surprised to learn that Lucía was swept away by Jack London's *The Call of the Wild*. She explained that she read occasionally during her niece's afternoon naps but one night she began reading and couldn't stop. Her mother found her at the kitchen table at 3:00 in the morning consumed by the adventures of the dog Buck. She finished the story that night and then used the next few afternoon nap sessions to copy and summarize her favorite scenes, eventually filling twenty pages of her response journal. It was *The Call of the Wild* that led to Lucía's reading transformation described earlier when she determined, "If I quit this book, I'm not going to read anymore. I said, 'No, I have to read and see if I understand.' And I understand and I feel good."

I did not suggest that students use response journals for copying and summarizing. I had instructed them to consult a guide for pre-reading, during-reading, and post-reading entries. The guide, adapted from Berger (1996), offered the following post-reading prompts: *What do you notice? What do you question? What do you feel? What do you relate to?* Lucía made prediction-oriented pre-reading entries but for post-reading entries she re-immersed herself in the story and relived the storytelling by sampling the writing. She recreated the story by borrowing the author's language and at the same time using her own words to explore the potential of the English language for herself. While many ESOL students find rereading necessary to comprehension, Lucía determined that rewriting would guide her understanding and expose her to new storytelling techniques. The following response journal entries, though they may not be exact quotes from the author, reflect her sampling of London amidst her twenty journal pages.

Buck's first day on the Pacific Coast was like a nightmare, he had been suddenly jerked from the heart of civilization and flung into the heart of a primitive world. There was an absolute need to be always alert, f or these dogs and men were not town dogs and men. They were savages, all of them.

Buck got a frothing enemy by the throat, and was sprayed with blood when his teeth sank through the jugular vein. The warm taste of it in his mouth urged him on to greater fierceness.

Such response writing illustrates what Lucía describes with regard to her learning process, "It's more difficult because I have to think about things, but it is better. I have to use the language for thinking, not wait to use it for the future." Rewriting, copying, and sampling helped her to think about the story—the language of the author—and to identify those features that she considered worth thinking about.

Following her breakthrough with *The Call of the Wild*, Lucía became an ardent reader of English. She jokingly complained about those afternoons when her niece's abbreviated naps robbed her of fifteen or twenty minutes of reading time. Though they were beneath her reading level, she turned to the collection of short, high interest-low readability novels available in the classroom. With several of these she wrote predictions, responded to and revised her prediction after each chapter, read to the end, and then copied excerpts that helped her to summarize the story. However, her samplings of texts changed with different stories. For instance, after reading the story of an elderly Chinese man who immigrated to the United States (*Honorable Grandfather*, Keller, 1992), she summarized the story mostly in her words. Then she copied a poem written by the character in the story and made

CHAPTER 7

comments alongside it. With each story, Lucía added more of these evaluative, thematic interpretations.

"A New Chinese Saying"
-by an old chinese man

New land, new friends, new customs
Old is not bad. New is not bad.
Both old and new are good.

New food, new clothes, new jobs.
New is strange, New is exciting.
There is comfort in the old,
But we must find joy in the new.

It is good to be needed.

He signed the paper in English: 'Honorable Chinese-American Grandfather.' He wanted his son to be proud of him. But more than that, he wanted his son to be proud of himself.

As I read through her response journal and then wrote back, I encouraged Lucía to continue exploring the language. But as her comfort with the language and stories increased, I suggested she respond with more critical and evaluative stances and consider the prompts I had provided. She did write more critically, including a few short essays. She titled one such essay, "'Growing Old" response to *The Granny Group*". In this essay, she continued to copy excerpts but also made comments at the end of the excerpts.

It is really unfair when young people don't value the intelligence and wisdom of the old people. It's really unbelievable that young people don't know how to give them love, tenderness or company. . . . But, remember that how you look now they used to look too. And, how they look now is how you are going to look. So think about it and don't be so pig-headed.

In another response essay which she titled, "'Facing a Change' response to the story, *The Kite Flyer*" (Keller, 1992), Lucía did not copy any text but wrote an opinionated response. She opened her essay:

All the parents have to face a change in their life when their kids get married. That moment is very difficult for them because they know they are going to lose them for ever.

. . . Fathers always are hiding their feelings because they don't want nobody sees their real feelings. They think the men have to be strong, and have to have the courage to pass all the difficult and sad things that could happen during their lives.

She ends her essay with the following declaration:

The ability of expressing tenderness and passion. The right of showing their sensations. They should stop wasting their time trying to be strong and insensitive. They should accept that they could be as sentimental and tenderness as the women are.

As she continued reading stories on her own, Lucía expanded her approach to the readings. When she left the low readability stories behind and began reading more difficult texts, as with Rudolfo Anaya's *Bless Me Ultima* (1972), she wrote predictions and revised prediction entries, but summarized the stories by following a story grammar approach, identifying the setting, characters and conflicts, as we had done with our first story in class, "The Battle for Farm Workers' Rights." Then, secure in her comprehension, she was able to write critical and evaluative responses as I suggested. With this development, Lucía had traveled a great distance from her anxiety over whether or not she could read English stories on her own. She learned to strategically approach a story with expectations about how the plot would unfold and about how the author's unique voice will emerge. She also learned to engage with English literature with expectations that she would be responding with her own interpretations. Initially, her interpretations were recorded in her journal. Later, her interpretations would be exhibited in original essays and classroom presentations.

READING AND RESPONDING WITH PERSONALLY SELECTED INFORMATIONAL TEXT

Because Lucía had hopes of attending college and studying medicine, I encouraged her to read informational or expository texts in addition to stories. I suggested that as her comfort with the English language narratives grew she might select some of these texts now and then. However, I was unaware that she had begun to do so until I read her eight-page response journal entry titled, "The Dangers and Effects of Alcohol and Other Drugs." She had read an article in a magazine and, as with the stories she had initially read, copied it into her journal. But in this case it appeared that she copied the entire piece word for word. The entry had several sections, "Alcohol," "Marijuana," "Cocaine," "PCP," "Heroin," and "Designer Drugs." It was encyclopedic in format, presentation, and detail. Each section identified the chemical properties, psychological and physical effects on the user, potential dangers, and side effects of each drug. When I asked her about the entry, she simply informed me that she wanted to learn more about the topic, so she read the article and copied it. It was then that I suggested the use of information gathering strategies, note-taking methods, and graphic organizers.

Following her entry about alcohol and drugs came a new entry a few weeks later which she titled, "Conception and Destruction of a Life," *response to Abortion: A Citizen's Guide to the Issues*" (source unknown). Lucía had already begun writing essays in response to stories and to my suggestion that she add evaluation and judgment to her information gathering with the texts she selected. With the essay excerpted below she used a mix of approaches. She sampled the original text by

97

CHAPTER 7

copying it in places, rewriting it in others, and sprinkling in evaluations and judgments, albeit with rhetorical twists and turns:

The book Abortion -- A Citizen's Guide to the Issues says that during the first twelve weeks of pregnancy the little portion of texture is in a condition like gelatin, and it is very easy to eliminate. Can we say that the abortion is just an act of "eliminating a little portion of texture?" That little portion of texture that is not desire is a live. It is growing, feeling, and it has cromosomas.

The majority of abortions are practicing during the first twelve weeks of the fetus life. At that time the little fetus already tries some movements of breathing, eating and its little heart is already palpitating. It can move its little toes, it can close its little hands, it can give some tumbles in its liquid environment and it can feel pain, too.

Lucía closed her essay with the following paragraph:

What do we really obtain destroying millions of lives? In the Bible says "the life is a gift that God give us, and you are not God. So you do not have the right to take away the life of anybody. And think about something "Are you a mother or a murder?" Only you have the answer.

If submitted as an independently written essay—not a response entry—Lucía's position regarding abortion would seem clear, despite the fact that she never directly stated her position in the essay. Instead, she moves from a touching description of the developing fetus to a harsh indictment of murderous mothers. The message is clear and strong, though it might not reflect Lucía's beliefs. When the topic of abortion came up in class discussion earlier, she asserted, "It is the body of the woman and she has the right to decide," leading most of us to assume she was pro-choice. She ends her essay by offering a choice that is really no choice at all. The decision for the reader of her essay is already prescribed. It is likely that the informational text she read, despite its title, promoted an anti-abortion stance but presented its subject matter with enough rhetorical devices to make it appear as if it offered a balanced argument about abortion. As she considered the many issues she would confront in her future in medicine, Lucía apparently found many of these rhetorical devices to be worth sampling. On the other hand, Lucía might have agreed with the essay. Perhaps, the pro-choice sentiment she shared in class was only an exercise in rhetoric for Lucía. What is clear is that her essay enabled her to learn and adapt the rhetorical style she encountered in *Abortion: A Citizen's Guide to the Issues.*

Lucía wrote one more such essay that I was privy to through her journal. This one was titled "The AIDS Children" and came in response to information she found on the Internet. In this piece, as in her later narrative responses, it appears that she wrote with due consideration of the information gathered, but without the rhetorical piracy that had been her practice. In a rather straightforward manner, she discussed medical symptoms and treatment, hospital and home care options, and the frequency of foster care placements for children born with AIDS. As the essay proceeds, however, Lucía describes the social pariah status that the children must confront. She presents an increasingly morose and despairing picture of child AIDS victims until her final two paragraphs, which, with a rhetorical flourish that more closely reflected the poet-doctor that I knew her to be, called for social change:

> *If all the people become more open minded about all sorts of things "biracial couples, gays, lesbians" and other people who are different from what society calls "normal," we could help each other to avoid so much suffering and pain that many times it's not need it. Everyone should be responsible for his own actions. This sickness is mortal. If you think that you are safe, then you are in danger.*
>
> *The AIDS doesn't forgive. Not even the unprotected children, the injury that AIDS snatch us away our family, our friends, our future, our dreams, and our life. It is still time to protect your life. Think twice why are you going to do something silly and principally don't hurt innocent people.*

RESPONSE TO IN-CLASS READINGS

To be clear, I should claim some responsibility for Lucía's continued development as a reader and writer, aside from my contributions during our writing conferences (which included numerous mini-lessons on revision, editing and grammar) and journal exchanges. With each of our reading-response centered class units, constructed, in part, to meet the interests of Leadership students, I encouraged students to write in response to readings and class discussion. Each of the readings prompted critical evaluation and argument. The personal scrutiny and cultural and political analyses brought forth by students in response to the readings were complex and wide-ranging. Following each unit, I suggested a variety of writing options for students to consider. Since Lucía was one of a few to write so diligently, I took the time to encourage her rhetorical investigations. In each case, I pushed Lucía to take more chances with her expression.

Lucía's response to "The Battle for Farm Workers' Rights" was largely a summary of the plot. But she also took my suggestion to write, in relation to the story, a piece about someone she admired. She wrote of the magical transformation and triumph of a tragically blinded friend from her childhood. In response to "Yo Soy Chicano" (Gomez, 1993) (see chapter 11), a story of a young man who is confounded by his Mexican heritage in an Anglo society, Lucía wrote an essay titled "A Confused Personality." In class discussions, she was initially disdainful of immigrant children who reject their heritage. But in her essay she describes the angst experienced by such children and writes with empathy. She finishes with the following advice:

> *It doesn't matter how they look like. It doesn't matter the language that they speak. It doesn't matter the color of their skin. The most important thing is*

CHAPTER 7

> *that if they really want to be somebody in their life, they should be proud of what they are. It doesn't matter what others think about them. In this life if they really want to become somebody important, they don't need to imitate nobody. They just need to be what their feelings tell them. They just need to do what their thoughts show them. They never have to forget that they are already very special people.*

After reading the piece, I met with Lucía. We reviewed grammar and discussed her presentation of the many emotions that can grip children. But I challenged the conclusion of her essay suggesting it was too simple. With any other student, I would likely have left well enough alone. But Lucía had argued forcefully in class that the color of skin, for example, does matter. In fact, she established to everyone's satisfaction that skin color is a determinant of one's identity and treatment in the United States. As I pointed this out to her, reading back to her the last sentence, "They never have to forget that they are already very special people," a smile of recognition washed over Lucía's face. I had caught her being Pollyannaish and she knew that I knew she was anything but and I wasn't going to let her get away with it.

As described earlier, reading *The Call of the Wild* marked a turning point for Lucía's relationship with written English. I believe that my writing conference with her regarding "A Confused Personality" also marked a turning point, though of a more subtle nature. It was after the conference that she began to examine her writing more critically, that she began playing with argument for argument's sake, but also exploring new pathways for expression of her ideas, however tentative and inchoate. She continued sampling authors' writing styles. She even continued copying their text into her journal, but did so in an effort to construct a point of view. At the conclusion of our fall semester, in response to a statistics-laden demographic study titled *Latinas in Chicago* (*Mujeres Latinas en Acción* & Latino Institute, 1996), Lucía constructed an essay in which she compared and contrasted the effects of economic development, health, education, and the prevalence of female-headed households on the status of Latinas. She evaluated these effects and argued that education should be the top public policy priority for Latinas in the city of Chicago. She continued this type of integrated, multi-factored analysis with other units, one of which focused on poverty levels, livable wages and labor market projections.

A SHY, COLLEGE-BOUND STUDENT

By the time she left my class, Lucía was ready for college. Like many ESOL students she felt insecure about her speaking abilities, but her anxiety was compounded by her shyness. Lucía was not comfortable communicating with anyone, in Spanish or English. I informed her that of the four communication domains—speaking, listening, reading, and writing—speaking was often the least required in college. She could attend classes, listen to lectures, complete her reading assignments and write papers while making new friends with similar interests and developing her confidence about speaking. Moreover, I informed her that most colleges in Chicago had support services for ESOL students and cultural programs for Latino or Mexican students. During an annual winter college fair held in Erie's gymnasium, Lucía was surprised to find that the majority of the fifteen information tables were staffed by Spanish-speaking representatives. Still, Olivia had to drag Lucía from table to table introducing her to the college representatives as a promising future student. Shy, occasionally giggling, but increasingly conversant in Spanish and English with the representatives, Lucía walked away with brochures and applications from several institutions.

At the end of our year together, class members elected to read a collection of historical narratives in a book titled *Us and Them: A History of Intolerance in the United States* (Carnes, 1995). The choice resulted from ongoing class discussions related to recent welfare and immigration reforms. The text covered more than three hundred years, with specific stories describing the hatred, oppression, and violence that are woven into the fabric of the U.S. Discrimination based on race, religion, immigrant status, gender, and sexual preference, the students learned, has always been present in the United States. The students selected stories to read on their own or in small groups and reported on them to the class. Lucía read several stories, but chose to report on a story called "Blankets for the Dead," about the Trail of Tears, the forced migration of the Cherokee Nation from the Smoky Mountains to Oklahoma. Lucía copied much of the story into her journal and read an excerpt to the class. When finished, she quietly closed her journal and turned to the next student, Gloria, who had read a story called "A Rose for Charlie," which is about a young gay man who in 1984 was thrown off a New England bridge to his death in the river below. The story prompted one student to describe the treatment of her gay nephew by his parents. They had kicked their son out of the house and my student took him in. She had difficulty forgiving her sister for rejecting her son.

Listening to these stories, Lucía, on our last night of class, uncharacteristically volunteered a story from her past in Mexico City. Some friends there had opened a beauty salon and marketed it as a place operated by and for gays and lesbians. After months of verbal abuse from the community, the salon was firebombed, killing a few people inside. Lucía described at length the destruction of the building and the injuries to those who survived. It appeared Lucía had finished, but then she pressed on with the story of her best friend in Mexico City who had also been kicked out of her house at a young age when her parents discovered her to be lesbian. The friend suffered from depression, and after months living on the street committed suicide. Lucía's storytelling continued with calm and determination. When a few students attempted to interrupt with comments or questions, she kept talking, just a little louder, a little more forcefully. She explained to us that she also read the story of Charlie Howard and found it compelling. But she thought it should be clear to everyone that the intolerance we were discussing was not unique to this new country. "It is part of our pasts too," she told us.

After nine months, on our last night of class together, Lucía had finally spoken more than a few sentences that were not first written in English. She held forth for about ten minutes, speaking in English, speaking from the heart, revealing some of

CHAPTER 7

the pain she had kept hidden. Previously, she had shared in the readings and joined sparingly in class discussions, calculating her thoughts and words for maximum impact. Outside of class, she escaped to the safe refuge of her books and journals. But on that last night of class she moved beyond her shyness and fear. She was reading and writing in English, as she had wanted, and she was prepared to raise her voice among peers in college.

CHAPTER 8

LA MARCHA

A text, whether written on paper, on the soul (Plato), or on the world (Freire), is a loaded weapon. The person, the educator, who hands over the gun, hands over the bullets (the perspective), and must own up to the consequences. There is no way out of having an opinion, an ideology, and a strong one—as did Plato, as [did] Freire. Literacy education is not for the timid. (James Gee, 1987, p. 162)

DOWN IN THEIR SHOES

During the two years I spent teaching at Erie Neighborhood House, I met regularly with a group of adult ESOL teachers from different Chicago community based organizations. The purpose of our meetings was to design immigrant rights curriculum for adult ESOL students. One of our priorities was to include writings from adult students in our programs. The essay below was written by Lucía and submitted to our working group for consideration.

"Why Immigrants are Important to the U.S.A."

Immigrants are important for this country because we can do the hardest and dirtiest work, and we never complain about anything.

The government can make any law it wants. The politicians know that no immigrant is going to bother them because an immigrant is just another number in the statistics.

It doesn't matter if we have legal documents or not. It doesn't matter where we are from. The point is that the government knows that an immigrant doesn't have the courage to fight against it. Immigrants don't have the courage to defend our rights and our freedom.

Immigrants are always going to be down in their shoes. That's why the U.S.A. loves immigrants.

Maybe someday we immigrants are going to take off our blindfolds and are going to make a big group that is going to defend our own ideas and beliefs.

CHAPTER 8

> *Yes, someday . . . the day that we discover that we have the talent and ability to transform our future to change the way we have been living until now.*
>
> *Yes, then we'll see that we have the magic and power in our hands to fight against any roadblock that the government puts in our way.*
>
> *I know that very soon we are going to have the courage to protect our own freedom and we are going to prove that immigrants are not a group of mediocre people.*

Though she authored the essay above, Lucía frequently professed to care little for politics. But she did care about her writing and she was developing her appreciation of the rhetorical role that audience (including her teachers) plays in a writer's work. For Lucía, politics served as another context within which she could explore her voice. The adult ESOL teachers' group liked the essay and wanted to include it in the curriculum, but we exhausted nearly an entire meeting debating Lucía's phrase *down in their shoes*. What were her intentions with the phrase? It was not familiar to the Mexican teachers in the group as a Mexican idiom. Was she attempting use of some American expression? Was she coining a new phrase? Should we seek clarification and revision? Should we edit the phrase or let it stand as an example of creative language use by an ESOL student with the potential to make a contribution to the evolving English language? With this latter possibility in mind, I argued to leave the phrase as it was written. Eventually, it was decided that Lucía should be consulted and the decision should be hers. Without much deliberation, Lucía offered a revision that she assumed would interest her liberal teacher audience. She revised the sentence to read, *Immigrants are always going to be <u>under the government's shoes</u>*.

After one month in my class, Lucía had written more than any other student. With the secret tale of how her father chose her name, she immediately attracted notice as a creative and reflective writer. After reading a short story about drug abuse, she wrote a mysterious piece that described the appeal of drugs, the process of becoming addicted to them, and the scourge of drug abuse. The piece was narrated from the bedeviling perspective of drugs themselves, which called out to and attempted to captivate potential users. In response to "The Battle for Farm Workers Rights," she wrote about a childhood friend who was blinded after a fall from a horse. The friend overcame her blindness, had a successful academic career, and eventually became a medical doctor. The students were amazed at such accomplishments, but when Lucía described her friend learning to drive a car and navigating the streets of their Mexican village, the amazement changed to disbelief. "No, that could not be possible," they claimed. Lucía calmly insisted that, though seeming a bit magical, the story of her friend was indeed real. "If you don't want to believe it, that is fine with me," she responded. Later, in a writing conference, Lucía confided her pleasure in having elicited such a response with her piece of magical realism.

LA MARCHA

READING WORKSHOP

During a pre-class conference in early October Lucía and I reviewed much of her writing. While I worked with Lucía, other students arrived, opened books they had selected and settled in to read quietly. When the conference ended, I looked around the table to find five students reading books and one writing. I announced that it was Talk time, but few looked up from their reading. I mentioned a few items from our wall chart of "Personal Interests and Community Concerns" but all eyes remained focused on the texts.

After a month with the students, it had become clear that most, unlike Lucía, were not likely to carve out time in their lives for reading. While our in-class reading and discussion of Jesse Lopez de la Cruz was fruitful, the students had not been getting very far with individual selections. I was surprised to learn that they wanted time in class to read their books. A spontaneous Reading Workshop had emerged during Talk time and that was fine with me.

Scanning the room I found Luis reading *Macho* (Villasenor, 1991), the story of a Mexican immigrant who, at seventeen—the same age Luis was when he came to Chicago—journeyed to California to work the farms there in the 1960s, but became disillusioned with the life and work. Justine was reading *Last Chance for Freedom* (Stadelhofen, 1990), a work of historical fiction about an escaped slave. Timoteo was reading his Spanish and English language book about Rudy Lozano, the progressive Mexican Chicago alderman. Lucía had selected a high interest-low readability story and had already opened her response journal. Amalia had flipped through a collection of short stories and settled on Alex Haley's "A Different Kind of Christmas." Cyntia, at my suggestion, was thumbing through an autobiography, *I Rigoberto Menchu: An Indian Woman in Guatemala* (Menchu, Burgos-Debray, Wright, 1987), deciding whether or not to devote her energies to the story. Meanwhile, Brisa, a new student, decided to follow the lead of the other students who wrote in response to "The Battle for Farm Workers Rights." Brisa composed an essay about someone she admired, her mother-in-law. While writing, she paused occasionally to consult with Luis; he wanted help with the English words in *Macho*, while she wanted support in writing more coherent and successful sentences.

The students read for nearly an hour while I consulted with each individually regarding response journal entries and other writing submissions. Jacinta had coupled my suggestion to read biographies of community organizers with a recommendation from her Leadership teacher to visit the local library to collect two books about Dr. Martin Luther King Jr. At the end of the workshop time, Jacinta volunteered to tell u about her reading.

> I was reading about that he learned a lesson from his mother. At the time when he was living, when he was like six or seven years, and there was a South segregation system. This means like black and white, they cannot be together. They have to be separate. So at this time, Martin Luther King was six or seven years and he had two friends that was white, white friends. He can't stay with them a lot of times. One day his mother didn't know about

this kind of friend. Some people who was racist was talking to his mom about him playing with white boys in the street. And his mother went there and take Martin Luther King away. He didn't understand this kind of system, why he can't be all the time with the white people. But his mother told him: "You have to know that you are as good as anyone." And he kept playing with the white people, but not all the time because of the system, you know. When he was growing up he was thinking how to help this country, how to make up a solution. . . .

Jacinta continued, telling us about King's college education, mentioning that he discovered another leader through his reading. "I don't know what his name, but he was some kind of minister. So the way [for King] to help people was as a minister. He fight a war but the war was non-violent. So that's something I agree too."

I asked what Jacinta knew about King previous to her reading. She said she knew only that he was a "black leader and did not use guns." She was surprised to learn of his vision for a more integrated society, that "he wants to be close, the black and white people." Having completed her summary, Jacinta looked at me, seemingly for acknowledgment that she had followed my suggestion to read biographies of community leaders. "So," she said, "I'm reading. I have two books." A week later, Jacinta was searching the internet to learn more about the civil rights movement. I met with her to share a modified KWL (Ogle, 1986) method of taking notes to support her inquiry.

THE MAGIC AND POWER IN OUR HANDS

I followed the class session described above with another short story for the class to read and discuss, Nicholasa Mohr's fictional "An Awakening Summer, 1956" (1993). In contrast to the Jesse Lopez de la Cruz colloquial narration, Mohr's writing is more descriptive and intentional, cultivating the reader's enthusiasm for the climax and resolution of the story. Lopez de la Cruz's story, on the other hand, ambles along from one problem and resolution to the next. Most of the students' writing, like Jacinta's story of her friend Annabella in chapter 5, did the same. But Mohr is a professional writer and knows how to construct a narrative. From the opening sentences of her story, we sense a buildup to some significant event:

> *The young woman looked out of the window as the greyhound bus sped by the barren, hot, dry Texas landscape. She squinted, clearing her vision against the blazing white sunlight. Occasionally, she could discern small adobe houses clumped together like mushrooms, or a gas station and diner standing alone and remote in the flat terrain. People were not visible . . . . (p. 51)*

I wanted the students to appreciate a different kind of narrative construction, one that centers on a particular event with all of the plot elements building to that event. In the story, a Puerto Rican woman travels to the United States for her first time. She flies to Texas where she boards a bus to her friend's rural town. Arriving early, she approaches a diner to wait for her friend but is stopped short by the sign on the door, "No Coloreds, No Mexicans, No Dogs Will Be Served On These Premises." Despite this, she enters, orders a drink, and steels herself for a confrontation.

With this story, I sought to elicit the students' appreciation for the passion people bring to community leadership and struggle. Indeed, Mohr's story is also a tale of a woman coming to a greater consciousness of intolerance and the need for action. The story nears its conclusion with the following lines:

> *She understood quite clearly in that summer of 1956, that no matter where she might settle and which direction life would take her, the work she would commit herself to, and indeed her existence itself, would be dedicated to the struggle and the fight against oppression. Consciously, for the first time in her life, the woman was proud of all she was, her skin, her hair, and the fact that she was a woman. (p.59)*

At the end of the story, Jacinta proclaimed: "That was a good story!"

"Why?" I asked, hoping for some appreciation of the writer's craft.

"She fight for her rights," Brisa responded. Brisa was a Honduran woman in her early thirties who had recently passed her citizenship test. She was interested in improving her English with hopes of expanding her day care business to include more English speaking clients. "That's something that still goes on today," she added.

"Yes," Lucía confirmed quietly, yet firmly.

Victoria then mentioned an occasion in which a waitress in a coffee shop ignored her for over ten minutes serving a succession of white women before finally getting to Victoria.

Brisa described a visit to a suburban seafood chain restaurant where she was made to wait an hour while newly arrived white customers were seated. Explaining again that she is Honduran and her husband is dark complected, Brisa told us the story and concluded, "That was a horrible experience and we experience that everyday in life. . . . It happens in the workplace. It happens in restaurants. It happens in little cafes. It's everywhere." She mentioned that the restaurant chain had recently been sued for discrimination.

Luis asked, "What is *sued*?" Victoria offered a translation and Luis was satisfied.

Brisa regretted the experience. She sighed, "I always wanted to go to [that seafood restaurant], but they are so far away from here, out in the suburbs. But when I see the shrimps on TV, oh, I wanted to go."

I asked the students, "Were there any particular parts of [Mohr's] story that stood out for you, that made you angry, that made you feel—"

"I like the part where she broke the glass." Jacinta interrupted before I had completed my question.

The students' excited laughter confirmed their agreement that this was the most memorable part. Lucía proclaimed with enthusiasm: "Yeah, I liked that!"

Lucía identified the passage and Jacinta re-read it aloud:

CHAPTER 8

> *Jesus and Virgin Mary . . . what was she supposed to do? Colors flashed and danced before her, embracing the angry faces and cold, hateful eyes that stared at her, daring her to say another word. Anger and fear welled up inside her and she felt threatened by even the shadows set against the bright sun. They seemed like daggers, menacing her very existence. She was going to fight. She was not going to let them cast her aside like an animal. Deeply she inhaled searching her voice, for her composure. And without warning, she heard herself shouting . . . . (p. 56)*

Jacinta continued reading rather excitedly. The Puerto Rican woman demanded a Pepsi but the merchant denied her request. She shouted at him again and again until he brought her Pepsi unopened, declaring there was not a bottle opener on the premises. While Jacinta reread, the students around the table grinned with anticipation of their character's moment of liberation.

> *Her eyes watched him and just for an instant the young woman hesitated before she stood, grabbed the bottle and lifted it high above her bringing it down with tremendous force and smashing it against the counter edge. Like hailstones in a storm, the glass flew in every direction, covering the counter and the space behind her. The warm bubbling liquid drenched her. Her heavy breathing sucked in the sweetness of the cola. (p. 57-58)*

Jacinta read these last words and looked up smiling.

"Yeah, that's the good part," Luis confirmed.

All of the students agreed. The buildup and release of tension was palpable. I then explained how Mohr set the stage for the showdown, beginning with descriptions of the hot, lazy Texas countryside in which she was abandoned, and providing just enough of the protagonists' background to let us know she was young and determined. I described my feeling of excitement over the escalating tension in the diner, and the release, the joyous sense of victory I felt when she smashed the bottle, despite what might happen next. The students confirmed that they had similar reactions to the story. When I asked them about their own writing, they acknowledged that they were not accomplishing as much as Mohr. But they might try.

The next week, many of the students were to travel to Washington, D.C. for *La Marcha* in support of immigrant rights. In class, we had had a few discussions about the trip and the planned demonstration. The Leadership students' excitement in anticipation of the trip was high. I suggested to the students that they keep a journal of their trip and write about memorable and inspiring moments and events, as the march among thousands of other Latinos and some of the speeches promised to be enthralling. Following Nicholasa Mohr's story, I suggested to the Leadership students that they attempt to describe their trip or some aspect of it with a passion similar to that of our heroine who shattered the bottle on the counter. Again, a few said they might try. But as I studied their faces, I wasn't sure they were ready to believe in, or even recognize, the possibility of their writing and *La Marcha* being connected.

TO TRANSFORM OUR FUTURE

A week after reading Nicholasa Mohr's story, the Erie students and I found ourselves among dozens of Latinos swarming a Bob Evans Restaurant in Breezewood, Pennsylvania at 5:00 in the morning, speaking Spanish and English, greeting each other, proclaiming, *La Marcha*! No bottles were broken, but much coffee was purchased and consumed. We were on our way to Washington, D.C. Midwestern Latinos had driven through the night in order to reach the nation's capitol by 10:00 a.m., when the march would begin. A seven van caravan had departed Erie Neighborhood House the night before. At each rest area along the way, Midwestern Latinos, previously unknown to one another, congregated and greeted each other by saying, "*La Marcha?!*" In Indiana, "*La Marcha?*" was a question about destination. By Pennsylvania, the greeting "*La Marcha!*" had become a statement of solidarity.

We arrived in a Washington D.C. neighborhood similar to Erie's, an ethnically mixed, port-of-entry neighborhood called Adams Morgan. Dozens of demonstrators pushed through the neighborhood ushering us to Meridian Hill Park, also known as Malcolm X Park, where the march would begin. From the park the students marched down 16th Street carrying an Erie Neighborhood House banner that spanned two of the four traffic lanes. Jacinta and Timoteo held the ends while Justine supported the middle. From the Scott Circle overpass that crosses 16th Street one-quarter mile north of the White House, the Erie banner was barely discernable among the throng of demonstrators streaming down the hill to the White House. It took two hours for the Erie group to march the twenty-five blocks and reach the Ellipse on the south side of the White House where the afternoon rally was held.

In preparation for *La Marcha*, and with Jacinta's research on Dr. Martin Luther King Jr. in mind, I presented a videotape of King's 1963 speech at the Lincoln Memorial. At that class session, Olivia joined our class for the first time. She had been living in the West Town neighborhood for only eleven days, having recently left her home and family in Brazil. She had studied English since childhood and had previously spent six months in England. An oral language assessment administered by Erie staff landed her in my advanced ESOL class where she discovered a group of aspiring young activists getting ready to march on Washington. For a newcomer to the country and to our class, such activity, I assumed, was just a little bewildering. After all, she signed up for and expected ESOL instruction. Therefore, I called on the students to explain why they were marching. I turned first to Timoteo and Jacinta.

Jacinta, in turn, looked to Timoteo, "Timoteo?"

Timoteo looked back and with false politeness responded, "Jacinta, ladies first."

Jacinta launched in, "OK, well, we are going to Washington for how you say, *La Marcha*. OK, we are going to march. This march is going to be—we are going to protest for immigrants' rights. And what else? Timoteo knows more about it."

I asked if Olivia understood so far. She responded, "You said that you go to Washington because...."

CHAPTER 8

"We are going to have a march, like a protest for immigrants' rights," Jacinta repeated.

"Immigrants?" Olivia wondered.

"Immigrants' rights," Jacinta clarified.

"Rights? Oh, rights," repeated Olivia. Olivia knew what immigration authorities told her and what she had read about when she decided to come to the United States. To her, immigration policies were intractable rules she expected to follow, not subjects for debate. She later explained to me how surprised she was to discover this small band of mostly young, Mexican immigrants thinking they were going to change the laws of the United States. And this was her first day of ESOL class!

Timoteo continued, "We're going to protest, too, about the reforms in the laws, the welfare, and the schools for kids whose fathers are illegals, and all this kinds of rules they are making against the immigrants, especially against the Mexicans."

"No, it's about the whole Spanish people." Brisa responded.

"Yeah, I think they say everybody from different countries," added Justine.

"It's not just Mexican. It's the whole Spanish people, Latin American, Central American, and the Mexicans." Brisa repeated. Brisa knew that while immigration policy often varies by country of origin, the new policies would, in fact, affect immigrants from all countries.

"They care more about the Mexicans with the laws," Jacinta said.

Brisa held her ground, "No, because if they find a Mexican, if they find one from Honduras, one from Guatemala, whatever, all of them are deported. They not gonna deport just the Mexican."

Jacinta agreed that new laws and proposals would impact all immigrants but most of these, she maintained, would be Mexican. Clearly, California's Proposition 187, many provisions of the recently passed welfare reform, and the pending immigration reform were undoubtedly designed to curtail Mexican immigration and foil the aspirations of Mexicans already in the United States. The students found much of the public rhetoric accompanying the new policies to be insulting. Not unlike Nicholasa Mohr's protagonist, they were ready to vent their pent-up fury over the relentless condemnation and defamation of Latinos hurled their way. Brisa and Justine were beginning to feel the impact of the anti-immigrant fervor sweeping the country and they were correct—the backlash would impact all Latino immigrants. Still it was also safe to say that a primary target of reform legislation was Mexican immigration; therefore, Timoteo and Jacinta were also accurate.

On Olivia's behalf but also in an effort to help the students clearly voice their positions, I asked, "Let's say I just came to this country eleven days ago (as Olivia had). I don't know about any problems in this country. Maybe I think everything in the United States is good. What are the problems here and why are you going to protest?"

Timoteo responded first: "Because the people here are getting tired of all the laws they are making, the welfare reform, the 187, and all the laws they are making. The immigrant won't receive welfare benefits. Only the citizens. Only the citizens can receive benefits and Medicaid, and all of this."

"Like food stamps," Lucía said.

"What are food stamps?" I asked, still trying to guide them toward careful explanations of their cause.

"The government gives you food stamps but it's like money," Jacinta said.

"But you can't buy anything. Only food," added Luis.

"The government gives this to American people?" Olivia looked at me, her eyes wide in a look of surprise.

Jacinta continued, "Not Mexican people. [They give it to] Puerto Rican people or the other people who need help."

Again, Brisa countered Jacinta's assertion, "It doesn't matter. It's if you need it. If you working and you don't have enough to eat for your family or yourself, you go to a public department and they give you food stamps."

Despite Brisa's correction, Olivia was captivated by Jacinta's comment and asked, "But they don't give it to Mexican people?"

Jacinta clarified that prohibitions applied to those who were not citizens. Brisa, a quick study, further explained the different provisions as they related to the undocumented, legal residents, and citizens. Timoteo and Jacinta congratulated Brisa for being so knowledgeable.

Olivia, however, had a puzzled look on her face. I asked about any lingering questions and she responded, "Well, I thought that the Mexican people—Mexican people, it is right to say?"

Several students confirmed that "Mexican" was an appropriate term.

Olivia continued, "I thought the Mexican people was legal here because I have seen, I think, 70% of the population here is Mexican. I haven't seen American people here."

"Where do you live? Do you live on 22nd Street?" Luis asked, prompting laughter from most of the students who knew 22nd Street as the heart of a Mexican neighborhood on the southwest side of the city.

Olivia identified her neighborhood. Justine informed her that they lived a few blocks from each other and should walk home together. Brisa, from the same neighborhood, suggested that Olivia was confusing many Central Americans with Mexicans. She described her experience, "When somebody sees me the first thing they say is, 'Are you Mexican?' It's confusing. They say, 'Oh, you must be Puerto Rican.' 'No, I'm not Puerto Rican. I'm from Honduras.' I explain to them where is Honduras."

The students told Olivia that there were many different Latinos living in her neighborhood, but they did not comprise 70% of the population of the Chicago region. They said she should travel more, go downtown or out to the suburbs. Brisa also suggested that Olivia might also be confusing Mexicans with Puerto Ricans who were already citizens and not affected by many of the reform policies, a fact that perplexed her. "I always wanted to know. Did the United States buy Puerto Rico?"

Luis knew some history. "[The United States] just went over there and sat down on those people. Like Spain did with Mexico. . . . Spanish people from over there,

CHAPTER 8

they came here and they start to steal our gold, to steal our wealth. I'm talking about Mexico and all the rest of the countries."

"Because Spain is our mother country," Brisa said. "It's like England with the United States except—"

Justine interrupted. "You pointing at me. Why you pointing at me?" she complained to Luis.

"Because you from Haiti, right," Luis explained.

"Yeah, who discovered Haiti? Who stole your country?" Brisa added.

"France, it was France, right?" Luis answered.

"Yeah, they like it better than we like it," explained Justine, perhaps alluding to the importation of Africans and the history of slavery in Haiti, or maybe explaining why her father moved his children to the United States, or possibly both.

Additional questions were raised about the hemisphere's history and the students' many heritages, including Olivia's, whose complexion was similar to the others but whose native tongue was not Spanish. Using a map of the Western Hemisphere, I presented five hundred years of colonialism in twenty minutes and segued to the videotape of King's "I Have a Dream" speech and the students' trip to Washington. I explained that the civil rights movement was a response to a history of intolerance. I described the movement as a point in time when the country was called on to clarify its values and principles. I wanted the students to know that people like them fought for those principles, and more than thirty years later, we were going to Washington to reassert their relevance amidst the recent backlash and assault on immigrants.

Just before viewing the tape, Brisa asked, "Teacher, did whites march with the blacks to Washington?"

Timoteo added, "Did Mexicans march with the blacks? Was it only African Americans and whites?"

I explained that the march was comprised primarily of African Americans and some whites. I wasn't sure about Mexicans. But I explained that the civil rights movement prompted several liberation movements, including the struggle for Chicano rights staged mostly in California. I recalled the United Farm Workers movement that we studied through the story of Jesse Lopez de la Cruz and that Dr. Martin Luther King Jr. had a relationship with César Chávez. I mentioned that while we clearly understood Jesse's motivations, it was crucial to appreciate that a larger movement existed, making it possible for Jesse to add her voice to the cause of full democracy in the U.S.

Timoteo nodded, "And Martin Luther King was the leader of the movement. Maybe later they are gonna be talking about rights and we are gonna be in a book or something."

Several smiles surfaced as we savored the possibility of a place in history.

The black and white "I Have a Dream" video opens with a crowd in Washington singing "We Shall Overcome." The anthem fades as Canadian Peter Jennings begins his narration, "It's the greatest gathering of its citizens the republic has ever seen. Three hundred thousand come to march on Washington. The theme is integration. The mood is optimism."

UNDER THE GOVERNMENT'S SHOES

More than thirty years later on Columbus's Birthday, October 12, 1996, the mood among most of the Erie students at the Ellipse for an afternoon of music and polemics combined hope and weariness. It had been a long trip with very little sleep for most. We tried to pay attention to the activities on the stage, but grew tired as the day wore on, napping intermittently in the afternoon sun. The march to the White House and Ellipse was exhilarating. The mass of demonstrators covered the entire length of 16th Street, from Meridian Hill Park to the White House. They were "at least one-hundred thousand" strong the students repeatedly told each other, feeling bolstered by the feeling that such numbers heralded the beginning of a movement. When the *Washington Post* reported the next day that the march drew 25,000, mostly from the East Coast, the students were disappointed but certain that their struggle would endure.

The midday rally at the Ellipse opened with a choir singing "The Star Spangled Banner" in Spanish and English. Soon after, the Erie students heard from their own U.S. Representative, Luis Guttierez, a Puerto Rican. Several other politicians spoke throughout the day. By day's end, we would also hear from actor Edward James Olmos and actor-musician-politician Rubén Blades. Vietnam and Gulf War Latino veterans took to the stage to denounce anti-Latino fervor as unpatriotic. Timoteo recalled one of the veterans complaining, "The government doesn't ask if we speak English when they send us off to war." Assembled in class the next week, many students recalled the speech from a Latino carpenter whose twelve-year-old son was killed in a racially-charged police scuffle to be the most memorable.

While Brisa and Timoteo might have hoped for greater participation from blacks and whites with regard to the 1963 march, this did not appear to be a goal of *La Marcha*. The aim, rather, was to serve notice of an emerging Latino political force in the United States. The platform for *La Marcha* had been identified months earlier, prior to the passage of the welfare reform bill with its anti-immigrant provisions and prior to resurrection of Wyoming Senator Alan Simpson's immigration reform legislation. The platform called for increasing the minimum wage to a livable one of $7.00 per hour. It called for free public education from kindergarten through college, universal health care, and citizen-comprised police review boards. The organizers demanded reform of international labor laws, expanded human and constitutional rights, and amnesty for all undocumented or illegal immigrant workers. Clearly, the agenda for *La Marcha* embraced traditionally progressive, Democratic Party values. There were few provisions with which President Clinton would have disagreed four years earlier before the Republicans took control of the House of Representatives or two years later when the economy scaled unimaginable heights and the public's anti-immigrant zeal was beginning to subside, having left a devastating immigration policy in its wake. However, as described in the Introduction, the Democratic Party at the time was waging a campaign of division and marginalization of its traditional constituencies as it embraced a conservative agenda in a strategy to secure the presidency, though it ultimately lost more congressional seats in the process.

CHAPTER 8

There was little doubt among the Erie students who was the better choice for president in 1996. Though he signed the welfare bill that proved so discouraging to many of the students, Clinton was clearly the lesser of two evils.

Justine opined, "Clinton is gonna be the winner because we don't like Bob Dole. They say if Bob Dole is president all the people gonna have to go back to their country. Because even if you Mexican or Puerto Rican, whatever you are, he don't like them. He only like whites."

"He like Puerto Ricans, of course," Luis responded without explanation. I registered Luis's comment among an emerging chorus of similar complaints. The Mexican students, seemingly in a defensive posture with the imposition of new federal laws designed to thwart their ambitions, were disgruntled that the other major Latino group in Chicago did not share victim status.

Justine continued, "He don't like them. He don't like all the Mexican or Puerto Rican. . . . I don't like him. I don't want him to win. I don't like him. . . . No, everybody not gonna vote for him, even me. Clinton have the most people. Because he don't care about Mexican or Puerto Rican, black, whatever you are. He don't care," Justine responded.

It was not clear if Justine was casting a negative attack on Bob Dole ("*he* don't care"), suggesting that Dole ignored Latinos, or if she was granting Clinton a more positive characterization ("*he* don't care") as, perhaps, a "color blind" politician. I assume she was referring to Bob Dole, but considering the stance of the Democratic Party at the time and the welfare and impending immigration reforms Clinton eventually signed, in retrospect this question seemed prophetic.

"He just care about rich people," Luis responded.

"Who?" I asked, needing clarification.

"Bob Dole," Luis clarified. All of the students agreed that Dole was the worse of the two candidates.

By the time Clinton won the election, the new immigration reform policies had taken shape and as far as the students were concerned, there was little point in siding with either candidate. As noted earlier, Clinton signed into law and then denounced the provisions for immigrants in the welfare reform legislation. The country would just have to suffer the collateral damage in order to win the battle against welfare as we knew it. But if the provisions of the welfare reform for immigrants were collateral damage, the antiterrorism and pending immigration reform legislations were direct hits. The antiterrorism law provided summary exclusion—there would be no court hearing or judicial review—for undocumented immigrants, regardless of employment status or a lack of criminal background if they were found in the United States. These individuals could be—and were—jailed for an interminable amount of time without any judicial hearing. The Supreme Court eventually ruled such actions unconstitutional though they were later resurrected by the U.S.A. Patriot Act following September 11, 2001.

Senator Alan Simpson's Immigration Reform Bill had lingered in Congress for some time before it gathered momentum in the fall of 1996. Once again Clinton signed the bill while vowing to amend it later. Under a new legal paradigm that lumped enforcement and residency policies together, immigrants were now viewed first as potential candidates for deportation rather than residency (the implementation of this new paradigm dramatically escalated under the Patriot Act).

Border enforcement funding would support triple fencing of the border near San Diego, California, and double the number of border patrol agents from California to Texas. The dramatic increase in the number of Mexican deaths at the border (Bailey, Eschbach, Hagan, & Rodriguez, 1996) exacerbated by previous stepped-up border patrol measures, had come to be viewed simply as the price paid by risk-taking immigrants. For those who might gain passage to the U.S., additional provisions were being considered. Detained immigrants would lose the right to challenge INS decisions in a court of law. The U.S. Attorney General would be granted discretionary power to have local law enforcement agents perform INS duties, thus thwarting a local executive order by the politically astute mayor 0f Chicago Richard M. Daley that prohibited such communications between city agencies and the INS. The minimum annual income of immigrant sponsors would be increased to 200% (in the House bill) or 125% (in the Senate bill, which eventually passed) of the poverty level, roughly $19,500 for a family of four. The types of allowable documents used for determining work eligibility would be reduced from twenty to six. Undocumented people found residing in the United States more than six months after April 1, 1997, would be deported and barred from re-entry for three years; those found extending their stay beyond one year would be barred from re-entry for ten years (see the Introduction to learn more about the effects of these policies).

The legislation described here, as well as some harsher provisions that did not pass, were on the congressional agenda when the Erie students marched in Washington. The organizers and politicians speaking at the rally were aware that the antiterrorism law and welfare reform were just the tip of the iceberg. They made reference to the pending legislation in a few of their speeches. As mentioned, however, the students had grown tired after a long trip and paid little attention to the speeches. If anything, they were more excited about being among so many other Latinos at a national event in the nation's capitol. During the long, hot afternoon the students frequently ventured from the Ellipse to discover many Washington, D.C. attractions. Timoteo visited the White House, but was unable to join a tour. He jokingly identified President Clinton's hiatus from Washington that day as a personal affront. Jacinta and Cyntia reported their visits to the Jefferson and Lincoln Memorials, the site of the 1963 demonstration we saw in the video.

The Washington Monument, standing at the crown of a hill, overlooked the Reflecting Pool and Lincoln Memorial to the west, the Latino rights demonstration and White House to the north, and the Mall and Capitol Building to the east. To escape the dense pack of demonstrators during the day, the students found themselves wandering to the top of the hill, where to the east a massive blanket and swarms of people came into view. The blanket appeared to cover the entire Mall, from the Washington Monument to the Capitol Building. The students were inevitably drawn down the slope to the blanket, which upon closer inspection was found to be a collection of thousands of quilts made in memory of people who died from HIV/AIDS. The quilt display known as the "Names Project" and the

CHAPTER 8

candlelight vigil held later that evening were later described by Jacinta and Justine as the most memorable feature of their weekend. The Names Project drew far more people than *La Marcha*. Jacinta offered at least one reason for its powerful attraction. "Each blanket tells a story of someone's life," she said.

There were many different stories being told in the capitol that day. Still, back in Chicago, Timoteo couldn't help but wonder why the two demonstrations did not draw more people. When we viewed the Martin Luther King speech before *La Marcha*, he wanted to know if Mexicans had supported African Americans thirty years earlier. In 1996 he was disturbed that Latinos marched seemingly alone. Was there not a common set of principles that might unite the victims of HIV/AIDS with the victims of immigration policy? Could they not, at least, lend their support to one another through a shared vision of a more hopeful, caring and just future? Timoteo was not alone. I had similar questions. I contemplated how Latino immigrant pride should be asserted while still embracing a wider audience? Given the progressive platform, where was the rest of the politically progressive population—why only 25,000? While *La Marcha* was a significant event, Timoteo and I felt a little down in our shoes.

THE TALENT AND ABILITY TO TRANSFORM OUR FUTURE

Back in Chicago I considered how to steer the curriculum in light of our trip and some lingering doubts. None of the students wrote about *La Marcha*—at all—let alone with the passion I previously imagined a-la-Nicholasa Mohr. Instead, they turned to other projects. Timoteo, Jacinta and Cyntia prepared to attend a union organizers' institute in Minnesota. Jacinta also began participating in a "Community Dialogues" series with several West Town groups, a project initiated by Erie's Community Economic Development program. Many students would attend at least one of a series of demonstrations to promote affordable housing in West Town. Hovering over the local action were the new federal policies. The Erie Adult Education staff monitored and provided frequent updates on the new laws in community forums.

A week after *La Marcha*, Erie hosted Chicago's Annual Hispanic Literacy Coalition meeting in which staff and students from several community agencies gathered for dinner, student readings, and performances. Jacinta, Timoteo, Cyntia, Tim and one other Leadership student performed a one-act play created in their Leadership class. Tim and Timoteo performed the roles of Spanish speaking Immigration and Naturalization Service authorities (*la Migra*). Their job was to raid Chicago factories looking for undocumented workers. Once the workers were identified they were interviewed and if it turned out if they did not strategically exercise their rights they would be deported. The first detained worker—played by a student I did not know—answered all of the questions from *la Migra* and signed the form she was given. She was promptly led away and deported back to her home country. The second worker, played by Cyntia, refused to answer any questions or sign any forms. Frustrated, *la Migra* then turned to Jacinta's character and began hollering at her in Spanish.

Jacinta yelled back, "I don't understand you. Speak English. Do you think I don't speak English just because I am Mexican? I don't know Spanish." Jacinta turned away from *la Migra* and winked to the audience. Like Cyntia's character, Jacinta's refused to answer any questions or sign any papers.

Their frustration piqued, *la Migra* departed the workplace complaining, "Estos obreros mexicanos conocen sus derechos." [These Mexican workers know their rights.]

Later in the Literacy Coalition program, Lucía read her revised essay, "Why Immigrants Are Important to the U.S.A." I encouraged her to select a more recent piece but upon review of her portfolio, she decided that the old essay would best suit the occasion. She read the revised essay, proclaiming that "immigrants are always going to be under the government's shoes," before continuing with her call for immigrants to "take off our blindfolds," to see "the magic and power in our hands," and "have the courage to protect our own freedom."

Through the first half of Lucía's presentation, the audience listened quietly, perhaps bemoaning the current state of affairs regarding immigrant status in the U.S. But as Lucía proclaimed greater hope and encouraged the immigrant community to fight back, a few stood to listen more closely. By the conclusion several more had risen to join the entire audience in applause for Lucía's conviction and to proclaim their solidarity.

During the fall of 1996, it may have been true that the Erie students were increasingly feeling the pressure of being "under the government's shoes." But they did not feel hopeless or "down in their shoes." The Erie students continued to act locally while keeping an eye on federal policies. As it turned out, *La Marcha* left a mixed yet accurate message. The Latino voice was muffled but getting louder. A groundswell of support might yet emerge. The students saw that a rising Latino immigrant voice required continued cultivation in their Chicago community and they were preparing to lead the effort.

Observing the new Latino political activism of the late 1990s, Tichenor (2002) offers a hopeful perspective for all of us:

> If we are lucky, new immigrants may do much more than give new life to the nation's troubled cities and graying labor force. They may demonstrate that participatory democracy and partisan competition still have vibrant possibilities in American politics. (p. 296)

At the time, I wondered if history might mark the autumn of 1996 as the last period of anti-Mexican immigrant intolerance and the beginning of a new era in which white Americans would have to reconcile themselves to the presence of millions of Mexicans living in their midst. The outlook for immigrants did, in fact, change. By the end of the decade, the courts had struck down numerous anti-immigrant laws while the Congress rescinded others. Both political parties altered their previous stances and began courting Latino constituencies. In the first six months of his administration, President George W. Bush established a new, stronger relationship with his Mexican counterpart, Vicente Fox, and charted a path for a more hospitable environment for immigrants. All this occurred before

CHAPTER 8

September 11, 2001. Since the terrorist attacks, however, the intolerant climate and harsh tenor of the immigrant debate has returned and grown stronger than ever.

PART IV

RACE AND AMERICAN DREAMS

CHAPTER 9

CRITICAL ENGAGEMENT WITH RACE AND MULTICULTURALISM

CRITICAL PERSPECTIVES

Polling throughout the 1990s showed that the American public was conflicted over immigration. Support for increasing border restrictions and for a reduction in legal entrants to the country reached historic highs (Tichenor, 2002; Zolberg, 2006). Just prior to the 1996 election when welfare reform, with its numerous provisions curtailing benefits for legal residents, and immigration reform were being moved through the Congress, 72% of poll respondents saw immigration as a threat to the United States (Tichenor, 2002). Interpretations of public opinion often focused on concerns for economic insecurity. In the wake of the 1994 World Trade Center bombings, other explanations of anti-immigrant sentiment identified apprehension over public safety among an increasingly isolationist public.

U.S. immigration policy has historically been framed in zero-sum terms with admissions criteria favoring applicants from one country of origin at the expense of those from other countries. Hence, we find competition to enter the country among the economically distressed, politically victimized, and those seeking reunification with family. Occasionally, the pie is expanded to grant increased opportunity across countries and interest groups. But illegal immigration from Mexico has tempered interest in expanding the pie and has generally pitted many in the U.S. against immigrants. Survey data from the 1990s on the desirability of different immigrant groups showed that Latin Americans and Haitians ranked far below European and Asian immigrants (Zolberg, 2006). Coupling these data with a proliferation of anti-bilingual and English-only proposals, Zolberg concludes that the American public's greatest concern regarding immigration in the 1990s was the perception of a cultural threat posed by immigrants. He explains that despite a general decline in prejudice during previous decades Americans' opposition to new immigrants was significantly related to their ethnicity and Latinos were among the least desired. These immigrants had come to "replace blacks as the 'other'" (p. 389) in the U.S. Zolberg explains that anti-immigrant attitudes in the 1990s were fueled by conservative treatises from the likes of Alan Bloom and Peter Brimelow who proclaimed a crisis for Western culture and, specifically, for white America. These and other polemicists pointed to predictions that by 2050 whites would compose less than 50% of the population. They lamented the decline in the white population and proclaimed that the American identity was at risk. The new immigrants with different complexions and an interest in maintaining their native language while learning English were not assimilating like white Europeans in the

CHAPTER 9

past. Appeals for a more multicultural society, many claimed, only exacerbated the cultural degradation and decline.

These polemics fostered anti-immigrant sentiments among an anxious public throughout the 1990s and were revived a decade later. Still, only three years after the September 11th terrorist attacks on the U.S., the public had returned to fairly balanced views regarding immigration (NPR/Kaiser/Kennedy School, 2004). A comprehensive immigration reform policy would likely have been satisfactory to the general public in the new century but border patrol vigilantes like the Minutemen and anti-immigrant zealots like television's Lou Dobbs and Congressman Tom Tancredo, Republican from Colorado, continued to stir up public opinion and to cause conservative congressional representatives and senators to oppose comprehensive reform efforts.

In such an environment, critical educators are called upon to identify the specific forms of intolerance that their students face and to support those students in the effort to confront the forces that oppress them. As previously discussed, critical pedagogy has expanded its reach beyond a traditional focus on economic or class determinism (Bowles & Gintis, 1976; Willis, 1977) and sought to include matters of gender, religion, sexuality, race and ethnicity in the examination of education in society. Ogbu (1978) identified race and ethnicity as being major determinants of one's place in American society. He discerned differences between "caste-like" minorities and "voluntary" minorities. The former are forced to reside in the U.S. (e.g. African-Americans brought here as slaves). The latter are immigrants who have chosen to live here. Ogbu explains that caste-like minorities are typically unable to assimilate and, consequently, develop resistance to the dominant culture and construct non-mainstream identities. Critics of Ogbu's dichotomy argue that it is incomplete, overly deterministic, and inflexible. Some point to the U.S. usurpation of western lands from Mexico, its possession of Puerto Rico, the international trade policies and joblessness that foster mass migration, and they expand the identification of caste-like minorities. Others identify the fact of persistent racial and linguistic differences exhibited by Latino immigrants in the U.S. to argue that different Latino immigrants and their successive generations are both caste-like and voluntary immigrants (Matute-Bianchi, 1991; Spener, 1996; Suarez-Orozco, 1991). Spener (1996) contends that voluntary immigrants have willingly reproduced a subordinate role by measuring their material situation within the hegemony. They attempt to climb the economic ladder but find their ethnicity denies them access to the top. Spener explains that material access is limited by an ambiguous social contract that fluctuates with the political winds and leaves many immigrants struggling just to secure their place on the bottom rungs of the social and economic ladder.

Most members of Chicago's (and Erie's) Mexican community could be considered immigrants with voluntary status. But the anti-immigrant attitude of the public and policies of the 1990s repositioned them and other immigrant groups at the lowest echelon of American society. Previously, federal policy permitted immigrants to occupy low status jobs that sustained their hopes (Spener, 1996). But the new immigration and labor policies attempted to close the door on those who worked ten hour days and still attended English classes, like my students. They alienated Mexican immigrants and much of the Latino community as a whole, imposing upon them something more akin to a caste-like status.

In an atmosphere where a particular ethnic group is ostracized so directly, calls for assimilation have little merit. In such an environment, pushing a multicultural agenda absent a critical perspective is naïve. Likewise, critically neutral language and literacy policies lose merit. Amidst the debates over English only or variations on bilingual education, Spener (1996) argues that the education system is set up to provide Latino immigrants with an inferior education and to create "a pool of adults who are qualified to be economically exploited, unemployed or underemployed" (p. 78). Spener continues,

> In the United States, where race and ethnicity frequently form the basis of low-status . . . the assumption [of compensatory education] does not hold true. Educational advocates for immigrants and language minorities must look beyond strictly academic themes and examine the adult roles open to these students in order to determine whether such programs do indeed facilitate both their advancement and mobility in our society. (p. 80)

In chapters 10 and 11 Olivia, a Brazilian student on a six-month tourist visa and a not-so-secret quest to find permanent legal status in the United States, receives an education about the roles of race, ethnicity, and opportunity in the land of her dreams. As part of her journey she strives to obtain a driver's license in the state of Illinois but finds the road to licensure obstructed by a racist, capricious and corrupt bureaucratic system. In chapter 11 Olivia joins other students in reading and discussing literature related to the Chicano experience. With the support of her classmates, who had already had numerous discouraging experiences in the United States, Olivia discovers that assimilation into the dominant culture let alone acceptance are uncertain outcomes for her or others who look like her.

Olivia discovers what critical race theorists argue to be the historical reality of the United States: racism is a common, ordinary, pervasive feature of our existence, not an aberration from the norm (Delgado & Stefanic, 2001; Dixon & Rousseau, 2006). Initially the province of legal scholarship, critical race theory (CRT) has recently found advocates and an audience in education (Ladson-Billings, 1999). CRT is related to traditional critical theory but narrows its focus to race matters. In an effort to further understand race as it relates to immigration, and to shed a brighter light on the experiences and perspectives of my students, an examination of CRT, though not an exhaustive discussion by any means, is offered here.

Most evolutionary biologists and sociologists agree that race is a social construction. There is little biological or genetic basis for identifying ourselves by racial categories. While our identities are shaped by far more than skin color and national origin, the social construct of race is still highly deterministic in our treatment of one another. Societies often use race to categorize people and address shifting priorities and episodic inclinations (Delgado & Stefanic, 2001). U.S. immigration history is replete with periods in which racial quota systems,

CHAPTER 9

sometimes construed as county-of-origin policies, have been used to secure admission for some (most notably, Northern Europeans) while denying admission for others (Southern Europeans, Asians, Africans, South Americans). As discussed above, many interpret the anti-Latino/Mexican fervor of the past twenty years to be a targeted rejection of these non-white, non-English speaking peoples, principally because they are less likely to assimilate into the white culture.

Critical race theorists explain that our liberal tradition founded on universal principles of western societies inevitably serves dominant members of society while constraining others. CRT challenges claims that objectivity, neutrality, colorblindness and merit can be trusted in creating a fair and equitable society (Dixon & Rousseau, 2006; Delgado & Stefanic, 2001). Contemporary immigration control advocates argue that their stance against illegal immigration rests on common principles concerning international borders and law abidance. That immigrants cross the border in search of food, housing, work and education is immaterial. Anti-immigrant advocates relegate such human rights to the realm of inconvenient truths. Similarly, immigration opponents may contend that race and ethnicity play no part in their position but the law and order stances they take are hardly race neutral. They may identify Middle Eastern Islamic terrorists as their greatest enemy but those most harmed by labor and immigration policies are Latin Americans generally and Mexicans specifically. What critical race theory calls for in such cases is, in fact, greater race or ethnic consciousness so that human rights injustices are clarified and the polarizing effects of public policies are more clearly understood. Then we may appropriately target remedies for social ills and inequitable policies.

Critical race theory also examines the historic tension between property rights and human rights. From the constitutionally sanctioned identification of Africans as human property to the confiscation of Native American lands to the removal of Japanese from their homes, racism and property rights have been intertwined throughout U.S. history (Ladson-Billings & Tate, 2006). Throughout the last century, zoning regulations and real estate interests restricted blacks and other peoples of color from purchasing homes in white, middle and upper class neighborhoods. In education, efforts to provide equal opportunity during the latter half of the twentieth century and now in the twenty-first century through desegregation, busing, or equitable state funding distribution formulas have not fared well given the entrenched tradition of property rights. Home ownership is generally a good thing. It is a remarkable achievement for many immigrants and others moving out of the lower classes. But those who live in areas with high property values secure for themselves the benefits of quality education virtually guaranteed through their rights as property owners (Kozol, 1992). If we expand the concept of property to a much larger context—that of a nation—we see how international borders outline national property and secure rights and opportunities for the people within them. When the U.S. wrested control of the West from Mexico in 1848 the line was drawn between those guaranteed protection and rights and those who would be excluded. A century and a half later, legislators rationalized the increasing number of deaths among border crossers at the U.S.

southern border by declaring the crossers to be undeserving of protection. They justified the elimination of benefits and rights for legal residents and further marginalized these people in U.S. society by emphasizing their alien status. The point here is not to disregard borders or to suggest that nations relinquish their responsibility for securing rights and privileges of their residents and citizens. But by dramatically increasing our southern border patrol efforts and targeting our anti-immigrant policies at Latin Americans, we have once again used property, albeit at a macro-scale, to justify race-based intolerance. We stand by principles of land ownership, property rights, and national sovereignty as we watch people of particular ethnic backgrounds struggle to survive.

As race and property are linked, whiteness and opportunity are also connected. Many in the critical race theory movement believe the privileges that come with whiteness (again, a social construct) need to be understood and that we should challenge those who readily use it to their advantage at the expense of others. Ignatiev and Garvey (1996) assert that "whiteness is treason to humanity" and call upon whites to acknowledge that throughout U.S. history becoming white has been synonymous with accessing power and privilege in society. Though some ethnic groups like the Irish, Italians, and Poles were initially discriminated against in the U.S., over generations they have gradually assimilated and gained acceptance in the white culture. They have eventually become white and secured greater access and leverage in the dominant spheres of society. CRT further calls upon whites to reject the advantages that come with skin color and to challenge the social structures that sustain their power and privilege (McIntosh, 1990). Whites are called upon to dismantle the numerous borders—from a fence in southern Arizona to the obstacles that prevent Olivia from obtaining a driver's license—that make white Americans feel secure while limiting freedoms and opportunities for others. Though white people always have the opportunity to return to their comfort zone, they too must be willing to cross and dismantle borders if they are to work side by side with immigrants or other marginalized people.

Finally (again, this is by no means an exhaustive discussion of critical race theory), much of CRT turns to the stories of peoples of color that counter the dominant discourse (Dixon & Rousseau, 2006; Delgado & Stefanic, 2001). The aim is to insert stories of non-mainstream (non-white) people firmly into the historical narrative of U.S. history. If space is determined to be limited, then some of the redundant tales of white manifest destiny have to give way for they are only one version of an as-yet elusive and multi-voiced truth (Zinn, 2005). The narratives in this text prioritize the voices of my adult immigrant students. This construction does not just serve the narrative structure by fleshing out the many personalities and motivations of my students. It is also a critical and political stance that I take. As an author, it is undeniable that I maintain the privilege of rendering interpretations of my students' lives while securing my place in the story. As a white teacher, I strive to foreground the Latino students and their voices in the narrative. Situating the voices of my students at the core of each chapter and telling their stories of hope and struggle is just one small effort in a larger movement to expand and break through the borders that surround all of us.

CHAPTER 9

RESPONSIVE LITERACY INSTRUCTION

For the most part, the multicultural education found in most U.S. schools is superficial (Nieto, 2000). Rather than infuse multiple perspectives and experiences across the curriculum, American schools typically set aside different times during the year (e.g., February for Black History or early May for Cinco de Mayo) to decorate classrooms and sample traditional cuisine. We fail to recognize that a curriculum is itself a cultural product that reflects and reproduces dominant white, middle and upper class ways of knowing and communicating in the U.S. Multicultural education has too often failed to interrogate the hidden curriculum (Jay, 2003). Alternative discourses and viewpoints are so far removed from the socio-pedagogical consciousness that non-white American cultures and their practices are most often reduced to the superficial. Without leaving the classroom we take our students on the briefest of innocuous visits to distant lands and times where they experience a Middle Eastern Kasbah, a Mayan ruin, or a black civil rights march. They then return safely home to their standardized curriculum. Such contrivances reduce culture to a series of curious artifacts and colorful personalities rendered sufficiently palatable for general consumption by a white student body. They are devoid of any features that might threaten the dominant culture. They fail to treat culture as complex and intricate and fail to realize that culture is an unfolding process with real people struggling through its transformation.

Nieto (2000, 2005) contends that multicultural education must be anti-racist, pervasive in the curriculum, intended for all students, and be recognized as an ongoing process. Multicultural education, she asserts, should promote social justice and should be synonymous with critical pedagogy. Nieto (2005) describes the journey that multicultural education has taken in recent decades. In the 1960s, deprivation theories identified genetic and cultural inferiority as the cause of poor achievement, particularly among African Americans. In the 1970s and 1980s greater recognition was given to incompatibility theory or incongruence between the practices and discourses of homes and the schools that serve them. Incongruence theories were followed by calls for culturally relevant pedagogies that value the interests and backgrounds of students. In more recent years, cultural relevance has given way to culturally *responsive* teaching which explicitly challenges schools to expand the curriculum and employ pedagogical practices that reflect student discourses.

Gay (1993) explains that responsive teachers need to be cultural brokers who understand cultural systems, interpret symbols, mediate differences and build bridges across cultures of the classroom and social contexts. Ladson-Billings' descriptions (1994) of effective teachers of black students suggest how teachers of any ethnic background can provide such relevant and responsive instruction. Tatum (2005) offers an extensive list as well as classroom descriptions of culturally responsive teaching practices that include high expectations for black males. Likewise, Moje and Hinchman (2004) describe culturally responsive literacy pedagogy for adolescents across content areas that bridge the gap between students' lives and the subjects they need to learn if they are to be successful in school. A common feature in the literature on culturally responsive teaching highlights the caring relationships that teachers build with students. Students who are marginalized by school practices, the content of curriculum, and pedagogical discourses are more likely to respond when they believe they are genuinely cared for through responsive teaching (Noddings, 1984).

Unfortunately, caring and culturally responsive pedagogy seldom make policymakers' lists of priorities or curriculum standards. Tatum points out that educational administrators typically fail to recognize anything but universal, acultural notions of best practice (2005). Responsive teachers, therefore, must engage in their own struggle to challenge and reshape the sanctioned content knowledge and literacy practices of the curriculum (Moje & Hinchman, 2004). When considering responsive multicultural literacy instruction, teachers might advocate for pedagogies that are informed by critical race theory or critical pedagogy more generally. But they will come up against a tradition that has chosen to shield all of our children from critical racial consciousness (Ladson-Billings, 1999).

In the West Town community of Chicago served by Erie Neighborhood House, Flores-Gonzalez (2002) conducted research in the local public high school where she revealed how school practices were highly unresponsive to students and, consequently, instrumental in producing a group of street kids who gave up on school and dropped out. Some of these kids found their way to Erie where they enrolled in GED classes and other programs. As described in the Introduction of this book, West Town was one of the most diverse Latino communities in Chicago and in the nation in the 1990s, with large numbers of Puerto Ricans and Mexicans and significant representation from various Central American, Caribbean, and South American countries. Olivia, the Brazilian student featured in the next two chapters, frequently lamented what she observed to be aimless, gangbanging kids in the neighborhood. She thought she had left such strife behind her in Sao Paulo. Filled with the visions of prosperity she expected to find in the America of her dreams, she was surprised to find such a diverse America but even more shocked and discouraged to discover so many people struggling to live a good and fulfilling life in the U.S. Her negative experiences in West Town led her to seek a new place to live out in the suburbs among more white people. Though Olivia was secure in her identity as a Brazilian (likewise all of the students maintained that they would forever be Mexican, Guatemalan, Haitian, etc.), she was unprepared to find that her brown skin and Portuguese accent could play so prominent a role in her quest for membership in U.S. society.

The question over appropriate language and literacy curriculum looms large in Olivia's case but also for all those kids who dropped out of the local high school. They require a caring, culturally responsive pedagogy that helps them to better understand their circumstances and take steps to a better future. Helping these students to overcome major obstacles in their lives could include a critical examination of social, political, racial, and economic contexts that frame their lives. Such an examination might lead them to pursue educational opportunities

CHAPTER 9

with renewed purpose. Of course, school bureaucracies seldom sanction such critical inquiry. To problematize those school practices that alienate students or to investigate the sociopolitical contexts that marginalize people based on race, ethnicity or immigration status are not practices embraced by most educational leaders. The subsequent steps in critical inquiry—identifying injustice, transforming students' consciousness, charting a course for cultural and political action—are even more rarely accepted. Even in adult literacy and adult ESOL programs where educators frequently proclaim the need for authentic, adult-centered topics and themes, teachers seldom deliver life-contextualized instruction that engages adults in critical, dialogic inquiry (Purcell-Gates, Degener & Jacobson, 2001, 2002; Worthman, 2006).

The delivery of critically relevant and responsive curriculum is not only constrained by educational policy. Purcell-Gates and Waterman (2000) explain that progressive scholars and classroom teachers alike who possess knowledge of linguistic and cognitive dimensions of literacy use have seldom promoted best practices in a critical context. The few ESOL experts and reading specialists that exist in adult education find their bag of teaching tricks inadequate to meet the goal of transforming students' lives. Likewise, few critical pedagogues steeped in the Freirean tradition have seriously embraced the latest language and literacy practices that could elevate the status of reading the word to its dialogic counterpart, reading the world. Curiously, reading books and engaging in extended reading and writing are often deemed elitist activities by community-based, activist educators. In taking this position, however, they fail to recognize that culturally relevant literature in a responsive curriculum can be a powerful force in fostering students' positive self-identities (Acosta, 2007) and further interrogating race, power, and privilege in society (Stairs, 2007). Unfortunately, too much of critical pedagogy, especially in adult literacy and adult ESOL instruction, has been unresponsive to those students who require advanced level literacy engagements in order to access discourses and institutions of power and then work toward their transformation.

In my classroom I endeavored to engage Olivia and the other adult immigrant students in extended language and literacy transactions. Engagement theory, according to Guthrie and Wigfield (2000), aims to link motivation with cognitive development and strategy use and involves several integrated features: goal or theme orientation, authentic literacy interactions, interesting text, support for developing autonomy, strategy use and guidance, and collaboration with others (Guthrie & Davis, 2003). The goals of my classroom were initially established through the students' Leadership agenda but they were also the subject of ongoing negotiation with the students. Authenticity and relevance were likewise part of the ongoing negotiation though I maintained some authoritative discretion. I carefully selected texts that aligned with students' interests and goals and promoted students' sustained involvement with literacy so that they could develop autonomy and independent use of reading and writing. My objective was not simply for students to spend more time with longer pieces of text. By prioritizing engaged reading, I was able to guide students to become strategic readers so they could pursue their individual goals and engage each other in meaningful and challenging transactions. The critical, responsive literacy instruction I provided engaged the students in sustained literacy activities so that they could become independent readers and continue their pursuits outside our classroom.

TEACHER RESEARCH

As explained in previous sections of this book, my teacher research effort was situated in a qualitative, ethnographic paradigm. Qualitative research seeks to reveal and illuminate phenomena of the classroom. It delves into and clarifies researchers', teachers', and students' questions. It aims to expose the lives of these classroom participants and the interactions between them. If researchers could actually get inside teachers' and students' heads; if they could better appreciate the nuances of their individual pursuits and motivations, then researchers could find out what really makes these people tick. Through observations and interviews researchers can get close. But the moment research subjects respond, the researcher doubts the information that is collected and seeks to substantiate teachers' comments through triangulation or "structural correlation" (Eisner, 1991), because, after all, in the mind of the researcher teachers and students might not really know what they are talking about. In short, researchers do not and should not fully trust teachers. Teachers and students haven't been trained to know and inquire about educational phenomena the way researchers have. But teachers are also right not to trust that observers will expose what the teacher believes essential to understanding a classroom dynamic. Observers' questions reveal interests that do not necessarily correspond with those of teachers. The observations are hopefully useful to the educational researcher and practice, but they don't necessarily account for teachers' intentions with students. There is at least one other side to the stories that observers tell and those stories are best told by teacher researchers.

In the following two chapters about Olivia and her classmates, I wrestle with matters of race in contemporary U.S. society. Few people, let alone teachers and educational researchers, make many friends by alleging racism (Ladson-Billings, 1999). Even though the Southern Poverty Law Center has documented ongoing white supremacist involvement in sectors of the anti-immigrant movement as well as a proliferation of violence toward immigrants (Mock, 2007), I would not ascribe racism as a conscious, motivating factor for most who express concern over illegal immigration. But I do believe that the recent xenophobia and specifically the intolerance of Mexicans in the U.S. must be understood as a chapter in the historical narrative of a racist country. As will be shown, my Erie students who had spent more than a few years in the U.S. understood that race and language significantly shaped the identity they sought to construct for themselves. But race was also the basis for the identity that was socially constructed for them by the dominant culture. Olivia, who had only been in the country a short time, was mystified by the role that skin color could play in what she understood to be a fair and egalitarian society. Throughout our interactions, I welcomed the students' longing to be members of such a society but I resisted contentions that it actually

CHAPTER 9

existed. As their middle class, highly educated teacher who was able to traverse numerous cultural boundaries and was always able to return to my comfort zone, I could expound on educational processes for attaining access to privilege and power. However, as a white, male teacher who believes fervently that Latin American immigrants at the turn of the new millennium are often victims of racism in the U.S., I remain conflicted about the promise of literacy education and the opportunity it may yield.

In Part I of this text, dialogue was presented as the necessary point of departure for a critical inquiry and learning to take place. Teachers and students should engage one another with mutual respect and without a predetermined outcome. Freire (1970) writes:

> Knowledge emerges only through invention and re-invention, through the restless, impatient, continuing, hopeful inquiry human beings pursue in the world, with the world, and with each other. . . . Education must begin with the solution of the teacher-student contradiction, by reconciling the poles of contradiction so that both are simultaneously teachers and students. (p.53)

Many interpret dialogic pedagogy as a call for elimination of the traditional teacher. It would seem that the teacher has less of a role in the critical classroom than in more traditional models, where a transmission-oriented or banking model of instruction occurs. In recent years it has become popular, especially in community-based literacy education, to replace the word *teacher* with the word *facilitator*. Such a term suggests an embrace of constructivist or critical pedagogy. Purcell-Gates and Waterman (2000) argue that laissez-fair practices often associated with the term facilitator may be an abdication of responsibility to challenge injustice. I am not so quick to discard the term teaching, nor my identity as a teacher. I feel privileged to respond to the calling (Hansen, 1995). Moreover, I found that the students at Erie Neighborhood House looked to teachers as the ones primarily responsible for planning and delivering instruction. They treated my role with respect and sought my recognition, calling out to me: "Teacher!" when they wanted my attention. I accept that students look to teachers, want them in their lives and expect them to teach. Whether teachers facilitate, coordinate, guide, lead, encourage or even lecture, these are all part of the repertoire. The critical-dialogic classroom should have a place for teachers whose minds are occupied by good teaching, generally, and who take a stand regarding the knowledge and experiences most worthwhile for pursuing a just and hopeful world.

The chapters in this part of the book, particularly chapter 11, describe a teacher who expands the zone of proximal development (Vygotsky, 1978) beyond what some might consider to be warranted in a student-centered classroom. But I am not a student-centered teacher. I identify myself as a response-centered teacher who expands the boundaries of the curriculum in order to promote experiences and learning that may not have been previously anticipated. After two months with my students, I chose to explore the issue of race in a more focused manner than we had done previously. Familiar with academic literature related to Latino acculturation, I wanted to know more about how my students perceived their status in their newly-chosen country at a time when their acceptance by the dominant culture was a significant political question. I knew more than the students about the history of the U.S. and I possessed a more critical awareness, or at least a different perspective, about their opportunities for success. While the students had previously identified race as one factor in the oppression they felt and internalized, I directed our focus more explicitly. I selected a short story, "Yo Soy Chicano" (Gomez, 1993), to read and respond to in order to learn more about how race and ethnicity were present in their experiences, in their perceptions of the U.S., and in their continued hopes for the future. As their teacher, I employed engaged, strategic literacy instruction and guided their development of a more critical, race-conscious perspective. As a researcher, I better understood what was important to me as their teacher at that point in time so that I could make new and better pedagogical choices.

CHAPTER 10

OLIVIA: WITH DREAMS OF ELVIS

The goal, then, is to facilitate new ways of perceiving and discussing students, not only as individuals but also as situated or embedded within a broader educational ecology that includes their household's funds of knowledge, and the realization that these funds of knowledge can be accessed strategically through the formations of social ties or networks. Thus, the formation of such social networks can form part of any classroom pedagogy. (Luis Moll, 2005, p. 283)

WILD IN THE COUNTRY

Two or three mornings each week, Olivia and Justine walked together to Erie. Olivia attended an introductory ESOL class and Justine attended her GED class. Along the way, they decided who would attend an afternoon tutoring session with me. Hoping I would not be too unhappy about yet another of her absences, Justine usually deferred to Olivia who was anxious to receive as much English instruction as she could fit in during the short time her tourist visa permitted her to stay in the United States. One of her goals was to become an English teacher for professionals in Sao Paolo, Brazil, where she lived permanently. In addition to attending my class and tutoring sessions where we worked on writing, grammar, idioms and oral reading, she also attended the basic ESOL class in the morning, where she reviewed grammar and phonics rules in preparation for one day teaching them. She met once per week with a volunteer tutor for more grammar and pronunciation support and attended two sessions per week in the technology center to develop her computer skills.

After a week in my class, she announced her plan to move to suburban Schaumburg with a Brazilian acquaintance. There, she had hopes of experiencing what she considered to be a more authentic American environment, or at least something that more closely resembled her American dream. She enlisted my help in finding a suburban ESOL program. However, a few weeks later when her plans to move fell through, she decided it was just as well, since she had grown concerned that she might never find "wonderful teachers" offering all the support provided at Erie.

One afternoon, Olivia arrived for a tutoring session but found Justine and me reading together. Olivia waited, though rather impatiently, until we were finished.

CHAPTER 10

Only a few minutes before class was scheduled to begin, Olivia reached into her portfolio for a few pieces of paper and set them on the table with the writing face down.

"You always want us to show writing to the other students," she said. "But this one I don't want anybody to look at. Sometimes, the things we are writing are not for other people to see."

"Of course," I responded, as she pushed one of her pages across the table. I quickly, silently read a short piece describing loneliness and disillusionment but also a bit of hope for the future.

"Do you understand?" Olivia asked.

"I think so. Do you want to talk about it?" I asked her.

"OK, maybe later," she said and then turned over the other piece of paper. "This one I can talk about. Oh, this made me so mad. I was really mad."

"You were really mad and so you wrote?" I asked, thinking about her literacy practices.

"Yes. I wrote because I want to say what I didn't," she explained. I eventually understood that she wanted to express pent-up anger toward her landlady, but was reluctant to confront her directly. So she composed a letter.

"Have you always been such a writer?" I asked, still thinking about her use of literacy.

"Pardon?"

"Have you always expressed your feelings through writing?"

"Yes. I told you that I used to write in the past." Olivia realized my intent. While she wanted me to be her grammar teacher, she came to understand that I wanted to learn more about the role reading and writing played in her life. "I used to write my thoughts. So I have more than one hundred [poems and essays]. I have a lot. I told you. They are in Portuguese. They are in Brazil. And I did not have time anymore, so I stopped."

"Now you have time again."

"Yeah, I have lots of time," she laughed. "I have wrote something, but I am going to say all the things I wrote to this person. Read it." She pushed the paper toward me.

As I began reading, Olivia's frustration and rage were apparent. I was her teacher and, at times, her confidante. Now I was to be her sounding board. Olivia was furious. She could no longer tolerate her landlady, a Brazilian-American woman who rented out a bedroom in her house. Olivia complained, "The woman, she picks up the other telephone and she listens when I am talking. She goes into my room when I am at school. . . . I bring home somebody that is very light complexion and she is very nice. 'How do you do?'" she imitated the landlady. "The other day, I bring home another Brazilian friend who, she is black, like African, and she ignored her. She treated her so bad. So bad. I am so mad. I have to get out of there. Oh, she is so intolerable. I can't stand that woman. I have to get out of there. I can't stand her. "With new students beginning to file in, I did not get a chance to read beyond the title of her piece, "Respect."

Two weeks later she told the class about another incident that upset her. Olivia was passing a lazy afternoon looking at dresses in a discount apparel shop when two African American children caught her eye. Olivia couldn't resist smiling as she watched the kids roam beneath the clothing racks, the bottoms of dresses and shirts tickling their heads. Their mother acknowledged Olivia's appreciation of the children's joyful play with a warm smile. Minutes later, Olivia was startled by the bellowing of the Asian storeowner. He had apparently caught the mother slipping clothing into a shopping bag. The mother abruptly dropped the bag and gathered the children in her arms before rushing out of the store and down the street with the owner following her to the sidewalk, threatening to call the police if she ever returned. He returned to the store, pulled two tiny winter coats from the shopping bag, inspected them, and returned them to the racks.

Olivia watched all this transpire and grew upset. Those poor, lovely kids needed warm coats for the winter, she thought. Of course, their mother should not have attempted the theft, she maintained, but there was little reason to frighten and treat the children that way. She walked past the man without saying a word and vowed never to return to the shop. The other students in our class seemed to understand Olivia's exasperation, her sense that something was unfair. Still, they expressed little surprise regarding the mother's actions and the merchant's response. While Olivia was upset, she learned from her classmates that such was the world she had entered on the near northwest side of Chicago.

FOLLOW THAT DREAM

Olivia was among many students who joined the class for English instruction and discovered the focus on community leadership in the curriculum. To satisfy my writing requirements, but also to introduce herself to her new classmates, she wrote the following essay, which I helped her to revise. She read it aloud two weeks after joining us.

"Life"

Well, when we talk about personal goals what comes in our mind are many things like jobs, learning, etc. But at the bottom of our heart we have some secret, something that we wish. Since I was very young I used to watch TV. I watched films about Elvis, and I loved him. I started to think about it and how it would be fantastic to be in those beautiful places, where the films was going on. Hawaii!!

Then, I started to be interested in the English language, and the countries where this language was spoken. So, I entered the English school to learn. I used to read and look at different countries in many kinds of magazines. I started to love this language and I wished to talk it, and get married to an American! Why an American? You would ask. America started to be a dream for me. Everything happened in America. If I got married to an American my

CHAPTER 10

dreams would come true. I would speak only English. I would know all those places I used to hear and see on TV.

Then, the time went by and I went to England. When I arrived there I was so excited that I couldn't sleep at night. I couldn't believe I was there. I was at last speaking English in a place where nobody could understand my own language. I was so happy to believe I was there. I stayed there only for a short time, 3 1/2 months, and I came back to Brazil. After that I started to think about everything I had done and seen there: their customs, their way of being. I figured out: "It is not England." I want to know the USA. Now, here I am. After five years since I was in England. I am as excited as I was in the past. I got more experiences knowing people from different cultures. I am not flying. I am not dreaming. I have my feet on the floor. I want to stay here. I want to know the USA. I want to do my best in order to know everything I can to be helpful to me.

When life is boring and you have nothing more to do to change it, you change your life. You change the place where you live, you change the country. Thank God I could do it. My life was so boring, so routine that I couldn't stand it anymore. So now I can think about me, about my life because I am on my own. I don't have my mother to take care of. I don't have the obligation that I made with myself to be with her until she died. I have my other sisters and brothers who will take care of her. So, now I am free of this responsibility. I can live my life. I can make my dreams come true, "to get married to an American" and make him really happy, because doing this I will be happy too. I would feel myself so realized.

You see, life is so easy. You have only the opportunity to pursue your goals.

Olivia's tone and expression fluctuated while reading her essay. She was poised and deliberate through the first two paragraphs and excited when announcing her decision to come to America. She choked up when discussing her mother and was nearly inaudible as she approached the conclusion, almost mumbling about her dream to marry an American and her assertion that life is so easy. She read these words as if the ideas, so solid and unyielding at one point in time, now required more thought and reflection even as she read them. She put the paper on the table and scanned the faces around the table. "So that's what I wrote," she said.

The students were silent, thinking. Olivia was so unlike them. Her story was so distant. She came to marry an American! With the exception of Amalia, whose parents brought her to the United States at the age of sixteen because of her father's lucrative job, the mostly Mexican students did not know of such frivolity. They came to the United States not to live a fantasy but to make a living. None had immigrated to the United States in fulfillment of childhood dreams. They had little choice. The Mexican economy held little opportunity for their families. Some, like Lucía and Victoria, had seen the Elvis movies, too, but aspiring to marry an American was, to them, an insult to their culture.

When they finally did speak, the students were gentle. Some wanted to know about Olivia's mother, but she declined to discuss their relationship, suggesting she could write a book about that topic, maybe two. Regarding Olivia's dream of marriage, they were again gentle, but clear. Sure, they, too, might one day fall in love with an American, but that was not their dream. They would be just as happy, and more proud, to marry a Mexican.

On the other hand, most of the students, as legal residents or citizens, and with strong support networks in Chicago's Mexican community, were in the United States to stay. They were able to preserve their Mexican identities while attaining residency or citizenship status and privileges. Olivia's only hope to remain in the United States legally was to marry. Marriage and the prospect of citizenship were synonymous for her. The immigration laws were becoming more stringent and she could not obtain a work visa since she did not possess valued technology skills. Twenty years earlier, she had made the decision not to attend college, opting instead to study the flute during a brief stint at a music conservatory. Her work history in Brazil included a dozen years as a secretary—during which she endured repeated incidents of sexual harassment—and eight years in her mother's dress shop where she became a buyer, traveling the coastal cities between Sao Paolo and Rio de Janeiro.

Fitting in with the Mexican students at Erie House was not one of Olivia's goals. She repeatedly complained that their imperfect usage and Mexican accents inhibited her English development. She did not want to speak English like them, nor, she made clear, should they speak English like her. She desired the company of "Americans." This was certainly required in order to marry one, but if she struck out on that score, she still wanted to develop an American accent in order to fulfill her backup goal of becoming an English teacher in Brazil. She described the circumstances of her life as she saw them, saying "I once saw a film about an old Japanese man teaching a young man [I believe she was referring to *The Karate Kid*]. He told the young man: 'Your head is like a cup. It's filling and dripping too much. You have many thoughts. You have many dreams. But it's all going out.'" She further elaborated: "I have many things to do but first I have to study. Then, I have many things to do. Now I'm not dreaming, just thinking. And I don't want to stay among Mexican people. I want to go where there is more American people. I have nothing against Mexican people but I did not want to come to Mexico. I don't like this. It was not my goal. Even if I found many Japanese people I would hate it because I did not intend to go to Japan."

As far as I know, Olivia made such comments only to me during tutoring sessions and was always careful to add that she was not racist. She often felt the need to clarify that she had nothing against Mexican people. They were all so nice to her at Erie. Nevertheless, the students were aware of her feelings and ambitions, and occasionally informed her that she would likely meet with disillusionment. I occasionally responded that her dream of America might have been only that. This country, I informed her, is comprised of immigrants, and increasingly of those with complexions similar to hers and the other students in our class. While I did not deny existence of the white suburban America she was searching for, I suggested that in West Town, on the near northwest side of Chicago, she was sampling as strong and rich a taste of America as she might ever find.

CHAPTER 10

Still, Olivia was intent on pursuing her dream, and recognizing that she had traveled a great distance in its pursuit, I assisted her during our tutoring sessions to explore the United States. We consulted books and internet sites to investigate possible travel plans and destinations. When she received a letter from a friend in Brazil informing Olivia of a future trip to "Carolina of the North," I sat down at the computer with Olivia to learn about the state. She asked to look up demographic data and we found that the Mexican population in "Carolina of the North" was much smaller than the Mexican population in Illinois. Eventually, Olivia determined that she needed something that was quintessentially American in order to pursue her dream. She needed to drive and, therefore, she wanted to obtain an Illinois drivers license.

SPINOUT

After making a proper stop and yielding to traffic or pedestrians within the intersection, it is permissible for drivers on a one-way street to turn left at a red light onto another one-way street that moves traffic to the left. True or False? (Illinois Secretary of State's Office, "Rules of the Road," 1996, p. 35)

By coincidence, the Illinois Secretary of State's Office, which oversees the licensing of drivers through its Department of Motor Vehicles, was also the principal funding agent of community-based adult literacy programs in Illinois. Because state funds to support full-time teachers were restricted to the community colleges (see chapter 12 for more information), programs like Erie relied on volunteers who received training through the Secretary of State's Literacy Office, which provided oversight of the state library system.

The Secretary of State's Office, managing what amounted to a charity operation in adult literacy and having little expertise in language and literacy education, was likely unaware that reading *The Rules of the Road*, written to "assist you in developing safe driving habits," was frustrating for limited English speaking tourists, residents and citizens who hoped to drive safely. In the Secretary of State's Office, the division that promoted safe driving made the task more difficult than was perhaps necessary, while the division that might have addressed the difficulty and informed the licensing division about the reading challenges posed by the *Rules of the Road* appeared to have little influence.

A volunteer at Erie helped Olivia once per week with the *Rules of the Road*. But when she became desperate to get her license, Olivia also enlisted my help. For Olivia, an advanced ESOL student who had been driving for twenty years in her home country, the numerous syntactic and semantic shifts as well as unfamiliar vocabulary all displayed within a single sentence, were difficult to manage. Reading these sentences requires a constructive process of identifying the meanings of words and phrases amidst a fluent pace while attending to the broader meaning of a given sentence. Since each successive prepositional phrase in the sentence may alter the ultimate meaning of the sentence, readers must hold onto tentative meanings until the sentence is completed and then make a final judgment in response to the prompt in the *Rules of the Road*. While this challenge exists for all readers, second language learners can become easily confounded by the frequent shifts in meaning that accompany each prepositional phrase.

Critical analysis suggests that the syntax of *Rules of the Road* is governed primarily by the need for precise legal rhetoric and the desire to test the driving public on their understanding of that rhetoric. The concern for promoting safe driving appears to be a secondary matter. For an experienced driver like Olivia, one might be tempted to reduce the rule presented at the beginning of this section to: "At a red light, it's OK to turn left onto another one-way street." Olivia, or likely any reasonable individual, would assume that stopping first is expected, avoiding cars and pedestrian is prudent, and not driving against the flow of traffic is the norm, if not the law. But to be sure that the directives are made explicit, the language is more precise than that. Successful reading requires strategic approaches and a trial and error effort to navigate legal discourse.

Olivia's volunteer tutor took the approach of isolating each phrase and reconstructing the sentences as if they were stanzas of a poem. This syntactic focus worked to an extent but Olivia was impatient. While grammar, syntax and idiomatic expressions once interested her, now she wanted to pass the test and begin driving. Now, she needed to read in earnest.

I adopted a meaning-centered, constructivist approach. First, I scanned the text to identify the principle and rule being presented. Second, I sketched a diagram to highlight possible vehicle movements and contingencies presented by traffic patterns. With diagrams providing visual cues and background support, we discussed the possible traffic movements and how to approach different situations. I posed specific questions regarding a driver's decisions, questions that addressed the particular rules within particular contexts. For the most part, Olivia knew the correct responses but occasionally deviated from them, sometimes based on her experience rather than the rule. One question I posed concerned the following rule:

> *In urban areas, drivers moving out of an alley, building, private road, or driveway need not come to a complete stop before entering the roadway if the roadway is clear of traffic.* **True or False?**

Looking at my diagram and responding to my own question before actually reading the text, Olivia said, "I would stop, well not a complete stop. If you are coming out of an alley like this, if you are here you just look and if there is nobody, if there is no traffic, you go. You don't need to really stop."

"But the law says you do. If you want to pass the test you do," I replied.

"Well, I don't agree."

"Well, tell that to the examiner when you take the test or to the policeman when he gives you the ticket."

"OK, OK, you have to stop," she relented.

Moments later, after I read the text aloud and she reread it—the third step in our process—she answered correctly: "False." She would stop at the alley, building, or private road, at least for the test.

CHAPTER 10

The prereading discussion and diagramming helped Olivia to learn the material—to understand the Secretary of State's rules. But she still needed to read the text independently to perform well on the test. She asked during one session, "Do we have enough time to read carefully? Because if you read and just mark the test, you wrong. You have to read and read and read again." In a later session we attacked the text directly to prepare for the test. The text still proved confounding, at times, as the next example shows.

A driver must yield to cross traffic when on the terminating highway of a "T" intersection with no traffic control signs or signals.

"OK, so I'm here," said Olivia, pointing to a picture that already existed in the book. "Oh, what do they want?" She paused and then continued reading, "'*a terminating highway of a "T" intersection.*'"

I reread the sentence for her, pointed to the picture and added: "If I'm here and the traffic is going either way, before I cross over—"

Olivia interrupted my explanation with laughter. "Oh, that is so obvious. It is obvious, but they make it so difficult."

Another example of the text making the obvious difficult is illustrated by Olivia's response to the following statement.

A driver must yield to any authorized vehicle engaged in construction or maintenance of a highway that is displaying amber (yellow) oscillating, rotating or flashing lights. Yielding the right-of-way can help prevent accidents and save lives.

Olivia read the statement and responded, "No."

"No?" I was surprised, recalling that we had previously discussed the item. However, while I was explaining the scenario, she reviewed the statement and replied: "Oh, I see, instead of running into the truck, well, you have two options: you can run into the truck or yield the right-of-way. Oh my goodness, this is so obvious."

Yet another example of the difficulty an English language learner faces when reading the R*ules of the Road* is illustrated by Olivia's response to the following helpful hint:

Follow the general curve of the curb as you make the right turn. Stay as close as possible to the curb.

Olivia read the statements and then mumbled, "What's a curb?"

"Oh, a curve is like this," I said as I began drawing.

"No curve, curb. Curb!" she clarified.

"Oh, a curb," I responded popping the 'b' sound. We took turns popping the 'b' two or three times apiece. I resumed my drawing, identifying the street, sidewalk, grass and fire hydrants. But I only had two dimensions and cannot draw very well. "So the curb is the part that goes up," I informed her rather unhelpfully.

"The sidewalk? No, not the sidewalk," Olivia struggled to make sense.

"Between the sidewalk and the street, you step up on the curb to get to the sidewalk. Here's the street and here's the sidewalk. The curb is the part that goes UP," I explained, adding emphasis to the word "up" as if that would help to identify the second dimension.

"Look, this is the street," she said, pointing to my picture. "Then here is the sidewalk. This is the sidewalk. The little space here," she said, pointing to the line that I had drawn, "is the curb?"

"No, the part that goes up is the curb," I repeated, but suddenly realized that the curb probably included six inches of the horizontal dimension, in addition to the vertical. I then used my hands to form a right angle and re-attack the problem.

"Ohh," Olivia sighed.

"The sidewalk is higher, right?" I was not giving up.

"Hmm. If it is higher then it would be equal. It would be equal, no?"

"It's higher than the street."

"What? The sidewalk?" She was still confused.

"The sidewalk is."

"So this part here is the curb." She seemed to understand.

"Uh huh, yes."

"Oh, how strange," she sighed again. "OK, what do they want to know? '*Follow the general curve of the curb as you make the right turn.*'" She reread the statement.

I pointed to the picture again to identify the arc that the car should make, following the curve of the curb.

"Oh!" she responded, somewhat exasperated.

"Instead of driving from here to here and over the curb to get there, you stay on the road," I explained, trying to unlock the mystery behind the rule.

Olivia rolled her eyes, tugged the hair at the sides of her head and laughed—a healthy response, I thought. She exclaimed, "So this, they didn't need to put this. It wasn't necessary to put this, '*to follow the general curve of the curb.*' Of course, you have to follow. It's obvious you have to follow."

We then amused ourselves by discussing the inadvisability of driving over the curb, hitting pedestrians, fire hydrants, newsstands, parked cars, bicyclists, and possibly store fronts. I explained that they probably included the rule, in part, because it is against the law to drive on sidewalks and people need to know the law.

"So they can give you a ticket, right?" she asked.

"Well, then they could give you a ticket, yes. It's not just that it makes sense to stay on the street, but it is the law," I confirmed.

"So you are getting this ticket because the law is in the book," she said.

I nodded. It appeared that Olivia was mastering the legal and bureaucratic discourse. The privilege of driving in the state of Illinois requires candidates for the license to become proficient in legal rhetoric and bureaucratese. It would certainly be easier to study and learn from driving manuals that were written or revised (Hunt, 1982) for reading by the general population. Such a literacy experience may translate into safer driving. But the *Rules of the Road* and the written examination

CHAPTER 10

require that prospective and experienced drivers alike traverse unfamiliar discourses. Still, teaching and learning the privileged discourse of the text did not guarantee access to the driving privilege in Illinois in the late 1990s, as will be shown below.

GIRL HAPPY

Wearing a smile none of us could help but notice, Olivia arrived late for a class in early February. Taking a seat, she announced, "I got it. I got my driver's license."

"Let's see it," a new group of students responded.

Most of the fall semester students had moved to other classes. In fact, with the mobility afforded by the license, Olivia was to attend for only two more weeks before she moved to a southern suburb. The new students, with whom she was sharing her victory, had markedly less English proficiency and I had to adjust my literacy instruction accordingly. But it was these new students, most with little formal education in their home countries of Mexico, Guatemala, and Haiti (Justine's aunt had joined the class) and with a longer road to travel in terms of attaining English proficiency, who provided Olivia with the greatest boost in realizing her dream.

A couple of weeks earlier, Olivia had exhausted her study of the *Rules of the Road* and was determined to take the test. With a borrowed car, a friend escorted her to the examining station on the far northwest side of the city in a white-ethnic community. She stood in line for over an hour before reaching a clerk who told her she could not get a license. She could not even take the exam because, the clerk informed her, she was only a tourist.

Naturally, feeling dejected, Olivia told her new classmates of her dilemma. Immediately one of the Mexican students asked where she took the test. Shaking his head, he informed Olivia that she couldn't get a license from that examination station. She would have to visit a station on the southwest side of the city. Another student explained that Olivia would need to give the examiner a "tip." She should place twenty dollars—fifty to be sure—under the passenger seat where it would not be visible but would be easily retrievable. The student explained that upon entering the car, the examiner would pass his hand under the seat, feigning an attempt to adjust his position, and secure the money. If Olivia performed at a minimally competent level she would pass. Four or five students confirmed this to be the procedure for obtaining a driver's license in Chicago.

One week later, with her license being passed from one student to the next, Olivia was asked, "So, how much money did you leave?" She proudly stated that she did not leave any. She passed on her own merit. Just in case, however, she explained to the group that she rolled up three one-dollar bills and placed them just inside her hip pocket. The students laughed uproariously at the mention of leaving only three dollars for a tip. Olivia defended herself, explaining that since the bills were rolled the examiner could not have known how much he was getting. She then described what happened. Olivia traveled to the station recommended by the students. She arrived in the afternoon, as one student suggested, since at that time the examiners would be tired. "Everyone there looked more like we do," she said. "They were a lot of African American people and Latin people. They all had brown and black hair." Following a long wait in line she nervously approached the clerk, an African American woman, who took her information and without hesitation sent her to take the vision and written tests. Olivia spent a long time with the written test before finally submitting it to a Latino man. "He said I could get eight wrong. I watched him write on the test with the pen and I got nine errors." Olivia and I had spent hours preparing for the question and answer section but very little time on the roadway signs. Six of her errors were on sign identification. Olivia asked to see and was shown her incorrect responses. Twenty minutes later she was in line to retake the test.

"And, I passed!" she declared proudly.

"And you didn't even give them a tip?" one of the students asked for clarification.

"No, I did not need a tip," she beamed.

JAILHOUSE ROCK

In a very lengthy statement full of numerous prepositional phrases that would confound an advanced student like Olivia, not to mention native English speaking adolescents and adults with lower literacy abilities, the Illinois Secretary of State's Office website now includes the following notice under the heading "Bribery":

*Recent legislation authorizes the Secretary of State to deny for a period of **120 consecutive days** the issuance of a driver's license and/or instructional permit to any person who, with intent to influence any act related to the issuance of any driver's license or instructional permit, attempts to bribe or otherwise influence an employee of the Secretary of State's office, the owner of any commercial driving school licensed by the Secretary of State, or any other individual authorized to give driving instructions or administer any part of a driver's license examination.* (Cyber Drive Illinois, 2006)

After Olivia got her license, the Illinois media unearthed what it referred to as a "license for bribes scandal" in the Chicago metropolitan region. Secretary of State Office employees were caught in an insidious scheme of awarding commercial driver's licenses to immigrants and their employers in exchange for bribes. The bribes were turned over to Secretary of State (and future Illinois governor) George Ryan's political fund. Ryan denied knowledge of this and other corruption charges but was found guilty and required to serve a prison sentence. As the scandal surfaced, Chicago news media outlets reported stories of immigrant truck drivers threatening the safety of our highways. Indeed, at least one tragic accident in which several people lost their lives did occur. But the media seldom, if ever, looked at the lives of those who may have turned to bribing officials for the opportunity to work as truck drivers. To my knowledge, the media did not examine what it takes for foreign-born workers—legal residents, citizens, and tourists—to read and learn the *Rules of the Road*, which is provided to "assist you in developing safe driving habits" (Introduction). The use of literacy in the driver's license examination process is not unlike most conventional uses of literacy in testing. Literacy requirements work to either support or block access to the social privilege (or academic opportunity) and are typically accepted without critical appraisal of their sociocultural worthiness or pragmatic validity. That the process, in this case, is dominated by a legalistic, bureaucratic discourse at odds with the social good is a dilemma left to be resolved by those most needing to participate.

Though aware of literacy practice as a convention of social discourse communities, I was still amazed by what my immigrant students understood without much question: the literacy which proved so difficult to master, in the end, was insufficient. Attaining a license required the ability to work the system. Whether it is crossing the border, obtaining employment, attaining residency or citizenship, learning how to work the system to their advantage was the skill that proved most valuable to many of the students. The funds of knowledge (Moll & Greenberg, 1990) these students shared with each other situated the literacy practices associated with the drivers' examination—and no doubt numerous other social and bureaucratic literacy practices—within a more manageable and negotiable communities of practice arena. Of course, not all functional and sociocultural contexts yield the same opportunities to construct curriculum. As the circumstances described here suggest, teaching students which driver's license examination stations are more accepting of ethnic and linguistic minorities is not a topic for which teachers can be expected to prepare. But creating a classroom community where funds of knowledge infuse the curriculum ought to be part of the adult literacy experience. Olivia's experience obtaining a license offers a radical example of, among other things, how the pervasive practice of adult literacy education as discreet and decontextualized activity (Purcell-Gates, Degener & Jacobson 2001, 2002) is inadequate for addressing students' interests and needs.

Olivia entered an advanced ESOL literacy-focused class with a curriculum that examined sociocultural contexts of language and literacy use for adult immigrants. Within that framework, strategic literacy engagements linked personal experiences, social participation, and political realities with the many texts that were read, including those authored by students. Olivia's personal ambition to become American may, in the end, have been only a dream. But the identity she sought to confirm for herself was no less tangible than that of the other adult immigrant students whose goals were grounded in family survival. Each of the students, engaged in their own identity development work, appreciated literacy texts for their value in realizing short-term aims as they considered larger aspirations. In Olivia's case, strategic literacy instruction attended to the "general curve of the curb" while keeping an eye on what it might mean to become "American." In the process, both Olivia and I learned more about the twists and turns of the racial, ethnic, and bureaucratic terrain of the American landscape. Olivia, in search of her dream, heightened her consciousness of racial and ethnic tolerance and its role in shaping American identity. This most important of learning experiences did not come from me or any text we shared but from the classmates whose knowledge and insight clearly reverberated through their imperfect grammar and heavy accents.

CHAPTER 11

THE SKIN IS TALKING

I wrote this essay because I have a common belief in the liberty of man and also I think that some day the American Dream can become a reality and maybe not just a ideology in my mind. But more than that, I think that my essay provides a clear sight of the usual confusion that a immigrant have when they arrive for first time.

The dream of each hispanic is to come to the United States to verify whether or not all those wonderful things they saw in the movies are true. In their imagination they want to prove their chances in this country. They believe they be accepted in the United States and, maybe enjoy those beautiful places like the American people do. . . . (Amalia, Erie Neighborhood House Student, 1996)

GROWING UP

Until she submitted the essay excerpted above, titled "The American Dream," I was not sure if our critical inquiries held much interest for Amalia. She attended the majority of class sessions after joining us in October, but she did not talk much. Her journal writing and occasional comments reflected thoughtful engagement, but she expressed little of the motivation and passion of the Leadership students. After reading this second draft prior to a revision and editing conference with me, I realized she had seriously contemplated our readings and the Leadership students' concerns. In the opening paragraphs Amalia identifies the initial hopes and dreams of many immigrants but the bulk of the essay, which will be discussed throughout this chapter, unfolds as a scathing criticism of the treatment of immigrants in the U.S. Still, at the conclusion of her essay, Amalia's hope, enthusiasm, and desire to resurrect the dreams of her youth ultimately prevail.

Despite their age difference of twenty years, Amalia and Olivia had a lot in common. As Olivia's essay, "Life," and Amalia's "The American Dream" reveal, both women dreamed about the United States and about "those wonderful things" they saw in the movies. Both came from middle class families in their South American countries. Both were successful in their early years of school, and while Olivia opted not to attend college, both had the opportunity to do so. In these aspects, they were different from most of the Mexican students.

In Amalia's family it was always assumed she would attend college but Amalia thought that would be in Quito, Ecuador. She was shocked when her father, an Ecuadorian military officer, moved the family to Chicago when Amalia was just sixteen. Despite the move, Amalia's early ambitions for a successful business

CHAPTER 11

career and to make a lot of money persisted in the United States. She had an aptitude for numbers and had taken accounting courses in her private school in Ecuador. As mentioned previously, while waiting to enroll in a college she attended my class at Erie and worked at a downtown McDonald's where she was quickly promoted ahead of English-speaking Americans to a crew leader with responsibility for balancing the cash register receipts at the end of her shift.

Like Olivia, Lucía, and Brisa, students who joined our class for advanced English instruction, Amalia claimed not to care much for politics. She felt that while the world might be crashing down on immigrants that did not mean they had to either fight back or retreat into a malaise of despair. She would endure with her sights set on the future. During a discussion one evening of the presidential campaign, in which Justine adamantly declared her preference for Bill Clinton, a few of the non-political students also weighed in with their opinions.

"So, Clinton or Dole?" I had asked.

"Clinton! Don't even talk about Dole. I hate him!" Justine responded.

"I don't know. I don't know much about none of them, not Clinton or Dole. I don't like to hear about politics," declared Lucía.

"Me, too. I don't like it," Maya promptly agreed, leading me to wonder why she was a member of the Leadership class.

"They always argue but they don't find a solution," Lucía added.

"I think the same thing," Amalia announced.

Our classroom library offered many opportunities for students to explore their personal interests through a variety of genres. American and Latino classics offered an opportunity to read in English those titles that some students had previously read in Spanish or, in Olivia's case, Portuguese. U.S. Latino literature offered stories that mirrored the immigrant journeys of the recently arrived students as well as stories of those who had established themselves over generations. A collection of young adult and adolescent literature was available at various reading levels for students to engage and explore. As has been discussed in previous chapters, students were encouraged to read personal selections outside of class, to meet for conferences with me to discuss their readings, to discuss the books during our Talk time, and to make recommendations to one another.

Occasionally, to meet the interests of students like Amalia who professed to care little for politics, I introduced short stories like Gary Soto's "Growing Up" (1993), about a young adolescent Latina longing for independence from her parents. Such stories prompted students to talk about their adolescent lives, the differences between them and other young adult Americans, and the universal problems of adolescents. In response to Soto's story, the students engaged in protracted discussion of the tensions between them and their parents. Amalia complained about her curfew. Lucía complained about parental hypocrisy. Justine, as was to be expected, complained about her stepmother.

Maya, in turn, attempted to argue the parents' perspective, telling stories about her teenage sons who stay out too late at night causing her much consternation. "The parents don't want to see their children suffering," she offered in Spanish for us to translate.

In response to an assertion that he was lucky not to have a curfew, Luis said, "I wish I was to be with my mother," reminding us that he came to Chicago to work and send money home to his family in Mexico.

The group agreed that they should continue such discussions, to learn from each other how to negotiate their relationships. Still Lucía maintained a determinedly independent attitude that most agreed with: "I think it's our life and I think we have to live it, and we are going to have to make a lot of mistakes and we have to face them. We are not going to be always next to the fathers [parents]. We are going to go away from them. If we are going to be always next to our mommy or daddy, how are we going to live outside? We cannot."

TO BECOME AMERICAN?

After the opening description of immigrant hopes and dreams Amalia's essay takes an abrupt shift:

> ... *But the surprise come when [immigrants] arrive for the first time in the USA, and they see hatred in the North American's face. So in that exact moment they notice that their dreams were untrue and the reality is: "they're rejected in American society." Here, they're not welcome.*
>
> *Furthermore, this is the beginning of a disappointment for every hispanic and for an illegal immigrant too. They know that they need money to make a new life in the United States, having a disadvantage under North-American people, because they don't know English. For instance, they should be able to accept any job, surely with low salary. Day after day they come to know that they're having treatment as a minority racial, and that the government does not accept their stay in this country. For this reason, new laws would be created against immigrants, thus making a harder life for them. However, they have to live with all those problems and those problems will affect their children causing frustration and confusion in their life. ...*

Normally, I checked in with each student weekly to review their writing efforts, to explore new topics, to provide encouragement, to hold revision and editing conferences, and to teach grammar. For two weeks, Amalia put me off, telling me that she had a surprise in store and that she was working on something at home. When she finally submitted her essay, "The American Dream," I learned that Amalia's attitude toward political matters—at least rhetorically—had been transformed through increasing exposure to and consciousness of false promises and opportunities, the federal government's targeted assault on immigrants, racism, and intolerance. I speculated that, like Lucía, she might be trying to please an audience, submitting an essay she thought I might want to read—not a bad tactic for a college-bound student who would need to employ alternative perspectives in arguing her views. But Amalia assured me that while she was trying to address the course content she had gradually come to believe what she had written in her essay. She explained that our reading and discussion of David Gomez's short story "Yo

CHAPTER 11

Soy Chicano," helped to solidify many of the opinions she held. Despite the creeping sense of dejection unfolding in her essay, Amalia's determination to attend community college and then a university to pursue a business degree was as strong as ever. Her goal to become wealthy in the United States and someday return to Ecuador mirrored the longing of most of the students.

The majority of my Erie students maintained that if they ever became rich they would return to their home countries. Justine once explained that someday when she became wealthy she would buy everyone a flower and say good-bye. Back to Haiti she would go. Over time, however, the goal of returning home seemed to fade for most students. They realized they were not likely to become rich, yet the money they earned and the standard of living they established in the United States could never be obtained in their home countries. The younger students claimed that their parents, who brought them to this country, never gave up the dream of returning to their countries of origin. In contrast, the young adult students who had spent five or more years in the United States usually reconciled themselves to spending the rest of their lives in their adopted country. I had noted this phenomenon during my previous thirteen months at Erie and wanted to better understand it. I wanted to learn about stages of acceptance through which students commonly passed. I also wanted to understand their attitudes toward the dominant social and cultural values of the United States, especially at a time when the country was turning against those who aspired to embrace those values and, perhaps, assimilate. Finally, I was interested in how my students perceived the children of immigrants, including their own, those who would grow up more "American."

These interests led me to David Gomez's "Yo Soy Chicano" (1993) the short story that had such an influence on Amalia. I wanted to continue the exploration of relationships between youth and adults launched by our discussion of Gary Soto's story, "Growing Up," but with more attention to culture and race. The subject of race had arisen at various times in prior class discussions. During one discussion period the students debated the use of "Latino" versus "Hispanic." Most of the students used Latino. Hispanic, they argued, implied acceptance of European colonialism and the mistreatment of indigenous peoples. Still, most preferred to identify themselves by their country of origin: Mexican, Brazilian, Ecuadorian, Haitian, Guatemalan. On an earlier occasion, when comparing Jesse Lopez de la Cruz's story to contemporary struggles, the students identified race, specifically white America's fear of a burgeoning Latino population, as being at the root of recent intolerance of immigrants. The historical tension between descendants of white Spanish colonists and indigenous peoples in most of Latin America is often suggested as essential to Latino identity formation. Identifying one's membership in *La Raza* is part of coming to terms with this integration. Yet, upon coming to the United States, Latino immigrants confront a whole new construct of whiteness. Northern Europeans in the United States, perhaps to a greater extent than their Latin American counterparts, have a long history of condemning (or prohibiting) interracial and interethnic marriage and sex, as evidence by anti-miscegenation laws and other practices in the United States. This is not to suggest that the caste-systems found in Justine's country of Haiti or in many Central and South American countries were not cruel and despotic. But the students learned that white America can also be severely repressive when threats to its power are perceived.

As identified in the Introduction, a Chicano rights movement arose in the southwest of the United States in the 1960s. The movement exerted Mexican-American pride and political solidarity. It fostered a literary genre that continues to explore Mexican-American or Chicano identity. A common theme of the genre delves into the personal struggles of Mexican-Americans to reconcile their two cultural identities in the United States. While many of my students in Chicago, Illinois had heard the term "Chicano," none used it to identify themselves. The term belonged to a different place and generation. "Yo Soy Chicano" is an early chapter from Gomez's autobiography titled *Somos Chicanos: Strangers in Our Own Land* (1973). In the chapter, Gomez examines his early years at home and school in Southern California. An introduction to the chapter states,

> *It was not until he entered school that Gomez realized that mainstream society considered him inferior. Accepting mainstream standards, Gomez gave up his Mexican heritage. Yet he felt like an outsider among his white classmates and teachers. . . . In this autobiographical account, Gomez discusses the difficulties that arise from being caught between two cultures and feeling like an outsider in both. (p. 4)*

Unlike my students, Gomez grew up in the United States. As a child, he felt alienated from white society but as a young adult he attempted to gain acceptance in white society only to experience further alienation. He was uncomfortable with his family heritage but learned his options were limited to embracing or rejecting his culture.

I systematically approached Gomez's story with three objectives. First, as mentioned, I wanted to learn more about the students' evolving acceptance of life in the United States and their possible embrace of American values. Second, I wanted to learn how conscious of racial identity they were as they embraced those values, whether or not they felt conflicted by their acceptance of American culture and how they expected to relate to dominant white society. Finally, and specifically with regard to Gomez's story, I wanted to learn from their response to Gomez's portrait of himself as a child whose embrace of "American" values comes to include an embrace of whiteness.

I asked the students to write about their feelings during three distinct periods of their lives: the first year in the U.S., the second through fifth years, and the fifth through tenth years. With their written reflections completed we opened up our discussion. Luis began by describing his initial amazement at the size of Chicago. By continually expanding the space between his hands he illustrated how the more he traveled in Chicago the bigger the city seemed to become to him.

Brisa described her first experiences. "I felt lost. Cause I come from a small city [in Honduras] and I came here and I felt, 'Oh my goodness!' I have to ride [the bus], and the signs when I get on the bus, and when I get off, and I walk alone, and I would have to get off at the next corner. It feels so weird."

"Weird? What's 'weird'?" Olivia asked, and an explanation was provided.

CHAPTER 11

"You feel confused," said Amalia, referring to the size of the city.

"It's very different.... The sickness, the homesickness," said Timoteo.

"You miss your family, your friends," said Luis.

"Your girlfriend, your wife," Timoteo chimed in.

"We miss our home country. We think about moving back," Lucía continued.

"Oh, don't remind me. Don't make me sad," Luis sighed. "Sometimes you just want to buy a ticket and go home."

I asked about initial encounters with "North Americans," an awkward term, but one that a few students had used in recent discussions. We occasionally determined the need to avoid the term "American" when designating people from the United States since the Americas included much more than the United States. However, we usually failed to be consistent in our effort to avoid the term.

"Sometimes," Timoteo paused and looked around the table before saying, "I feel discriminated."

"The people who live here? They discriminate." Victoria added. "I came here in November and I went to spend Thanksgiving in the suburbs and the people who lived there, they didn't speak to me. They didn't say anything. They was white people."

Brisa's experience was different. "No, I was lucky that didn't happen to me. You know when we came here and I met some people, cause my sister-in-law do a lot of cleaning in downtown, and all them were nice to me. And I was like shy and I didn't want them to talk to me because I didn't know how to answer them in English. They were nice. They understood that."

Yet another new student had joined our class that evening. Pablo, a forty-year-old who annoyed many of the others by thumping his fist on the table in order to overcome his limited English and drive home his remarks had listened to the discussion and was ready to join. Thumping away, Pablo told us that he lost his job in Chicago after moving his family from Mexico. His Mexican landlord evicted the family, forcing them into a temporary shelter and dependence on the donated food and winter clothes available at Erie Neighborhood House. The donations, he insisted, were mostly from white people. A few years later, when Pablo was again out of work, his white landlord granted a few months rent reprieve. Pablo thumped his fist louder and cautioned against generalizations. In fact, he claimed, "You cannot always trust—how you say—you *paisano*, you countrymen."

I moved the discussion forward, though still quite a distance from the Gomez story, asking the students about their feelings and experiences during the second through fifth years.

Luis explained that he began to feel better. "I meet more people. I make friends with different kinds of people."

Victoria struggled a little more than Luis. "In the first year, I want to go back to Mexico. And in the second year, I still want to go back," she said. "But after three years I start to adjustment. But in the second year was terrible for me—the first and second year—cause I miss my family and friends. Here, I used to go out but not like in Mexico [where] every weekend I went to another place and socialize."

"It's better when you understand more English. It's more friendly the people with you," Pablo said.

Brisa agreed. "I feel like free, like I can come in and go everywhere and you know when I speak English I can answer them. I feel like you know, before [learning English], like a child."

Following a pregnant pause, I asked if the students had begun to feel like the United States was their country during that time frame.

"Yes," Lucía said.

"I don't think so," said Timoteo

"It isn't my country," Luis added.

Olivia, having been in the United States for less than one month, carefully employed an idiom to describe her expectations, "I think you always feel like a fish out of water." She looked around the table to gauge the success of her phrase. "I think so. Not only in the first year. I don't know how long you feel this way. I used to feel that way when I was in England because I was not one of them. I was different. So, I used to feel like a fish out of water."

"That's right. There are some people here who has thirty years or even fifty, and they still miss their country. They miss their culture. They not comfortable here," Timoteo said.

Everyone agreed that their feelings toward the people of the United States improved with their development of English.

Pablo summarized, "The magical word is English."

"Oh yeah!" Brisa agreed.

"After this you can do everything," Pablo continued.

Victoria said: "Oh yeah, when you can communicate, you can reply—"

"Or you can fight," interrupted Pablo, who again thumped his fist on the table as he related a story of having demanded greater respect with his white American boss. Pablo had challenged his boss's practice of assigning Mexican workers to simple tasks that the boss could more easily explain to workers who had limited English.

Only a few students had been in the United States for more than five years, but their stories were significant for the comparisons they were able to make to their home countries and to their first few years in the United States. Their material lives significantly improved and this change in circumstances was confirmed with each return visit to the home country. It was during such visits when they began to consider living in the United States the rest of their lives.

Brisa reflected on her first year, recalling her experiences with public transportation. "Thank God I have my car now!" she exclaimed. "I don't have problems getting around." She then made comparisons to Honduras. "When I go to my country for vacation I don't know what happened but I spent one month and I feel like something's missing. You know, missing something. After one month I feel like I am in jail. I just want to fly back. Oh my goodness . . . I went back two years ago. Gosh, just terrible. So, you know, you say, 'Why, I have a job [in the United States] and I live good and it is hard here [in Honduras].' And you think, 'Man, I don't have a house here and I don't have a job. How could I live here?'

CHAPTER 11

That's when we say, 'Well, at least we have over there something, you know, work, and we can do better living.' So it's then you realize that maybe you can spend the rest of your life [in the United States]."

Timoteo also described his return visits and an emerging appreciation of Chicago. "I have like seven years. The first time I come here was in 1989. But I went back for five months and then I come back. I went eight months and then I come here again. Since the last time, I feel that it's very different than the other times. Now I'm trying to improve myself, learning new things, going to different places. Like the first time I was here I didn't know any nice places in Chicago, like the Aquarium, the Planetarium, some nice parts out of the city. I'm taking English classes and Leadership classes. I think I am enjoying more. I am not wasting my time." Timoteo struggled for the word to describe his new outlook and desire to make good use of the opportunities available to him, repeating the Spanish *aprovechar* twice.

Lucía supplied a translation for Timoteo, saying, "to take advantage."

"I am taking advantage," Timoteo continued, nodding his gratitude to Lucía and perusing the faces of those students with less time in the country. "Because I think when I went to Mexico I came back with a different vision, with a different way of thinking. Like I want to save some money, but I want to enjoy it, to improve my living circumstance."

It seemed clear that the longer my students stayed in the United States the more likely they were to grow comfortable with the language, the economic and material opportunities, and the culture. One might be tempted to say they were becoming "American." In anticipation of the Gomez story we were about to read, we had laid some groundwork for understanding why immigrant children might embrace the culture of the U.S. and reject their parent's heritage. By the story's end, I would hope to see how the students understood their acceptance of the new country as compared to how a member of the next generation might feel about being American.

In fact, I wondered if my students would ever consider themselves American and decided to ask them. "Do you feel the longer you are here, you are becoming more American?"

"No!" Amalia responded without hesitation.

"We will never be. We are Hispanic," Olivia said.

"Hispanic-American, Latino-American. We are Americans right now," Luis reminded us.

"We are American right now. We are not North American," Lucía added further clarification to Luis' reminder that they had always lived in the Americas.

But Olivia was thinking of the common, easy-off-the-tongue use of the term American. "We will never be American," she said. "I think American people will never see you as American. They will always see me as Brazilian. I will always be Brazilian."

"How do you see yourself?" I asked, wondering also if she realized that in this country it was more likely that people—white people in particular—would usually look at her and label her as Hispanic or Latino at best, but seldom Brazilian.

"I am Brazilian," she responded with pride, yet with a matter-of-factness that allowed no other possibility.

Looking around the table, I asked, "So you could be here the rest of your life, but you will always be—"

"—Mexican!" Several voices responded.

Moving closer to the Gomez story, I seized this opportunity to move to the next stage of my inquiry. "What if you have children here? How would you like your children to feel? How would you like your children to identify themselves?"

There was some initial hesitation on the part of the students to speak their minds. Eventually Timoteo offered a measured opinion, "Some feel like American. Some feel like Mexican. It's kind of confusing."

Olivia provided her assessment, "Children don't feel the differences of race or difference of color. They don't feel anything. People teach the children how to feel. You can see a child—they go to black people. They go to Japanese people. They love all of them and after when time goes by, they grow and teach them how to feel. And then they separate their persons. A child is perfect in their feelings."

Victoria, who worked in Erie's day care center, added her observations, "I don't know how the little kids know there is discrimination because I work with little kids and they don't want to speak Spanish. They hear a lot of Spanish and they talk to me in English. I ask them to talk to me in Spanish. They say, 'Oh, I don't know how to say this.' So I tell them but they don't want to speak Spanish. I ask them why and they say, 'I don't like it.'"

The subject of children's refusal to speak Spanish was a sore point for most of the students. It was viewed not only as a problem within families but also a rejection of their cultural heritage.

"I don't like it," Luis said. "If I have children, even if I know English pretty well, they will learn English at school, but I'm going to help them with the Spanish. If I have someday a kid, what happens if I want to take them to my country and they don't know anything about Spanish? What are they going to do? They going to feel very afraid or embarrassed with their relatives over there. I know people who is like that." Luis mentioned acquaintances who do not teach Spanish to their children, but Luis was confused by such narrow thinking. "It's good to know English," he said. "But it's a lot better to know more than one language. If they can know English and Spanish it is better, so why not?"

Lucía indicated that she had something to say. "I have a cousin. He came here when he was like three or four years old and now he's nine years old. And he always say that he's not Mexican."

Timoteo gasped. The other students turned to each other muttering their disgust. To disavow ethnic identity was a distressing transgression.

Lucía continued, "He does. He say he's not Mexican. He doesn't want to talk Spanish because he says he hates Spanish. He hate the Spanish people."

Despite the bitterness felt by the students, their response turned from grousing to silence, conveying, it seemed, recognition but also sorrow, a personal hurt. Olivia's mouth dropped open and remained open: it seemed as if she could not find the words to express her feelings. Pablo stared at his hands resting motionless on the table, probably thinking about his own children and their diminishing Spanish, which he would later describe to us. Timoteo gazed over Lucía's shoulder, out the window, as he wondered about these children in his adopted country.

Amalia eventually spoke up. "I listened to some teenage boys who don't like to speak Spanish because their friends are American. They say Spanish is not important here. It's not the language of the future; English is the language of the future. And they feel embarrassing when they hear about Mexican and Ecuadorian customs."

"But if Spanish is not the language of the future, it is still not bad to speak two languages," Luis reiterated, appealing to common sense.

While the students felt dejected, no one else suggested how the children of immigrants might feel, how they had come to adopt such attitudes. I decided, finally, that it was time to read the story.

TO BE THE BLUE EYES

I read the first line of Gomez's story: *My early schooling was a terribly destructive experience for it stripped away my identity as a mexicano and alienated me from my own people, including my parents* (p. 5-6). Olivia responded immediately to the first sentence, declaring that schools would be the villain in our story. I asked how Gomez' identity was stripped away, but did not wait for a response. I let the question linger as I read Gomez's description about the privileging of everything white and European. I read about his teachers calling the children Spanish, not Mexican. Gomez explains that they wanted to *soften the ugly sound of Mexican by calling them Spanish*. He further explains that classmates called him a *dirty Mexican*. I read the last lines of the paragraph: *If we Mexicans wanted to survive at all we would have to become* white. *And I wanted to be* white (p. 6).

Lucía responded after listening to the first paragraph, "I think that's why he doesn't want to be Mexican or Latino. In the school the kids don't want you, nor the teachers. So he start thinking that Mexican or Hispanic is not good. Instead he being white."

Luis understood young David Gomez's plight but not his resolution, "He says they call him dirty because the skin is brown, right. So what could he do to stop them calling him dirty? He said he wanted to be white but how he change his skin?"

Pablo linked the story to our earlier discussion, "I think it continually happens today. The kids want to be like white people. They want to be like them today."

After I read the first paragraph, the students volunteered to read aloud. Their reading was fluent, interrupted only by classmates' comment on events in the story. The responses to the first pages were enlightening, not only for their interpretive insights, but for the immediate recognition of the impossible situation children of immigrants face. These children, we were learning from the story and the students were readily acknowledging, are often confronted with an irreconcilable dilemma yet forced to make troubling choices. Continuing our journey through Gomez's childhood, we learned of the humiliation he felt when his mother came to school and called to him in Spanish. We read about young Gomez's longing for white friends and his giving away a prized possession to a white boy he hoped to befriend who, in turn, continued to ignore David. We read Gomez's explanation of the incident, *Perhaps, I somehow knew all along that I could not buy his friendship and that all I would succeed in doing was to pay homage to the symbol of what I most admired and wanted* (p. 9). Olivia stopped us to find the definition of the word "homage."

Lucía then commented, "He wanted to be a gringo."

"He admired a lot to be the blue eyes," said Luis.

"He got a lot of problems in his mind," Olivia suggested.

"Not in his mind, in his life," Lucía responded.

I asked Amalia if she liked the young David Gomez. She shook her head.

Luis offered a more generous assessment, "As a boy all you want is to be playing with your friends. All you want is to go out during a break from school."

We continued reading the story, discussing vocabulary, commenting and sighing as we learned of Gomez's continued alienation through his elementary years. We learned, however, that in high school Gomez met another Mexican boy, Leo, who demonstrated by his own example that Gomez could succeed in the school and eventually attend college. Gomez went to a university where he enlisted in a Marine Corps Officer Training program but soon dropped out of the program. He explains, *My heart wasn't in the program and in that sense my failure was a fitting end to something I should never have attempted to be: a white Macho whom other whites would accept and admire* (p. 17). While Gomez continued at the university, his friend Leo attended a city college but dropped out after his second year. Gomez then ended their friendship. He writes at the end of the story, *[Leo] was the last Chicano I would have as a real friend for years to come. At least in the way I treated Leo, I had indeed become the gabacho I so desperately wanted to be* (p. 17).

Upon reading the final sentence, Olivia explained that she understood the story until the very end: "I did not understand this end. . . . What does he want to say? *At least in the way I treated Leo, I had indeed become the gabacho I so desperately wanted to be*? He said that he became a gringo? *Gabacho* is gringo, yes? He is saying about Leo or about the white world? He confused himself as gringo to Leo or to white people?"

"To white people," Pablo responded.

"He wanted to be white real bad!" Brisa added.

"Yes, but why put Leo here?" Olivia pressed.

I suggested we look at the last paragraph and reread from it in order to find an answer to Olivia's question. I read,

> . . . *I was also cut off from my Mexican roots. Nor was I able to look to Leo for friendship or emotional support. He had dropped out of college after the second year, and that, coupled with his being Mexican (a mirror image of what I had tried to put behind me) led me to have less and less to do with him until we were no longer friends. Leo was the only Chicano I knew who had gotten as far as college with me (a remarkable achievement for Chicanos!),*

CHAPTER 11

and it seemed almost natural for him, as a Chicano with his roots in the familia, to drop out. He was the last Chicano I would have as a real friend for years to come. At least in the way I treated Leo, I had indeed become the gabacho I so desperately wanted to be. (p. 17)

I turned to Olivia. "So your question: Was he acting like a *gabacho* or gringo to Leo or like a gringo to other gringos? So what is the answer?"

"Yes, I don't know," she replied, her eyes begging me to provide the answer from a teacher's perspective.

"That, I think, is for us to try to understand," I responded. I could have provided an answer that I believed was available from the evidence in the story. Implicit in the sentence, and consistent with the rest of the story, was the understanding that *gabachos*—a somewhat derogatory term used to identify white Americans—treat Mexicans poorly. Thus, Gomez would not be accepted by the white world. He could not be a "gringo to other gringos." However, I was hopeful that the students would explore Olivia's question with its relevance to their own lives. Based on their experiences what expectations did they have for David Gomez? Did my students ever expect to become *gringos*? Could they or their children establish membership in white America if they wanted to? With the students' perspectives still to be revealed, I refrained from answering Olivia's question with the response I believed to be obvious.

Olivia continued, "I think they mix understand. I think for me it's mixed here. I'm not saying his treatment. I'm saying his feelings. He felt: *At least in the way I treated Leo, I had indeed become the gabacho I so desperately wanted to be.* He felt like a gringo to Leo or to white people?"

"OK, that's one thing we cannot see. We have to interpret it," Victoria declared, thereby leading us back into the pages of the story to unravel the plot.

After a few passages were reexamined in an effort to gather evidence, Pablo attempted a thesis: "I think the problem was for him, the whole life he was fighting to try to come into the white people, to enter the group, no? And in the sentence in [the story] he is fighting with hisself because the white people don't accept him."

"So, is that the answer to Olivia's question?" I asked, getting a frustrated look from Olivia, who, I sensed, still wanted a correct answer from me.

"You want to know who is the *gabacho*, no?" Pablo asked Olivia.

"Yes, I did not understand [the sentence], *At least in the way I treated Leo, I had indeed become the gabacho I so desperately wanted to be.* He's gringo because of his treatment to Leo only? Or he felt gringo among the white people?" Olivia repeated her question, clarifying that she understood Gomez's attitude toward Leo.

Brisa weighed in, "What it say here . . . he putting the Mexican people behind him. He wanted to be accepted. Maybe he don't want to be Mexican. Maybe he wasn't that but he wanted to be accepted by the others."

"Yes, by the white people," Pablo responded. Then with a sarcastic tone, perhaps contemptuous of a course that he believed white America expected him to follow, he added, "After you resident, you citizen. Now when you citizen, you are American." But this scenario did not fit him. Thumping his fist repeatedly on the table, he declared, "Now, I am resident. But after that I am Mexican. When I born,

THE SKIN IS TALKING

I am Mexican. When I die, I am Mexican. It's very simple. One time a person told me, 'My heart I got in Mexico. My stomach I got in the United States.'"

Consistent with feelings expressed by most students before reading the story, Pablo asserted that he would always be Mexican, regardless of the lifestyle or values he adopted in the new country. There was no question of becoming a *gabacho* or *gringo*. However, maintaining one's cultural affinity with the home country was not so easy once it was left behind, as Brisa illustrated by recalling a conversation with her sister, "My sister ask me: 'Are you planning to go back to your country?' So I say, 'I don't know. Maybe when I die.' And she say, 'They don't want your stinking body.'"

A moment of silence passed before several students understood the meaning of Brisa's comment and laughed aloud.

"So then, back to Olivia's question," I said, attempting to return us to our discussion of Gomez's story. "In his treatment of Leo, he felt like a *gabacho*. But does he actually become one? The story stops there."

"No, I don't think so," Brisa answered.

Most of the students agreed that Gomez did not become a *gabacho*. Indeed, he could not become a *gabacho*.

Victoria, a college freshman, held out a possibility: "Not physically, but maybe emotionally or socially . . . he was accepted by the other world because he got more education. Maybe that's why he felt like a *gabacho* because he entered the other world."

"So this is what I'm [asking]. I understood he felt *gringo* to Leo, [but] not in the white world?" Olivia was in distress. As described in the previous chapter, she had come to the United States with visions of Elvis Presley movies in her head. She entered on a six-month tourist visa but hoped to marry an American and remain in the United States. Upon learning of this plan, most of the students rolled their eyes. Seeing the disdainful looks on their faces, Olivia assured us that she would marry only for love. But her plans were not panning out before her, at least not initially. America, from the vantage point of her Chicago neighborhood, looked nothing like the Elvis Presley movies. She had been considering a move to the suburbs. While Olivia had previously declared she would always be Brazilian, she wanted a clear understanding of her options. She wanted to know if she could pass in the new country. She repeated one last time, "He said: *I had indeed become the gabacho I so desperately wanted to be.*"

Our conversation continued for a few more minutes as Brisa and Victoria returned to the text and tried to interpret Gomez's feelings. Brisa decided, "He really wanted to feel like a white boy. He's frustrated. This guy, he's very frustrated."

By discussion's end, it appeared that the students were prepared to address only one facet of Olivia's question: Could David Gomez ever truly *feel* that he was a *gabacho*, a *gringo*, a white boy? The story suggested very strongly that the white community would never accept him unless he at least tried to become a member. However, there was nothing to suggest that making this attempt would guarantee acceptance, let alone an embrace of Gomez by white society. In the discussion

CHAPTER 11

immediately following the story, the students refrained from criticism of whites as a group. Gomez's characterization of white people's intolerance needed no further exploration. At the time, I made a pedagogical choice not to provide Olivia with the "correct" answer. I believed that Gomez's choice of words was deliberately ambiguous, though the context, as most of the students appreciated, made the meaning clear. I decided that the interpretive challenge was Olivia's, and I, therefore, refrained from providing the expected ESOL teacher response.

But my stance was not merely pedagogical. I did not feel prepared to speak on behalf of white America. I would not offer false assurance of acceptance and equality, nor did I feel that I could suggest multiculturalism as an answer. At a time when Latino immigrants were so clearly under assault, I considered such a claim to be naïve and inconsequential. Moreover, Gomez's story belied the hope of those who believe equality and fairness will come through a multiculturalism that is devoid of a critical perspective. I could not and would not tell Olivia that after she learned enough English, Elvis Presley would be waiting out in the suburbs with open arms. I never answered Olivia's question to her satisfaction.

INDIVIDUAL LIBERTIES AND THE LIBERTIES OF OTHERS

Though she remained mostly silent during the reading and discussions surrounding "Yo Soy Chicano," Amalia was certainly thinking. Her three months in our class marked a transition period from high school to college, from adolescence to young adulthood. She had some time on her hands before beginning college but nobody required her attendance in our class. She came and listened intently to the other young adults, most just a year or two older than her and who were making their way in the world without many of the opportunities available to Amalia. The ideas presented in her essay which was submitted two weeks after we competed our study of "Yo Soy Chicano" were taking shape in her mind as she pondered the literature, the response from the other students in class, and her passage to adulthood in the U.S. Her essay continues below.

> *... Well, anyways the immigrants wish of a better life has broken and now they're in such a humiliate position that the immigrant is able to accept all kind of aggression in order to earn money and try to have a better life, like a North American.*
>
> *You have to learn the rules of the game. You have to know the hard way that the Hispanics have and that sometimes the government can take the wrong decisions that affect you. And, also I believe that here the Hispanics are not living happy, and they are just surviving in a racist society.*
>
> *When you get involve in community problems like gangs, poverty, racism, etc., that perturbs my liberty. You find that people everywhere, trying to confuse your own beliefs. These people are persons who lost their individualism and the motivation to get to perform the American Dream.*
>
> *But fortunately many people think like me too. They have the same dreams and expectations. And it a hope for me and my individual choice and*

THE SKIN IS TALKING

goals to be against the people who want to destroy our dreams with illogic excuses. . . .

In the class session following our reading and discussion of the David Gomez story, I presented three lists that identified the students' feelings at different stages of their lives in the United States. The lists included the feelings students expressed about their first year, second to fifth years, and fifth through tenth years in the U.S. Each held eight or more descriptors and most of these pertained to economic opportunity. But when I presented a list that captured the students' feelings about children of immigrants born in the U.S. we saw that it only had three items and none included description of children's feelings. The three items are below:

- children don't want to speak Spanish in public
- children don't want to identify with parents' culture
- problems in home regarding language and culture

Pablo looked at the three items and was reminded of his fifteen-year-old son who was born in Mexico and lived in the United States for only five years but was already losing command of his Spanish. Luis again complained about young people who won't speak Spanish even with the family. I asked that the students think not just about the actions but also about the feelings that underlie those actions.

Luis remarked, "They are like the guy in the story. They want to be white maybe. They get embarrassed about the culture."

"I think he was not happy," Olivia said. "He wasn't happy. I think he used to feel small, less than everybody. He is very miserable. I think he feels he is nothing. He feels nothing, nothing."

Lucía agreed, "I think he was like that and I think he is confused. Because at home the fathers try to teach them how to be part of a culture, and the school, teachers and the other kids try to teach them how to be part of another culture. So we don't know what these children will be like."

After a few more comments were offered the students agreed to add the following cultural-psychological items to the list:

- feel discriminated against for speaking Spanish
- embarrassed about culture
- want to be white
- feel small, less than other people
- feel nothing
- confused over which culture to be proud of

With the chart completed, I explained that I was going to adopt a devil's advocate position. After explaining the term "devil's advocate" I pointed out the changes that the students had undergone by the time they reached the five to ten year period of residency in the U.S.:

CHAPTER 11

- trying to improve yourself
- not wasting time
- getting a car
- living better economically and emotionally
- getting used to the cold
- beginning to think you can live here the rest of your life
- realizing when you visit your home country it is not as good
- planning to buy a house

Considering these changes, I asked them, "The longer we live here the more we accept the North American values and we get accustomed to the way of life here. America is getting better and better and you're thinking 'This is where I'm going to stay.' But when you have children, what are they supposed to think? Why should we think they would respect your home culture if you've already left it behind?" I looked around the room to gauge the faces of the students. Most were pensive.

Lucía responded first. "We accept to be here and live here maybe the rest of our lives but we don't forget our home culture. We don't forget about our lives. I think we have to teach our kids that they have to accept the culture that they are in, but they have to respect our culture too. They have to be proud of what we are, not only of what they are here in this country." I did not realize it immediately, but Lucía had actually modified her opinion about adolescents' needs to be left alone by their parents, which she expressed in response to Gary Soto's story. Now she was stating that culture should serve as unifying force across the generation gap. Cultural pride was a lesson worth teaching and learning for both the parents and children's sake.

Luis followed Lucía saying, "Because if they are born here that doesn't mean they are white or that they won't eat the food we used to eat."

"But here I see many Mexican restaurants," Olivia replied, thinking about the food people eat in the United States and momentarily diverting the discussion. "When I was in Brazil I look in a book [about the United States] and I see *burritos*. *Burritos, tacos, tacos, burritos*. What are *burritos*?" she wondered at the time. In class, she repeated "burrito" several times, rolling the "rr's" like a purring kitten, elongating them like Spanish and Portuguese speaking children are taught to do, delighting in the evocative sound, revealing her eagerness to sample American cuisine. We all laughed along with Olivia, recognizing that in addition to marrying Elvis, Olivia's American dream included devouring an exquisite Mexican *burrito*.

I returned to my role as devil's advocate, asking, "Why shouldn't the child say: 'Well, you decided to accept American values and you decided to live here the rest of your life. Why don't I just take it all the way? Why don't I just become American?'"

"Because they cannot be. They are not white. They born here but they are not white. Their fathers are not white. They cannot do something they are not," Lucía again responded adamantly.

"But to live here you have to live as American," Timoteo replied before a puzzled expression emerged from his face.

"Yes, we cannot avoid that a kid wants to live like an American. But it's not fair that they don't appreciate the culture that their fathers are. And I think they have to respect it," Lucía said.

I reissued my challenge one last time: "What if the child says: 'Hey you brought me here. You brought me here to be an American.'"

"I think the child will always be half and half," Olivia said.

"I think depends the age, no?" Pablo said. "I've seen lots of teenagers who think a bit confused. But my daughter has four years and she say, 'Hey Papi, hey Papi, I born here. I'm American. I got papers.' She told me that."

"She's only four?" Olivia exclaimed amidst some laughter.

"Four years old," Pablo replied. "Let me tell you something. She's already practicing on the computer. And she say, 'I can go to Mexico, but you can't go. I got the papers.'" He compared his four-year-old to his fifteen-year-old, who was only concerned about getting a social security number so that he could get a job and go to college.

I asked how Pablo felt about his children's attitudes.

"Maybe it's OK," he said. "Because I told you before, my first thing when we come to this country was the kids learn English."

I turned back to Lucía: "I think you said something early on like you'll never be able to be American."

Lucía nodded.

"Why not?" I asked.

"Because if they want to do the things that Americans do or to feel like an American they cannot," she replied, disassociating herself from the question and choosing instead to refer to other immigrants.

"Why?" I asked.

"Because I think, like in the story, if you want to be a white boy, first of all the skin is different. You cannot say I am not Mexican or I don't have Latin American parents because," Lucía paused, "the skin is talking."

Looking around the room, I found most heads nodding in agreement. No one spoke after Lucía's remark about skin talking, about race in America. After reading the Gary Soto story "Growing Up" it was Lucía who had stated the need for adolescents to live their own lives which seemed to represent the ardent convictions of the young adult students in class. Now, she seized upon an interpretation of David Gomez's story that also seemed to capture the students' understanding of the reality of their adolescent and adult lives in the United States. On the one hand, parents need to back off and allow children to make their own mistakes. On the other hand, it is incumbent upon parents to teach their children well, especially in regards to cultural pride and diversity. Moreover, it is vital that children consider and embrace what their parents have to offer. For children to disavow their heritage places them on a slippery slope, for ignoring their cultural identity may lead to disillusionment and dejection.

CHAPTER 11

Having crossed borders themselves the students could gently mock Olivia's, and indeed their own, American dreams. They understood how Pablo's four-year-old daughter, simply by being born on U.S. soil, had advantages that were unavailable to them as adult immigrants. They recognized that their acquisition of American values resulted in permanent transformation of themselves and their families. But they were also secure in understanding that they would not attain full membership in white America and, therefore, they would not become American, even when they had secured citizenship. They were Mexican, Brazilian, Honduran and Ecuadorian. They were proud to identify themselves as such. In certain respects, their cultural pride and their appreciation that they would likely occupy a marginalized place in U.S. society made it easier to be the immigrant than the child of one.

With our students' comments about race and identify in mind, I suggested writing topics for the students to consider. Two weeks later, Amalia submitted her somber yet hopeful draft of the "The American Dream." The final paragraphs of her essay are below.

> . . . *Many experiences, relationships, and other facts with different people since my arrival in the United States influenced my thinking and did possible this essay for your dreams.*
>
> *Now, however, after all those good and bad experiences, I have in my heart a big enthusiasm that my words can become a fantastic reality in my life. I think that this piece show the influence that the society have in the development of man who take the hard way to the future. Sometimes the individual liberty depends on the liberty of others.*
>
> *In conclusion, with this essay, I wish that everyone can understand the great potential the immigrants have in our minds, and a sincere hope of a American Dream.*

PART V

THE ADULT LITERACY EDUCATION SYSTEM FOR LATINO/A IMMIGRANTS

CHAPTER 12

GLOBAL ECONOMY, CITIZENSHIP, AND EDUCATIONAL OPPORTUNITY

CRITICAL PERSPECTIVES

In Part I of this book, we looked at the evolution of the U.S. adult literacy education system since the 1960s. Evaluations of the system have repeatedly determined it to be ineffective (Cranney, 1983; Diekhoff, 1988; Fingeret; 1994, Foster, 1988; Guth & Wrigley, 1992; Kazemek, 1988; Purcell-Gates, Degener & Jacobsen, 2001, 2002; Sherman, Kutner, Hemphill & Jones, 1991). Programs typically identify grade level gains through pre- and post-testing but apart from anecdotal evidence systems have not demonstrated the ability to bring about large scale, practical changes in students' lives (Diekhoff, 1988). Most fail to deliver instruction that is directly applicable for students outside of the classroom (Purcell-Gates, Degener & Jacobsen, 2002). In such an environment, curriculum that aims to change students' lives by confronting intolerance, revealing inequality, and promoting social justice is even less common (Worthman, 2006) though examples do exist (Auerbach, 1992; Boudin, 1993; Heller, 1997; Power, 1995; Purcell-Gates & Waterman, 2000).

Seeking better employment opportunities and a better life for their families, immigrants participate in the adult education system and, like other adult students, find it can be lacking—with one notable exception. The system has generally been successful in preparing immigrants for the citizenship examination and attaining citizenship is, of course, a major life-changing event. Over the past century, the language and literacy requirements for passing the citizenship tests steadily increased but still remained attainable. Immigrant rights activists argue, as they did in the 1990s, that increasing language and literacy requirements for citizenship infringes on immigrants' civil rights, not unlike how literacy tests were used to prevent African Americans from voting during the Jim Crow era in the U.S. South. While the vast majority of immigrants, like the students at Erie, make learning English a high priority in their lives, there is still a preference among advocates to keep the language as well as content knowledge requirements for citizenship low. A result is that we often find citizenship classes that lead to success on citizenship exams but do little to prepare students for the full democratic participation that is required of a critical, enlightened citizenry. Citizenship curriculum often reflects the curricula commonly found in the rest of the adult literacy education system where we typically see a narrow, circumscribed set of practices that focus on lowest common denominator skill sets and, for the most part, fail to dramatically

CHAPTER 12

improve the lives of adult students (though, again, attaining citizenship is certainly life-changing).

In recent years, scholars and practitioners have made strides in situating adult literacy and adult ESOL instruction in specific contexts like the family and workplace. These approaches provide immediate and direct application of literacy, making it useful for adult students. Probably the most significant strides have been made in workplace literacy. Premised on situated cognition and activity theories (Chaiklin & Lave, 1993; Lave, 1993), literacy learning has been brought into the workplace to be provided in the context of workers' participation on the job. Instruction is situated in purposeful activities that engage the learners in cognitive and linguistic tasks that promote their development. Many researchers have made use of these and related theories to promote workplace literacy education that benefits both the worker-student and the employer (Jolliffe, 1994; Raizen, 1989, Stasz, et.al., 1992). The CWELL (Consortium for Workforce Education and Lifelong Learning) project offers a highly successful model for functional, workforce and workplace literacy education (see Sticht, 1987 for background). Still, some workplace literacy practices have been criticized for being irrelevant to workers' interests and exploitative of their participation (Gowen, 1992; Hull, 1992; Schultz, 1997).

In the past two decades, family literacy services have been implemented to help immigrant adults secure a more promising future, through education, for their children (Delgado-Gaitan, 1994; Mulhern, Rodriguez-Brown & Shanahan, 1994; Weinstein-Shr & Quintero, 1995). Though some of these efforts are coupled with bilingual education, ESOL, and GED instruction for the adults, the prospect of their advancing to higher education or employment through most of these projects is of secondary concern. Indeed, many parents participate in family literacy for the children's benefit. But there are others who witness social and economic possibilities and hope that adult-focused education will leverage greater opportunities. Such hopes characterize the students I taught during my two years at Erie.

In a global economy with increasing emphasis on information technologies and services, it is generally accepted that a high school diploma accompanied by specific vocational training or at least two years of college are required to access the higher paying, more secure jobs that are available (Carnevale & Desrochers, 2003; Suarez-Orozco, 2001). Unfortunately, the adult literacy education system as a whole has struggled to establish effective models for adults with low literacy skills who lack a high school diploma. Despite periodic commitments from politicians, funding for the services these students require has rarely been adequate. Adult education systems, like those in Illinois during 1990s, have been reluctant to commit resources to adults most in need: non-readers, low-level readers, high school dropouts and pushouts, and adult immigrants. Those students are left to rely on a "social equity" distribution policy that is primarily federally funded (Wong, 1990). Though the students served through this policy have always been the most in need, the peripheral programs that serve them have always been the most poorly funded. The conundrum of adult literacy education is often framed in terms of a circular argument. On the one hand, the system has not proven itself worthy of being funded. On the other hand, lack of funding inhibits effective service delivery models and the professionalization that many deem necessary.

For decades, the state of Illinois committed nearly all of its adult education funding to the community college system. In Chicago, the City Colleges of Chicago received the lion's share of state funds. Traditional community agencies that had endured over long periods of time like Erie Neighborhood House were granted little state funding beyond the Secretary of State Office's support for volunteer services. Malcolm X College, one of several City College campuses in the city, served the west side (predominantly African American) and near northwest side (largely Latino) of the city and placed more teachers at community sites like Erie than did any of its sister colleges (Illinois Community College Board, 1992). The large number of satellite placements was due, in part, to the reluctance of Latinos to leave their neighborhoods to attend classes at the main campus which was located near a poor, African American neighborhood. Still, Latinos comprised a significant portion of Malcolm X's Adult Learning Skills Program (ALSP) that served beginning literacy level, adult basic education, General Educational Development (GED) preparation, Citizenship, and ESOL students. Following passage of the 1986 Immigration Reform and Control Act and into the 1990s, Malcolm X dramatically reversed its previous steady decline in ALSP enrollment largely through participation of Latino, mostly Mexican, immigrants (Langan & Orfield, 1991).

In the 1980s and 1990s, the Illinois funding formula tied disbursements to student registration. Thus, the City Colleges and Malcolm X in particular benefited from the increased Latino enrollment in the ALSP programs on campus and in community programs. However, the City Colleges, striving to bolster its reputation as a legitimate community college with a strong undergraduate-level program, chose to allocate its financial resources to the college level, credit programs. Though the ALSP enrollments were nearly double the number of college-level enrollments the salary allocation for the non-credit ALSP faculty who were employed part-time declined to less than 10% of all faculty salaries (Langan & Orfield, 1991; Illinois Community College Board, 1992). The Illinois Community College Board (ICCB) concluded:

> There is strong, almost indisputable, evidence that the various components of the [City Colleges of Chicago's] mission are not perceived as having equal importance. In fact, there appears to be an inequitable, two-tiered system evolving: i.e., college credit and non-college credit programs, with a vastly different commitment to each. The two-tiered system resembles a two-class system in which learning, learners, and teachers appear to have different levels of importance depending on the level of instruction involved. (ICCB, 1992, p. 2)

It should not be surprising that a second-class system of education yielded dismal completion and graduation rates. In 1989, the City Colleges matriculated only 13% of its Adult Basic Education enrollment to the GED preparation level

CHAPTER 12

and from that pool only 4% subsequently passed the GED test (Langan & Orfield, 1991). Similarly dismal performance throughout the 1990s, reflecting a continuing spiral of decline in ALSP outcomes were reported despite repeated vows from the City Colleges to reform the system.

If the City Colleges operated a "two-class system" within its campuses, then by restricting the majority of funding to the City Colleges and providing minimal support through teacher placements in community outposts like Erie, the state was guilty of institutionalizing an underclass of adult "learning, learners, and teachers." The history of Chicago settlement houses and community agencies providing adult education is long and rich. But ever since the ICCB and City Colleges assumed control of the adult education system in the 1960s, community agencies have had little opportunity to compete for state funds, to exhibit evidence of superior performance (Hellwig & Wilson, 1996), and to prove their viability. By the end of the 1990s, the state had begun to respond to this criticism by directly funding community based organizations. However, those allocations remained relatively small.

In the 1990s the adult education system in Chicago was inadequate for adult immigrant ESOL students who hoped to pursue language and literacy education as a foundation for access to new opportunities and more lucrative employment. As the staff at Erie and other community agencies understood, the problems but also the solutions were political. Ramsey and Robyn (1992) compared the Miami, Florida system to other systems in the country and found it provided a superior education to adult immigrants. Compared to other systems, the administrators, teachers and students in Miami were more satisfied and more inclined to believe that the system met their needs. A critical distinction, they found, is that Miami's immigrants were empowered at the local and state levels. Because the politicians were beholden to the powerful Cuban immigrant constituency, adult education and training were given higher priority. Further, the Miami system linked its language and literacy curriculum to specific employment opportunities. Such a curricular policy coincides quite well with desires frequently expressed by Erie students that to succeed on their jobs they needed to learn relevant English. An appropriate response would be the contextualization of language instruction for the workplace. But in light of the changing education and training demands of the future labor market, it is irresponsible to provide only workplace literacy or to provide ESOL services that attend only to oral communication. On this point, Ramsey and Robyn concur:

> The newest wave of immigrants . . . may be less content simply to make things better for the second generation. These immigrants are much more likely to enter the system of adult education and seek skills to compete for higher-paying jobs. (1992, p. 1)

The City Colleges of Chicago sustained a virtual open admissions policy, much like that of the system in Miami, Florida. However, with few exceptions the curriculum was lacking. An appropriate state educational policy for adult immigrants and poor Latinos living in the West Town community, a policy that promoted contextualized English and Spanish literacy instruction and could lead to higher education and training opportunities, would have been welcomed by Erie Neighborhood House and other community agencies. But in the 1990s, when long-term, sustained educational activity was devalued in federal welfare-to-work policy, and severe restrictions were being placed on recent immigrants, the odds were stacked against those who tried to untangle the system and take advantage of the educational opportunities that did exist. Fortunately, Erie Neighborhood House, continuing its 125 year mission, was there to support those immigrants who were determined to try.

RESPONSIVE LITERACY INSTRUCTION

The research on Latino immigrant literacy and educational achievement presents a daunting challenge. Latinos are among the least educated group in the country (Chapa, 1991, Suarez-Orozco, 2001). They are among the least likely to graduate from high school and the least likely to enroll in college and receive a degree (Carter & Wilson, in Gandara, 1995). Perez and Salazar (1995) identify the illiteracy rate of Latinos in the 1990s as being higher than any non-Latino group, with 12% of Latinos over the age of 25 having attended less than five years of schooling. Among Mexican-Americans the rate is even higher at 15.6%. The English literacy skills of Latino adults are generally lower than those of other groups. In the last twenty years, the population of Spanish speakers in the United States, over age five, nearly doubled (Macias, 1994, Wiley, 2005). It appears that the age of arrival in the U.S. is the greatest determinant of English literacy; those arriving beyond age 12 participate far less in formal education and attain much lower levels of English literacy (Greenberg, Macias, Rhodes & Chan, 2001). Many recent immigrants come from rural villages in their home countries where they had little opportunity to develop literacy through formal education in their native language (Guth & Wrigley, 1992). Paral (1994) explains that among the Mexican, non-citizen population of Chicago in the 1990s, 48% spoke English well, 25% had a high school diploma, and 3% had an undergraduate degree. These data approximately reflect the population that attended Erie Neighborhood House for native language literacy and/or ESOL instruction during the years I taught and conducted research.

Most research literature that pertains to Latinos pursuing higher education or training focuses on the children of immigrants, the first generation born in this country (Gandara, 1995; Torres & de la Torre, 1997). The educational aspirations of adult immigrants, we are left to assume, are limited to short-term objectives and life-skills competencies even though formal education and English literacy are significant factors in the wage earning potential of immigrants (Greenberg, Macias, Rhodes & Chan, 2001). Kaestle (1988) suggests a "history of frustration and bitterness" among adult immigrants to the U.S. as they realize "the necessity of acquiring literacy and then higher education as a resource to confront economic and occupational inequality" but realize that such benefits are more likely to be obtained by the next generation (p. 116).

CHAPTER 12

Farr (1994b) cautions scholars and practitioners with an agenda to promote advanced educational opportunities that many Mexican immigrants are "transnational." They maintain family in Mexico and the U.S. and travel back and forth. Through the support of extended family networks many spend only short periods working in Chicago and other regions of the U.S. Thus they do not need to participate in academic literacy instruction. This also rings true of many who participated peripherally at Erie. But it is also important to consider that while immigration by adults has increased, the Mexican immigrant population in the U.S. (as well as other Latino groups) is still relatively young (Paral, 1994). Many young adults evaluate their long-term prospects for remaining in the U.S. and determine that the labor market requires education beyond the citizenship classes and the basic, functional, oral communication-focused, ESOL classes that are pervasive. As presented in the previous chapters, many of my Erie students claimed that they never intended to live permanently in Chicago, but five, ten, fifteen and even twenty years later, as in Maya's case, they determined it was time to improve their English literacy in order to stake a better claim in the West Town community of Chicago. To be sure, Farr does not suggest that the *mexicano* transnational families that were the subjects of her long-term sociolinguistic analysis reject academic literacy completely; rather, their existing contexts of family, community and workplace participation have not required extensive textual engagements. They live in a commercially robust community that plays a significant role in the Chicago economy while thriving on Mexican cultural practices.

Ramirez (1994) found a greater linguistic insularity among Latinos in Chicago than in ten other cities with large Latino populations. Across generations, Chicago Latinos tended to speak more Spanish in the home than in the ten other cities. Likewise, in the community domains of neighborhood, school, church and recreation, the Spanish language was used more exclusively in Chicago than the other cities (Ramirez, 1994). Both Farr and Ramirez show that in Chicago, a city of ethnic neighborhoods, it has been very possible to survive and succeed without learning English and without using academic literacy, as immigrants from various countries who settled in urban centers did in the past. Despite public demands for English language and literacy, Latino immigrants in Chicago, as Farr suggests, do what makes sense to them to do. They learn enough English to succeed in venues where English is spoken and they continue to use their native language in venues where Spanish is the predominant language. In order for Spanish speaking immigrants to succeed within their ethnic communities and neighborhoods it may be just as valuable to promote Spanish literacy instruction for many students (Spener, 1994). But the West Town community that Erie Neighborhood House serves has always been more culturally and linguistically diverse than the community that Farr studied, which was predominantly Mexican. The Erie students have, perhaps, more reason for becoming bi-literate. Many of them—Lucía, Jacinta and Victoria, for example—obtained their GED's through Spanish instructional and testing programs before proceeding to ESOL studies at Erie.

Many of Farr's *mexicano* adults increased their literacy using *learning lírico*, an as-needed, written approach to representing speech through letters of the alphabet.

In *learning lírico*, spelling, grammar and punctuation serve little function as such skills represent schooled literacy practices. However, the literacy that most of Farr's *mexicano* families see as more valuable—the type they want for their children—is the academic discourse. But the ideological underpinning of schooling in the U.S. promotes individual and career advancement, and tends to ignore family-focused cultural values and practices. Intergenerational, cultural, and linguistic conflict between the school and home has been a common theme in Latino educational literature (Delgado-Gaitan, 1993; Gonzalez, Moll & Amanti, 2005; Matute-Bianchi, 1991; Moll & Greenberg, 1990; Suarez-Orozco, 1987; Valdes, 1996). The practice, content and purposes of schools isolate many Latino children from their home and culture. Both Farr in Chicago (1994) and Valdes in Texas (1996) found that the families of Mexican origin they studied expected literacy to be practiced as a social phenomenon. They believed that literacy is most important if used for living up to personal obligations and for supporting nuclear and extended familial relationships. This sentiment is echoed in Carger's (1996) study of one Mexican family in Chicago struggling across cultural barriers to maintain strong family values while promoting the children's educational advancement.

But again the story was different for most of my young adult, immigrant Erie students who examined the opportunities available in the 1990's labor market and decided that higher levels of literacy would help them. Many of my students wanted to go to college. Many thought they might advance their working lives through increased literacy use. Many of the students, like Jacinta who is the focus of the next two chapters, recognized the need to venture beyond the safety of their neighborhood enclave in order to seek new opportunities. The Leadership students came to realize that their aim to make a better life for their families and community would be enhanced through development of academic reading and writing. In fact, after I shared passages from Valdes's (1996) analysis of her Mexican informants' literacy practices with my students they argued that they should not have to choose between family obligations and individual advancement through literacy education. As will be shown in the next chapters, their American dreams included personal advancement as well as strong, family-focused values. They wanted American-style education and Mexican-style *educación*.

TEACHER RESEARCH

During my second year teaching at Erie Neighborhood House, I signed on to be a Malcolm X College ALSP Level 5 English instructor, though I still taught in an Erie classroom. In that role, I helped Erie to buttress its relationship with the City Colleges and garner extra support for its Advanced Level English offerings. As an ALSP instructor, I was required to submit attendance records and to participate in a yearly training symposium. I was also encouraged to select from several adult ESOL workbooks that were available and frame my curriculum through those texts. These were all consumable books focusing on oral language skills and grammar though a scope and sequence that assumed all Level 5 students (based upon a test of oral language use) to have the same English language proficiencies and developmental needs. But the skills and proficiencies exhibited by my students were wide ranging. Though they qualified for advanced level instruction, their oral communication abilities and interests varied greatly. Moreover, those who had attained high levels of schooling and achieved high levels of literacy in their first language far outpaced the students who had very little previous formal literacy education but had high levels of English oral proficiency. Like many who are proficient in literacy, the literate students exhibited different strengths and weaknesses in the domains of reading and writing. Thus, adhering to any of the workbooks as a curriculum framework for my advanced level students (and, I would also argue, students at any level) would have meant that at any given time only a few would have their language needs met. Of course, none of this skill and grammar-focused curriculum attempted to situate the learning in a meaningful, purposeful context, let alone a context that was oriented to meet the stated interests of the students and their need to confront the intolerance they encountered.

Qualitative researchers continually strive to get closer to phenomena by peeling away overlapping layers of the educational context to reveal meaning and significance. As a qualitative teacher researcher, I was engaged in the ongoing challenge to know my students better and to respond to them by expanding the curriculum to meet the developmental range and interests of each and every student. I will not suggest that I was always successful but the programmed instruction suggested by the City Colleges ALSP could meet none of these goals. The ALSP curriculum, in fact, served to distance teachers from their students by steering their attention to the workbook pages rather than to students' sociocultural and linguistic needs. While I constructed and reconstructed a critically responsive pedagogy in an attempt to meet the students' needs, the generic ALSP curriculum offered throughout the city treated teachers and students alike as pawns in a futile system. In chapters 13 and 14, we will see just how important it is to adult immigrant students (again, I would contend, for all students) for their passions and opinions about their educational pursuits to be fully considered in the formation and ongoing negotiation of curriculum and instruction.

Jacinta, one of the most dedicated of the Leadership students, will be the focus in the next two chapters. Jacinta spent two years in my classes and was the student I knew best at Erie. Still, there remained a distance between us that I was not fully aware of until one afternoon when she asked me. "Why are you teaching us?" She wanted to know why I spent time helping adult immigrants to attain their goals. She also needed to know why I cared about people who were so different from me. Such a question is profound though hardly earth-shaking. In fact, in my response to Jacinta, I told her that it was a good question and one that all teachers ponder from time to time but should probably be required to answer consistently throughout their careers. But Jacinta's need was to know if she should trust me as her teacher. Nel Noddings (1984) suggests that an essential philosophical grounding for good teaching is that teachers "care for" students and, in turn, the students feel "cared-for." In my relationship with Jacinta--and to different degrees with other students—my capacity and willingness to care for them and about the lives they led nourished the soil from which lifelong exploration and learning could grow. Caring for the students meant embracing the students' causes as just and worthwhile.

In chapter 14, we find Jacinta splitting her time between attendance at a series of Community Dialogue forums and our class. Each week Jacinta reported on the content and activities of the forum so that we would know what local community leaders were planning on our behalf. We, in turn, gave Jacinta feedback to take to the next week's forum. We also reached a point in the class where it was time for the students, both Leadership and the rest, to determine our next steps and choose our next readings. I had only one pedagogical requirement which was for us to read informational texts. While individual students had read informational texts on their own (and I had guided them to use specific information gathering approaches), as a class we had thus far immersed ourselves in reading and response to narratives. There were many reading strategies I believed necessary to teach in the context of informational texts. As a teacher researcher, my aim was to expand the collective zone of proximal development for the students, monitor how they employed reading strategies and responded to the text, and then continue with our negotiation of future topics and readings. But in contrast to my earlier selection of "Yo Soy Chicano" as an attempt to better understand students' dispositions toward race (chapter 11), the topic and reading selection for this unit were decided by the students. The give and take, the negotiation of our agenda made for an educational experience that most of the students had rarely encountered. The opportunity to establish their own inquiry, as will be shown, led the students to critically question the prospects for education in their lives and the lives of adult immigrants in their community. In taking up the cause of education for Latinas in Chicago, the students learned how they might take their agenda to community leaders and politicians.

CHAPTER 13

JACINTA: FEELING HER WAY THROUGH

Teaching is an interactive practice that begins and ends with seeing the student. This is more complicated than it seems, for it is something that is ongoing and never completely finished. The student grows and changes, the teacher learns, the situation shifts, and seeing becomes an evolving challenge. As layers of mystification and obfuscation are peeled away, as the student becomes more fully present to the teacher, experiences and ways of thinking and knowing that were initially obscure become the ground on which real teaching can be constructed. (William Ayers, 1993, p. 25)

WHY WE READ TOGETHER

When we met to discuss the first thirty pages of *Diary of an Undocumented Immigrant* (Perez, 1991) Jacinta lamented her initial struggles with the book. She had selected it from our classroom library two months earlier in January, 1997, but had yet to gain momentum in her reading of the text. Her many commitments in the community and her job at a Mexican-owned, neighborhood *taquería* on the first floor of the building where her family lived demanded most of her time. During slow periods at the *taquería* she pulled the book from her bag to read at the counter, but found herself turning back to the first page each time. Too much time lapsed between reading attempts. She explained that her feeling for the main character was not forming. Having read books in my classes for one and a-half years, Jacinta was familiar with the challenge of overcoming doubts during the reading of a first chapter and pushing forward toward greater satisfaction as the story developed. With this new book, she hadn't yet fully devoted herself to the challenge.

Jacinta had completed the *secundaria* (approximately equivalent to an eighth grade education) in Mexico, and obtained her high school diploma through an all-Spanish curriculum in a Chicago high school, but prior to my class a year earlier she never read an entire book in English. Following high school she attended Erie, which was her neighborhood sanctuary, for adult ESOL education classes and was eventually placed in my class designed for both ESOL students and native English speakers with low literacy levels. Following the completion of her first low readability-high interest novel she became a prolific reader, devouring the entire collection of these books, and then moving to the next level, abridged and

CHAPTER 13

unabridged young adult and classic literature. Throughout that year, she increased her involvement in Erie programs, eventually joining the Community Leadership class while continuing to work at the *taquería*. Though many other employment opportunities were presented to her, she declined them all. Tim believed that she was not yet ready to leave the *barrio*.

When the possibility of my complementary English class for Community Leaders was first raised, I consulted with Jacinta. She was encouraging, convinced that a class similar to what she already experienced, with students reading English stories and other texts about community activism, would draw all of the Leadership students. She promoted the class to her Leadership classmates. But she was unaware of how many of these students, with the same level of English language and literacy skills she had possessed one year earlier, were too intimidated by what others announced to be an advanced ESOL course.

As explained in the next chapter, Jacinta's work schedule and her increasing involvement in community activism eventually resulted in her declining attendance in my class. By January, her many commitments had become too much for her and she realized she would have to let something go. She had already decided to enroll in Erie's Pathways to Success program—a grant-funded program—to prepare for college or a specialized vocational training course. During an interview with the Pathways Coordinator two critical issues were clarified for Jacinta. First, the Coordinator helped her to calculate her real wages at the *taquería*. Often working seven days and more than fifty hours per week, she came to realize that she was making much less than the existing minimum wage. With a weekend union organizing institute and our studies of labor organizing behind her, Jacinta was incensed. She knew already that she was not earning her worth; she had been biding her time before taking her next step. But she hadn't realized that in some weeks her wages were as low as $3.00 per hour. With this information she quit her job the next day, and turned down the repeated requests from the owner to return at a higher wage. The second issue that was presented to Jacinta was that her reading level, according to the Test of Adult Basic Education (TABE) was in the eighth grade range. She would need to increase that level to eleventh or higher to pass the Pathways course. Having already discussed the possibility of my tutoring her, she became more determined and we resumed tutoring sessions.

In our first meeting, we decided on the following plan for our sessions: 30 minutes for Pathways homework, 15 minutes for grammar and vocabulary learning, and 45 minutes for reading and discussion. She had the same response journal I had given her in September, and had attempted a few entries on the book *Diary of an Undocumented Immigrant*. She turned the journal pages to exhibit her entries and then described her repeated halting starts with the book. I suggested that another book might be in order, but she disagreed. She wanted to read this story, to know it a little better. She noted that it was not the same as her personal immigration story, but it would help her to appreciate some of the other Mexicans at Erie who usually declined to share their border crossing stories. During the session, she read her initial entry aloud.

I selected the book because I hope to find a lot of experience about undocumented people. I would like to know more about what kind of problems they have to risk when they cross the border to the USA. The only thing I know is that it is hard to cross the river. The people have to run when the immigration comes. Some people die crossing the border and the family not know how they die. Some times the people are treated for exposing to the cold temperature when they have no clothes to cover their body or their wet clothes.

Jacinta set her journal down. She picked up the book and flipped the pages, front to back. She then turned back to her journal and flipped through a few more pages before closing it again and sighing. She explained that she had been reviewing her journal notes before the session and was thinking about me. "You are different from us, right?" she asked.

"Yeah, right," I responded, unaware of what she was after.

"And I don't know how you feel when I show you this. I don't know if you understand what I say about it. I'm not sure if you care about this kind of topic."

"Oh, yes I do, very much."

"Because I know some people that are from here. They don't like to talk about it."

"Why not?" I asked.

Jacinta described some people from the neighborhood who, though immigrants themselves, were not interested in such stories. They did not want to revisit them. Instead, she said, they focused their attention on moving to the suburbs or someplace nice. Then she re-addressed her concerns about me. "And I was thinking about you and I'm reading this and I say: 'Do you like it, to hear it?'"

"Do you want to ask me about my feelings?" I responded, wondering if she wanted to examine my commitment to Mexican immigrants.

"Uh huh."

"OK, what?" I wanted to understand more specifically.

"What do you feel about the immigration people who come here? Especially because you are a teacher, right. I was thinking why do you teach English to the immigrant people even if some people don't really care about it? Especially the poor people who are Mexican? I was thinking why are you teaching us? English? What do you feel about us? Or how do you feel to teach immigrant people? When I was reading this, I say, 'Oh my God. I'm saying a lot of things about it but I don't know how you are to feel. And that's why I have this question about teaching this to us.'"

I responded that with regard to the book, I was happy to read whatever she wanted to read, but also that I knew too little about the story and wanted to learn more. Teaching at Erie, I told her, I should know more about such stories.

"What I'm thinking," she continued, "is why you want to teach Mexican immigrants at Erie House?" She peered at me, waiting for an answer, though I'm not sure she expected one.

I fumbled about in my attempt to provide an answer. I talked at length about politics, about race, about the immigration reforms, about the history of the United

CHAPTER 13

States and our struggle in the 1990s. Indeed, I had put a lot of thought into the question but never clearly formulated the answer.

"I think it was a hard question, right?" she said after I began to repeat myself in search of connections among my different motivations.

"I think it was a very good question," I replied. "I think it is something that every student deserves an answer to. But I'm wondering, you've known me for almost two years. Why do you ask me this question now?"

Jacinta did not answer my question directly, but said: "I ask one teacher and he say he don't really care a lot about immigration." This was an ALSP instructor who had not taught at Erie very long. "He say, 'I teach English because it was an easy profession, an easy way to go because I know English.'"

In comparison to this teacher, I gave Jacinta an answer that left her more content. However, I was not satisfied. Her question, I believe, should be answered clearly by all teachers, and especially those in community classrooms like those at Erie. That evening I wrote a letter to Jacinta and gave it to her Pathways teacher for delivery to Jacinta the next day, since I would not see her for another week.

Dear Jacinta,

I wanted to write and tell you that I've been doing a lot of thinking since our talk and the questions you asked me about why I teach at Erie. The question you asked is one which I've been thinking about for past 1 1/2 years since I've been at Erie and known you and others. As you could tell by my response I still have not completely answered the question for myself. But below I would like to try, with the benefit of writing to help me make decisions about what I say since writing allows me to speak more carefully. I think that you and other students have a right to know why the teachers do what they do. It might be a good idea if more teachers had to answer that question on a regular basis. Anyway, my thoughts are below.

There are many reasons that I teach at Erie, that I teach immigrants from Mexico and from other countries. You mentioned that when you asked another teacher this question the person responded that he already knew English and so he thought it would be an easy thing to do, an easy job. This sounds strange to me because I have found teaching English to be quite challenging. When we talked, I mentioned that for me teaching at Erie has to do with politics and race, my feelings about this country and its history, my desire to learn more from the students at Erie, and my desire to teach in a place like Erie—a place that is committed to people and to justice. I will also tell you something below that I did not tell you on Wednesday.

On Wednesday I shared my feelings about being "white." I believe there is a problem with being "white." Let me explain: I believe that race is a socially constructed thing. In other words, I don't believe that there is any biological basis for us to think about ourselves as being necessarily different from each other. Because I believe that "whiteness" is not something I am born with but something that I get from my culture, then I also believe that "whiteness" is something I do not have to accept. The reason I do not want to accept it is because "white" people have used their power throughout history to oppress other people. "White" people, men, in particular, have acted as if they were superior to others and they have, in this country, been very ugly and inhumane to many peoples. I am referring to the genocide of Native Americans, the enslavement of black people, the theft of land from Mexican people, the jailing and confinement of Asian people, the suppression of women, and the constant ridicule and oppression of poor people. And these are just examples of a few wrongs that took/take place in this country, not outside of this country. "White" people have done these things because they believe they can get power and privilege by joining the "white club." The "white club" gives power and privilege. Now if I don't want to be "white" and if I want to become a better person in my mind, then I need to act as if my goals are not to join the power and privilege of being white, but instead work against that power and privilege. I do not teach at Erie so that the students can become more like me—the American "white guy"—but so I can contribute to helping others find the opportunities that they hunger for and to challenge the current system.

So in many ways I teach at Erie because it is a political thing to do, because I can help people, I hope, to succeed against the system that gives power and privilege to some and closes the door to others. The immigration reform is a terrible thing. It is a huge door slamming on the hopes of many people and there's no reason to close such doors. It's just that some people think that their power and privilege might be lost. They are wrong. I know they are wrong because their actions are not actions that demonstrate caring. You see, I teach at Erie, as I said, because of political beliefs, but I also teach because I care about people. I know that everyone can say they care. It is very easy to say this. But I care about other people and I care about the world that we live in, and the world that we are making for all of us. That is why I am a teacher. I believe we are all together, that we share a consciousness, and that our actions affect each other.

Your question, specifically, however, was why I teach immigrant people at Erie. Well, I teach because I care, and I teach at Erie because the system of this country is working against the hopes that I have to live in a better world. Therefore, I am political. There is a man from Brazil who Tim and Delores [the Leadership teacher] and others think is a very wise and important person. His name is Paolo Freire and he is very political in his reasons for teaching. Many people read Freire's writing and decide that because he is political, then that is the place from where they need to start with their teaching. They should teach because of political beliefs. I read Freire's writing and I understand that he is political because he has love and caring for the people who are oppressed, and also for the people who are the oppressors. He believes that we need to reach out past who we are and live with others as if we were sharing the same world and treating each other as ourselves.

I continued the letter noting an ongoing concern of mine, that many of the Mexican students in the class had expressed resentment toward Puerto Ricans who

CHAPTER 13

would not bear the brunt of anti-immigrant policies. Likewise, the students occasionally expressed disdain for Puerto Ricans and African Americans who received welfare benefits. As citizens, members of these ethnic groups had all the opportunities they needed to succeed, the students felt. I suggested that the Leadership students might investigate these matters more carefully and learn more about the history of Puerto Ricans and African Americans in the United States. Some of these concerns are presented in the next chapter. I concluded my letter to Jacinta:

> *Anyway, these are my thoughts for now. I'm sure that some of them will change but others will not change. I look forward to hearing back from you. I definitely look forward to reading, together, the book you have. I expect to learn a lot from the book and even more from you.*

I anxiously anticipated our meeting one week later. I envisioned a lengthy discussion, assuming I would need to further clarify my thoughts. I longed to know if my answer was satisfactory and how Jacinta might respond. In fact, her response proved entirely satisfactory. She acknowledged the letter, said she appreciated my taking time to write so much about her question, and . . . she was ready to begin working—nothing more. She wanted to begin reading. It seemed that we had developed an understanding and it was time to move forward. It was time to read the story to discover how it made us feel.

The first chapters of *Diary of an Undocumented Immigrant* introduce the protagonist, Ramón, and his decision to leave his Mexican village in search of lucrative employment in the United States. At the Rio Grande, he entrusts himself to a coyote, and, along with several others, makes repeated crossing attempts. He is caught by *la migra* (immigration authorities) twice before finally succeeding. Once in Texas, Ramón hides out in abandoned shacks and piles into the cargo area of trucks with numerous others and very little space to breath for transport from place to place. Throughout the first chapters, it is the coyotes, not *la migra*, whom Ramón describes as the most villainous. They abandon the weaker of Ramón's compatriots, leaving them to die, and they rape a Salvadoran woman who joined the crossing party.

Jacinta read the story aloud. Her word recognition was near perfect, though she stopped frequently to discuss vocabulary terms: "reconnoiter," "river swelling," "rusted." She had not fully comprehended the rape of the Salvadoran woman until we discussed the chapter. Somewhat to my surprise, Jacinta explained that she had not heard such stories before. As we began to read a chapter titled "Texas," I asked if she had ever been there.

"Yes, it's close to Ciudad Juarez." Ciudad Juarez, she explained, was where she crossed almost four years earlier at the age of fifteen. Unlike in Ramon's experience, Jacinta explained, "It was easy to pass." Jacinta then shared some of her story with me.

Jacinta's father had immigrated to the United States, settling in Chicago fifteen years earlier. Her mother later joined him, leaving Jacinta and her twin brother with an uncle in Durango, Mexico. In Durango, Jacinta had her childhood friends and attended school. After school and on weekends she and her cousins would pick crops for her uncle or follow him and his plow, planting seeds along the rows. When she was a little older she worked in her uncle's market, sometimes running the store for hours at a time while the uncle tended to animals on his small ranch. Occasionally, Jacinta explained, she gave candy away to other children, but she always confessed to her uncle who found such honesty amusing. She explained, "He believed in me. He would touch my head and tell me, 'You are a good girl, Jacinta. But don't give them too much candy.'" As a young adult working in Chicago, Jacinta frequently sent him money, helping him to maintain the ranch so that when he was old he would not have to sell his animals and move.

When her parents felt confident that they had stable employment and a suitable home, it was time for the children to join them in Chicago. Jacinta used the birth certificate of a cousin born in Texas when she crossed the border. She was told, if asked, to inform the border authorities that she was born in Texas but moved back to Durango as a baby and therefore did not know English. She was frightened at the time, but again, found the crossing was easy. Unfortunately, her brother had greater difficulty crossing separately, but eventually made it to Chicago without harm.

Listening to Jacinta, I realized that I had known her longer than any other student at Erie, but had never heard her story before. In fact, she had written the story of Annabella (discussed in chapter 5), but never shared her own. "I've known you as long as I've know any other student but I've never heard you talk about your past," I said to her. I guessed at the time, and came to appreciate more over the next two months, that my testimony of why I taught at Erie opened the door for her to trust me a little more and for us to share the experience of reading together.

"It's sad sometimes," she said, referring to being separated from her parents. "I just don't talk about it."

"It seems that you always talk about the future," I wondered aloud as Jacinta signaled that she was ready to begin the next chapter. We launched into the chapter and over the next two months continued reading Ramón's story, mulling over its relevance to our respective missions at Erie and in the community.

NO REST FOR THE ACTIVE

"I am so tired," Jacinta sighed. Jacinta explained she would do her best during our session but might falter occasionally. She had awakened early that morning to drive with Tim and a few others to Springfield, Illinois to testify before the state legislature. Out of the blue, a Chicago legislator managed to get a hearing for a proposal to award state community college funds directly to community-based organizations like Erie, without having to subcontract from community colleges or simply accept the teachers that community colleges placed in the community sites. Jacinta was ready to do Tim's bidding, accepting his contention that sites like Erie should at least be able to compete for funds. She was prepared to tell the legislators that Erie was where she learned her first words of English. She was prepared to tell them that with control of the funds, Erie could create courses that focused on

CHAPTER 13

specific topics that students wanted to learn about. She would have included Geometry, Immigration, History, or Jobs as possible classes. Though scheduled to testify, the Erie group never did. The session was hectic. "It's like a war or something because they start asking so many questions," she said. The bill did not pass; it only received one vote in its favor. During our session that afternoon, Jacinta's reading was off. She made occasional miscues, could not recall some vocabulary terms previously reviewed, and had more difficulty comprehending. She was tired but, we agreed, her day was well spent.

Though she had quit her fifty-hour-per-week job, Jacinta was not one to relax. She fit in the trip to Springfield at a moment's notice, amidst her classes and job search. Although her Pathways class met four nights per week, she enrolled in a morning ESOL program in a distant neighborhood. She initiated a job search downtown, a search that included asking fellow passengers about potential job leads while riding the bus. She continued with all of her commitments to Erie's recreation program and the Leadership program at Erie. She found a different church group with which to affiliate and pursue her faith. She and her sister bought a car for $50.00.

As we had agreed, during our tutoring sessions I helped Jacinta with her Pathways homework which included a vast array of topics. One week, I helped her to prepare a five minute oral presentation of a "memorable incident" in her life. She selected a weekend union organizing institute she attended in Minnesota. Another week I assisted her in analyzing fifteen and thirty year mortgage tables and performing related calculations. Throughout the program, she was given various grammar lessons. The grammar topics ranged from recognition of past and present participles to mastery of a list of contractions to identification of palindromes. Whenever possible I connected the grammar studies to our reading and journal writing. For example, I identified, to her surprise, places where she had already used the active and passive voices in her writing. However, we did not encounter any palindromes in our reading and writing. One afternoon Jacinta informed me that she would not be attending her Pathways class that evening. "It would be dishonest," she said, explaining that a "professional" woman wearing a skirt and heels was delivering a series of workshops on self-esteem. Jacinta described the woman's attitude toward the class members as demeaning and opted not to attend rather than feign interest.

Eventually, Jacinta dropped her morning ESOL class in the distant neighborhood. She endured three days of testing before the program finally placed her in a level six English class, which I found intriguing since my Erie class was at one point designated as level five though I did not design or teach it according to traditional ESOL proficiency levels. For the first month Jacinta liked the other class, trying to learn all of the grammar she could. However, she eventually grew tired of the daily mastery tests that were administered without much instruction from teachers. When she was absent, as she was when she went to Springfield with Tim, for example, she received zeros on her tests and was told that she risked failing the course.

The most notable of Jacinta's life changes during that spring season were her new job and new church. Tim had once explained that Jacinta was scared to leave the *barrio*. She clung to Erie and her neighborhood, like so many did, postponing the day when she would branch out and investigate opportunities available in Chicago. After Jacinta left the level six ESOL class she went in search of work downtown, perhaps in a small shop or restaurant. Following one interview, a prospective employer informed Jacinta that knowing Spanish and English as well as she did would be an asset to the restaurant. She took the job, assuming it would be temporary, while she waited to complete her Pathways class and then enroll in an office technology training program. Work as an administrative assistant would be still another short-term measure with the eventual goal of obtaining better employment and wages in order to some day pay for college tuition.

Meanwhile, Jacinta had grown tired of her youth group, with whom she had taken her vow of premarital abstinence, in the neighborhood Catholic church. She still wore a ring to symbolize her commitment but the kids in that group, she eventually decided, were not very serious. She began visiting another church and spending time with older, "more mature" people in their twenties and thirties. They met regularly to discuss their spirituality. This group helped to prepare the liturgical service every Sunday. Some of them stood before the congregation and delivered the Old and New Testament readings prior to the Gospel reading by the officiating priest. Jacinta hoped to someday read in the Sunday mass and began preparations with the group toward that end. She informed them of the commitments she made with the youth group. They asked her to work with them to promote the cause among youth in their church. They gave her a new Bible so that she could read and study with them.

LIKE TO TAKE A BATH

As mentioned, Jacinta had little, if any, difficulty reading and pronouncing English words accurately. Her previous ESOL instruction had served her well in that regard and her Spanish literacy supported her English literacy development. When the Pathways program determined her reading level using the Test of Adult Basic Education (TABE), it found her vocabulary score to be lower than her comprehension score, with the two scores factored together to derive an eighth grade reading level. This was no surprise to me, given that she was an ESOL student. Though I recognized that it was not an appropriate ESOL test, I had, nevertheless, once administered the TABE to a group of my ESOL students after two months of instruction—just to see how they would fare according to adult education standards for native speakers of English—and found, consistently, that their vocabulary scores were below their comprehension scores. The importance of vocabulary to second language literacy learners is well documented (Carlo, et. al., 2004; Lesaux, Geva, Koda, Siegel & Shanahan, 2008; Nagy, Garcia, Durgunoglu, Hancin-Bhatt, 1993). Based on the Pathways assessment and her need to score well on a post-test, Jacinta wanted to focus on vocabulary and comprehension. We started a word bank, and I introduced different approaches for learning vocabulary in the context of our story. Of course, translation using a Spanish-English dictionary was also helpful. While reading together we developed a practice of stopping after every four to five paragraphs to review plot and character developments. During our first four sessions, I prompted and guided her with questions designed to look at the story from different perspectives. The questions focused on setting, character motivations and developments, and plot events. Eventually, Jacinta took over, stopping intermittently to identify events that she considered significant to her.

I had supplied Jacinta with the same response journal guide adapted from Berger's work (1996) that I had given all of the students for individual reading outside of our class. The guide included a variety of prompts: What do you notice? What do you question? What do you feel? What do you relate to? Increasingly, Jacinta responded to her chapters by focusing on the feelings she had developed for the characters. Early in the story she responded to an account of the immigrants being piled into a truck for an overnight journey. "I could imagine the truck they were in, a full truck, a lot of people, with ladies and men. And it's like feeling something like sad for the girl. And still they want to get to the United States to start their life." In one chapter, she described her strong feeling that a miracle from God led to Ramón's finding a job. But in the subsequent chapter, while reading about a magical, fantastic event, Jacinta lost interest. She had no feelings toward the characters Ramón encountered and no interest in learning more about them.

As Jacinta continued through the second half of the book, with Ramon moving from Texas to California to Washington and finally back to Mexico, she refrained from writing in her journal unless, she explained, she had a strong feeling about the story. Those feelings were governed by how she related to the characters. If their immigration struggles helped her to imagine the experiences of people she knew at Erie or elsewhere, then she felt strongly about the characters. She would write. If she could not envision the events of the story taking place for anyone she knew or might encounter, then she refrained from response writing and moved on to the next chapter.

But the story also provided her with new insights and new feelings for people she might meet. "Sometimes when I see a lot of people like Hispanic people, I feel with them more seriously," she explained. "If they say something like, 'I am illegal people,' I know already how they came. . . . I understand more because I'm reading a lot of experience about it. In the past I didn't feel like from my heart how did they feel when they came here."

Jacinta struggled to describe the feeling that washed over her while reading. "And when I'm reading I feel, I feel when I'm reading I try to, how you say like, it's like to take a bath, like you are really full of the experience. Like now you are strong because you have a lot of experience about how they came here. I'm full about it. I feel like I'm strong with those feelings. And if they try to speak to me about it, I know already, how they feel or what are their dreams when they came here. I feel like from my heart. If they say to me, 'Oh, I came here to look for a job,' I already know how this person feel because I have the experience reading."

Finally, Jacinta described how her reading experiences helped her to feel what the rest of society seldom could. Speaking about her empathy for immigrants enduring difficult border crossing she said, "You know sometimes we see from TV what is going on with the immigrants, sometimes they show on the TV how the police talk, or how *la migra* took them and started hitting them. And I was watching and I was thinking: 'Oh, it's so hard.' But then I didn't feel like that weak feeling, like I'm going down on my knees, like I'm gonna die. And with this book I feel these things. I feel like I learn a lot of experiences and when somebody talk about immigrants I understand more about the way they feel."

NOT A FANCY STORY

Though we met weekly for three months, it still took me by surprise when Jacinta would arrive for tutoring, plop her books down on the table, sigh, and then launch into a story of the busy week she had. I was still getting used to her being so open with me, but I enjoyed her weekly reports. By May, she was working her new job and earning more money Monday through Friday than she had when working seven days per week at the *taquería*. She was soon to graduate from Pathways to Success with, among other accomplishments, a higher reading score. She had completed a student loan application and was preparing to start her office technology training program in the summer. Representatives of different city parishes had invited her to speak with their youth groups about the abstinence vow. She was meeting regularly with her new church group and was preparing to read at a Sunday mass. Her $50.00 car was in a constant state of disrepair. She finished *Diary of an Undocumented Immigrant* and was learning to juggle more than one book at a time.

"Is that the longest book you've read?" I asked when she had finished.

"Yes."

"What do you think about that?" I asked.

"It was hard to concentrate on the book. It was really interesting, but in the final chapter I was thinking about in church I have another book to read. I was thinking: 'Oh my God, I have two books to read at the same time.' And it was hard for me to read this and read the other one. Sometimes, I would read the church book and sometimes, 'Oh my God! I need to read the other one.'"

Like many devout readers, Jacinta found herself needing her book when her life slowed down. She regretted those times on the bus when she found herself without a book. Before work in the morning or sometimes during her lunch break she read at the restaurant. Her coworkers would say, "Oh, you like to read. Oh, don't talk with her, she likes to read." She did not let these comments, made in jest for the most part, bother her. She just smiled and returned to her book. Such feedback was not unlike the comments she received from friends at Erie regarding her renewed spiritual interests and her vow of chastity. She related their conversations and their teasing her about the ring she wore to symbolize her vow, saying, "'Jacinta, we are going to a picnic with a lot of people and dancing. Don't forget to put a lot of rings

CHAPTER 13

on each finger.' I say: 'Yeah, OK, don't worry.'" These comments were made by friends who knew her well and respected her tremendously.

On warm evenings, she liked to sit on her front stoop and read. Once, while she was reading *Diary of an Undocumented Immigrant*, a neighbor asked her about it. "Why you want to read this book?" Jacinta described that neighbor as politically active but also cynical. "OK, when you finish it," he said, "we are gonna see that now he's a lawyer and he's got a big house and a lot of money and he lives in the suburbs." The neighbor couldn't fathom that a realistic story about the immigration experience might be written. No one wanted to know the real story, he told her.

Since she had completed the book without me, I asked, "So, he didn't become a lawyer?"

"No, she responded. "That's why I think it is a real life experience. It's not now he becomes a smart student, he learns a lot of English, now he has an easy job.... [Instead] he goes back to Mexico to be with his family. It's not a fancy story."

I wanted to learn more about the end of the book. After all, I had been reading along with her. Jacinta explained that Ramón grew tired of always being on the lookout for *la migra*. He narrowly avoided being apprehended while working at a factory. His California roommate had been caught and deported. But Ramón was not very happy about being a dishwasher, his last job before returning to Mexico. Jacinta noted that the dishwashers at her restaurant never appeared very happy either. "I think there's a lot of angry dishwashers," she said. Finally, Ramón grew tired of the routine, she explained. She showed me the passage in which Ramón explains that people in Mexico work hard but always have a festival to look forward to. In the United States life was a routine. You work all day, come home, drink beer and watch TV with nothing to look forward to but another day, week, month and year of the same thing. Ramón earned his money and returned to his family in Mexico, just as he originally set out to do. He writes: *To stay the rest of my life is to live a routine until my last day.*

I asked Jacinta what she thought of Ramón's decision to return. She said she understood. He had earned money to send home, like he wanted, and besides, his family was in Mexico. I asked what she thought of his contention that life in the United States was a dreary routine. Regarding that complaint, she was less sympathetic.

"I don't see my life as a routine," she said. "I have work and other things. I have activities like here in school or in the church. I feel like I have to work because I need the money, no? But in the meantime, it is not routine. I can do a lot of things here [at Erie]. But these guys," she said, referring to people she knew who were like Ramon, "I think they used to work and go back home, and like he say, drink beer and watch TV. And this is a routine. . . . I think [Ramon] is closing his mind. Like all his thoughts are in Mexico. I think he feels a little bit of racism. Like he feels, 'OK, the American knows English and I don't know so I'm going to stay home.' Like very closed is his head. It don't open. He needs to learn English. He needs to learn other customs, like, to mix. You know, like 'I have my custom. I would like to know how is the custom of him.' He doesn't do this. If he were trying, I think he would accept to stay here in the United States, but he is a little bit down. His feelings are down."

Jacinta reflected on her own experience. "Before, when I was here the first year, I feel like I didn't know English and I feel, well, that's my custom. My custom is the Spanish language and I feel like [Ramón], like I didn't open my mouth to other people because I didn't know English. But if you learn some of the culture, if you learn we are the same people, just with a different language. If you learn something, you can be equal. And I started learning English and I get friends and I am getting more friends."

Despite her appraisal of Ramón, in the end, Jacinta agreed that he probably made the right decision. After all, his family was in Mexico and he should be with them. I asked Jacinta if she thought her parents would some day return to live in Mexico. She said that they planned to do so. They did not want to grow old in Chicago. I asked if she would follow them. She doubted that she would. She explained that she understood why her parents would return, but they were of a culture different from the one she was beginning to understand and embrace. She had recently begun to explore life outside the *barrio* and, meanwhile, had discovered the sage voice that lay within.

CHAPTER 14

EDUCATION/*EDUCACIÓN* FOR LATINAS IN CHICAGO

Latinas face a dilemma between cultural values and assimilation. Neither alternative is acceptable since women are subordinate to men in Latin America, and in the United States. Assimilation means at least becoming a part of the underlying sexism in society, and at worst, the triple oppression of gender, color, and class . . . still women do not surrender. Latinas, above all else, seek out family relationships to help with daycare, job searches, finances, and other forms of mutual assistance. (Latino Institute, 1987, p. 1)

COMMUNITY DIALOGUES

The rectangular table barely fit into our small classroom, leaving little space to squeeze between students and the walls and book cases. Early arrivals took seats at the far end of the room leaving the chairs near the door vacant for those coming to class late from work. But there was one seat at the far end, which, without discussion, was often left empty for the daring student who chose to hold forth on a subject. Arriving late from work and out of breath on an early November evening, Jacinta jostled shoulders and bumped heads as she made her way to that remaining seat. Finally settled, she looked my way to determine whether or not I would hold her to our agreement: If she missed our Wednesday class to attend the Community Dialogues meetings, she would report on those meetings to the class each Monday.

After a brief discussion about gangs had run its course during our Talk time, Jacinta took my nod in her direction as a signal to begin. "Well, we are living here and we know the problems we got here," she said. "So we can report ideas how we can solve these kinds of problems, especially for us if we have even three years here. We know that a building is going to be constructed to make a new home. So we can talk to him about the house, the building, or the owners. They cannot destroy them or something like that. So they want to get ideas from us because we live in the community that they are defending, no?"

Confused, but trying to make sense of what Jacinta was talking about, Luis asked, "Who wants to get ideas? Who's 'him'?"

"Carl. He's a leader in the community from Erie House," Jacinta continued. "But some people are from Holy Innocents who go there. And from Santa María is one people or two. So they all are around here so they can come to Carl or to other people. I don't know what are their names. They are important people that are taking our ideas and our problems. I think it's good to be, how you say, like, together in the community. For example, the church, Santa María and Holy Innocents are included, and Erie House. We are working together with our ideas. For example, to solve problems at the school. When the kids get out from school at Carpenter School, one people have a program after school, like basketball."

"So what are the goals of these meetings?" I asked, trying to help Jacinta make herself clear to the other students.

"To get united with the community!" Jacinta responded more confidently than before. "Because all the Latinos, the Puerto Ricans, Polish—I think if we are together we can make something."

"So you want to make changes in the community? How can you make changes by getting together and having meetings?" I continued in my effort to foster communication between Jacinta and the students. I was sincere in my desire for them to believe community meetings and organizing could make a difference.

Jacinta responded, "I think getting ideas from us. We say we need materials for [Erie] so maybe they can get money or something like that. It was my first meeting but it's good because we have all the communities together from each church and the schools, public schools. They are people from there."

While she wasn't very clear regarding the objectives of her Wednesday meetings, Jacinta was sure they were worthwhile. As she explained, it was her first meeting. In time she hoped to understand more and become more active in the organizing. When she explained that there was good food and English-Spanish translators a few more students expressed interest in attending the meetings.

SEEKING A CONFLUENCE OF INTERESTS

The five-year effort of Erie's Community Economic Development Department to build new and affordable housing for local residents was nearing its end in the autumn of 1996. Months earlier, the local alderman had retracted his campaign pledge to support the initiative. Most of the subsequent legal and bureaucratic alternatives had been exhausted. The community activists, with a few of my students among them, were left to engage in public demonstrations in hopes of getting Mayor Daley's support for their cause. Following Thanksgiving, the group protested at Daley Plaza during the city's annual Christmas tree lighting ceremony. They paraded with a larger-than-life turkey carcass, symbolic of the scraps of housing that were being left for low- and middle-income residents in many Chicago neighborhoods, especially West Town. In early December, Jacinta and I joined the group singing Christmas carols outside the mayor's new townhouse in a gated community on the near south side of downtown. One of the group's often repeated favorites was sung to the tune of "Rudolph, the Red Nose Reindeer:"

> We want to live in West Town
> In an Erie Co-op home
> But one of your alderman

Won't even throw us a bone.

Despite the on-going protests, Carl, who for years led the Erie Housing Coop initiative, had already begun to turn his attentions elsewhere. The neighborhood was rapidly gentrifying, yet numerous other issues confronted West Town. Carl launched the West Town Community Dialogues Initiative and invited my students to attend the weekly meetings. The Dialogues Initiative, as Jacinta struggled to explain, was established to bring community residents and leaders together to identify local problems, determine and prioritize solutions, and then take action. The meetings were held on Wednesday evenings during our class time. I presented my students with an alternative schedule so that they could attend. We could all attend the Wednesday meetings and hold our regular class on Mondays. However, only Jacinta and Timoteo, the more resolute of the remaining community activists in the class, expressed interest. So our class continued to meet on Mondays and Wednesdays.

Two weeks before the first Wednesday Community Dialogues meeting, Jacinta and Timoteo accompanied a handful of Erie representatives to a weekend union organizers' institute in Minnesota. At the institute they were grouped with "Asian people" and "white people," which was fine, they said, except that these people spoke fluent English. Some in the Erie group were initially intimidated but after adjustments were made, and some translation services were provided, Timoteo and Jacinta emerged as full participants. At my suggestion that it might serve her interest in meeting new people, Jacinta carried the biography of Mother Jones that I had given her. Though she hadn't yet opened the book, she informed me that it did prompt some introductions and yielded a few conversations during the weekend.

Upon their return to Chicago, Timoteo and Jacinta were ready for more political activity. Timoteo was soon offered an opportunity to travel to New York for the second stage of the union training—a two week session—to be held in January. Completion of the training would lead to more travel throughout the Midwest. He eagerly accepted, but decided that with such a commitment looming he ought to make his annual winter visit to his family in Mexico a little earlier. Thus, Timoteo would leave our class by mid-November. Jacinta did not receive an offer to attend the second training but was only slightly disappointed. She was not ready to leave her family and neighborhood in Chicago. The West Town Community Dialogues surfaced as a valuable outlet for her. However, she would miss our class on Wednesdays.

Though my students were drifting along different streams, I felt compelled to find a confluence of their interests, a place where the three groups of students—the community organizers, the full-time workers, and the college-bound—could meet and continue their individual studies for the next month. I presented these three categories to the students and my thoughts on where each was situated. They appeared intrigued by my classifications of their agendas and the possibility that we might venture forward with common interests.

I also met with each student in early November to establish individualized plans for language and literacy skills instruction. I would meet with them in tutoring sessions and writing conferences, and give each individualized homework

CHAPTER 14

assignments. While I had always looked for grammar challenges shared by most of the students that I could address through formal, full-group instruction, there were few grammar topics common among most of the students that made grammar instruction in the class worthwhile. As the chapters on Justine, Lucía, Olivia and Jacinta show, the students' language and literacy skills varied greatly, as did their motivations for improving their English. While my class was seen by many as the fifth level of ESOL instruction, the host of grammar problems the students exhibited ranged across several levels. The students' wide range of educational backgrounds and the varieties of formal English instruction they received placed them all over the map with regard to English grammar. Yet all, including Maya, who dropped to a lower level class, could participate in guided reading and discussion.

The remaining pedagogical concern I had in crafting curriculum for our next unit was that from "The Battle for Farm Workers' Rights" to "Yo Soy Chicano," we had read primarily narrative texts during our two months together. College-bound students, full-time workers, and community organizers need to be familiar with the forms and varieties of informational or expository text, as well as the strategies and reader stances that such reading requires. I selected three different texts that I hoped would capture and unite the students' interests and serve the pedagogical objective of exposing students to informational text. Each selection was a research and public policy document concerning Latino issues in Chicago. Each was published by Chicago's Latino Institute, a nonprofit research and advocacy organization. Through these reports, I hoped to learn from students' response to research and public policy written about them, but that did not include their voices. The first report was *Hopes and Dreams: A Statistical Profile of the Non-citizen Population of Chicago* (Paral, 1994). The second was *Chicago's Working Latinas: Confronting Multiple Roles and Pressures* (Latino Institute, 1987). The third selection was *Latinas in Chicago: A Portrait* (*Mujeres Latinas en Acción* & Latino Institute, 1996).

Latinas in Chicago, a compilation of data taken from Public Use Microdata Samples (PUMS) extracted from census data, had only recently been published. The report was a collaborative effort between the Latino Institute and *Mujeres Latinas en Acción*, a neighborhood-based organization on the southwest side of the city. The fifty-three page booklet, including a focus group section, is comprised mostly of charts and tables with interpretive essays in the introduction of each section. The principle chapters examine economic self-sufficiency, employment, education, immigration, health, and domestic violence, as they relate to local Latinas. The report also includes an executive summary, policy recommendations, methodology, a glossary and references. *Latinas in Chicago* included a variety of expository forms.

Seated at the table, the students passed around the three texts, flipping through the pages, comparing the thickness of each booklet, examining the density of text per page, and reading introductory remarks aloud. Victoria suggested that we could read all three and compare the information, but the other students rejected this idea. That would be too much work. Pablo acknowledged that most of the class was female, so a report on Latinas would be appropriate. Luis preferred *Chicago's*

Working Latinas but without much debate agreed with the rest to read *Latinas in Chicago*. Timoteo and Victoria immediately recognized the organization, *Mujeres Latinas en Acción,* since their Leadership instructor, Delores, was a member. The report appeared to contain information on numerous topics and, moreover, it was the most current data available on Latinas in Chicago. Most were excited to have a publication hot off the presses. Our class would be on the cutting edge in understanding issues related to Chicago's Latina population.

In the "Findings and Recommended Policy Directions" section of *Latinas* the authors write:

> *These findings and recommendations are offered in the spirit of eliciting dialogue which will lead to narrowing the gap that exists between Latinas and larger society. They are purposely broad in order to provide a framework by which various publics may craft specific strategies which target the challenges of the Latina community.* (pg. 4)

As our class ventured forward with reading and discussion, I had a sense of clandestine pride, believing we were doing something important. Our journey paralleled those that were taking place in different, more prominent and public spheres. The publication of *Latinas in Chicago* was an effort to reach policy makers, prompt city-wide discussion of existing problems, establish priorities, chart new directions, and take action. After the demise of the Erie Housing Co-op, which only compounded the effects of the backlash against Latinos epitomized by the immigration reforms, the West Town Dialogues was established to regain some footing and proceed with objectives similar to those in *Latinas in Chicago*. In our own little corner of the world, in our cramped, secluded classroom space on the third floor of Erie Neighborhood House, my students, too, were preparing to confront the issues, discuss and debate them, and make their voices heard in the workplace, in college, and on the streets of Chicago.

WHAT DO WE KNOW ABOUT LATINAS IN CHICAGO?

We started by asking what we already knew about Latinas in Chicago. The range and depth of response could have been overwhelming. Nevertheless, that is where I decided to start. Having surveyed the text in advance, however, the students understood that their responses were bounded by the types of information they might expect to find in the text. I listed the students' responses to the question on an overhead transparency.

What do we know about Latinas in Chicago?
- Some or most work.
- Some are immigrants.
- Some are the only people in the family who work and make money.
- Some are abused by their husbands [a response that clearly reflected the survey of the text with its section on domestic abuse].

CHAPTER 14

- Some abuse their husbands [a somewhat defensive response from Luis, though he wasn't married and intended the remark to be humorous].
- Some have good jobs and education.
- There are increasing numbers of single mothers.
- There are increasing numbers of teen mothers.
- Some are citizens.
- Many work and take care of children.

I chose the KWL (Ogle, 1986) method as a strategic reading and note-taking approach to guide our initial forays into the text. This method encourages students to ask themselves the following questions, before, during and after reading: What do you Know? What do you Want to Know? What are you Learning? The KWL method is among the simplest of strategies, yet also the most elegant. It captures those cognitive and meta-cognitive activities that reading scholars have long believed essential to effective, strategic reading with informational texts. From experience, however, I knew that KWL also required some guidance and manipulation in order for students to generate questions that would yield answers from the text and satisfaction for students. In my experience, it was too often the case that the items students listed under "What do you want to know?" were never addressed in the text.

I introduced a web diagram with "Latinas in Chicago" at the center, surrounded by chapter topics and student interest topics.

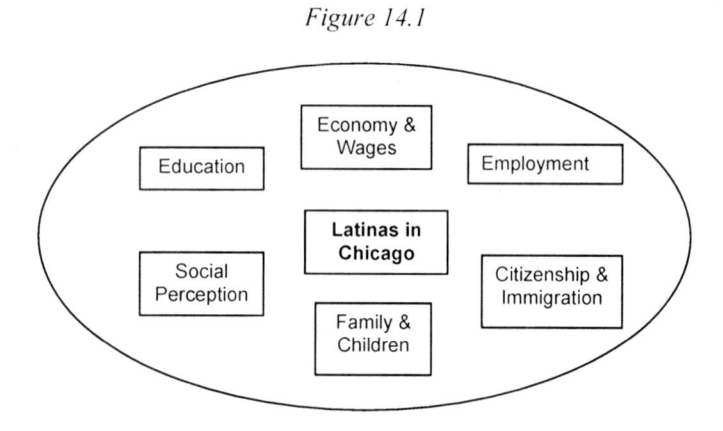

Figure 14.1

We used these topics to help frame and guide our purposes for reading. When identifying what they *wanted* to know, the students understood that their questions should reflect a preliminary understanding of what would be presented in the text. Moreover, when developing the questions, we also identified those categories from our web (which was derived, in part, from our survey of the text) under which we expected to find answers. This procedure, I suggested, would help to focus our information-gathering processes and would help the students to organize ideas when they later wrote essays. The numbers in the right column below correspond with the web diagram categories and show where we would expect to find answers to our questions.

What do we want to know about Latinas in Chicago? **Chapter in Text**
1. How can they improve their lives? 1, 2, 4, 5
2. Do they want to go to school? 1
3. How can they get legal help? 6
4. What types of employment to they have/want? 3
5. What kind of government help do they receive? 4, 5
6. What are their hopes and dreams? 1, 2, 3, 4, 5, 6
7. What kind of help does *Mujeres Latinas en Acción* give? Intro. to text
8. Are they involved in the decisions of the country? 4, 6

With these prereading activities completed, we read the "Executive Summary," after which I asked the students to individually write what they learned. They reported the following and I, again, listed the information on an overhead transparency for them to see.

What are you learning about Latinas in Chicago?
- The difference for Latinas versus other people regarding social and economic issues. It is worse for Latinas.
- Language, poverty, few resources, isolation create barriers.
- They have low paying jobs. They have the worst jobs.
- They feel invisible.
- 20% of Latino families are headed by women alone.
- Latinas are confronted with negative social perceptions.
- Puerto Rican women are the poorest.

We briefly discussed these claims, identifying the few that served as preliminary answers to questions previously posed. I then explained that the more we learned, the more questions we would want to have answered, and asked the students for new questions to add to our "What do we want to know about Latinas in Chicago?" list.

Jacinta asked, "Why are Puerto Rican women the poorest?" As I listed her question and she watched it appear on our chart, she added, "If they are single mothers?"

I asked how to put that into a question and Luis responded, "How much percent of Puerto Rican Latinas are single with kids?"

I added Luis's question.

Jacinta posed a third question: "Do Puerto Ricans want public benefits?"

Because Latinas in Chicago had just been released, the Executive Director of Mujeres Latinas en Acción had been promoting the report in the media. I was fortunate to hear and record an interview with her from the radio, and I played it

CHAPTER 14

for the students. While I was excited to add the interview to our study of *Latinas in Chicago*, the students were not impressed.

Jacinta's response seemed to capture the majority sentiment: "Well, the information she was talking about was in the book, in the first page. We already read something like that." Though I had high hopes that the alternative multimedia presentation would be appreciated, it offered little more to the students' information gathering.

Luis heard something new from the interview, however, "I didn't know that only four out of ten Latinas finish high school. I thought there was more, most of them finished high school."

Though we had already established that Puerto Rican women were the poorest as a group among Latinas, Lucía remarked, "I didn't imagine that the Puerto Rican women were the poorest. Because they are already citizens here."

"Yeah, that's another one that surprise me," Luis said. "Because if they are able to work anywhere they want, I don't know why. For a lot of people who is not able or does not have the paper it is difficult to find the job. There are these people who have good education but these people don't have papers and they're working in restaurants or doing less than their capacity—I don't know how to say—because of the papers. And the Puerto Ricans they don't have this problem, this big problem."

"I think most Puerto Ricans are single mothers," offered Jacinta.

"Is that a question or something you know?" I interjected a pedagogical query with some concern that the discussion might proceed toward the negative characterizations of Puerto Ricans I had previously observed in class.

"It's my thoughts," Jacinta replied. "I think most Puerto Ricans are single mothers because the Latinas, the custom is to be at home. The Puerto Ricans doesn't care."

"Why they doesn't care?" Justine asked.

"Because they let the kids go in the street." Jacinta replied. "The Latinas doesn't let the kids to go because the tradition is to stay at home or something."

I was confused by Jacinta's use of the word Latina. After I noted and explained correct use of the terms "doesn't and don't," I asked whether or not she included Puerto Rican women among Latinas. She responded that she did not. Luis explained to her that Puerto Rican women are also Latina. I added that there were several cultures grouped among Latinas, that Olivia (a Brazilian) and Amalia (an Ecuadorian), were Latinas. Jacinta said she understood, but in subsequent discussions she continued to differentiate between Latinas and Puerto Ricans.

Luis continued the discussion: "I don't know, but I think I see many Puerto Ricans they are, actually when I'm coming here I know I always see like three ladies they are working and three or four childs to keep, but I never see man or the husbands. So maybe they are lonely."

I responded that the complex connection between poverty and female-headed families was one we might also investigate in our book.

"Maybe they say so [in the book] because I seen also my point of view is that many of them are very, they like to go a lot to welfare," Luis said. "If somebody goes to welfare that means he's poor, but I know people that get these benefits and these people have cars, good cars, and even their own houses."

"Is that something you know or a question?" I asked again, employing my teacher role in an effort to suspend, though not disregard, some value judgments until, at least, we had more information.

"It's not a question," Luis responded. "I know these people that have good cars. And you can see them."

SUPPORTING LATINAS

The next section of *Latinas in Chicago* was titled "Findings and Recommended Policy Directions", which provided more details about specific issues related to economic self-sufficiency, employment, education, immigration, health and domestic violence. The topics were presented in separate tables, each with columns for findings and recommendations. I previewed some vocabulary terms: *eliciting, framework, philanthropist, ignorance, focus group*. We then proceeded to read the three pages of tables with one student reading the findings and another reading the accompanying recommendations for each section. We also read the two-page "Introduction" to the report. While reading the introduction we needed to stop and discuss complex concepts such as: *lower socioeconomic status in a nation stratified by class; gender in a patriarchal system;* and *ethnicity in a race-conscious society* (p. 8).

When we finished reading, I asked for responses, included anything that struck the students as important or surprising.

Jacinta was first, "I think we answered, they answered what we have before: 'Why Latinas are the poorest?' It's because the Latinas doesn't have voice, cannot vote." She found the information in the Education table. "The Latinas, it say the voices are not heard. . . . When they say that the Puerto Ricans are poorer than Latinas it's because I'm sure that Latina voices are not heard. [But] I think that Puerto Rican voices are heard."

I asked, once again, if Jacinta was distinguishing Puerto Ricans from Latinas. She responded that she understood the relationship. However, she continued in the same vein, interchanging Latinas for Mexicans, or perhaps even undocumented Mexicans.

"Because the government didn't see the Latinas because they don't have the rights to have welfare. This is connected by when the Latina didn't vote. We don't hear the voice," Jacinta explained. "And the Puerto Ricans has that right because they are citizens and when they go to welfare they count the Puerto Ricans."

"She saying the government counts only the Puerto Rican women and the government counts only part of the other Latinas but not all of them because a lot of them don't have papers. And they don't go to welfare," Luis said.

"Uh huh." Jacinta nodded her agreement.

"The Puerto Rican citizens they go a lot for welfare. So the government thinks they are poor," Lucía added for clarification. "The other group, they don't have papers. They don't go."

CHAPTER 14

"So you think that maybe Mexican-origin-Latina women," I wanted to clarify our terms, "are just as poor as Puerto Rican-Latina women, but the government doesn't know about many Mexican women?"

Nodding her head enthusiastically, Jacinta added, "That's why the Puerto Ricans are connected to society, because they have rights. The government sees the Puerto Ricans in society."

Justine was confused, "How come they have the rights and the Mexicans don't have the rights too?"

"Because [the undocumented Mexicans] are not citizens," said Lucía.

Olivia, who read two of the tables aloud but had remained silent since, asked, "So to have benefits you have to be citizen?"

Lucía answered, "Under the new law they have to be citizens." In fact, undocumented immigrants have never been eligible for benefits though legal residents were eligible before the new laws.

"Oh yeah, the new laws," Luis added, speaking softly and reservedly, realizing that he had temporarily forgotten the welfare and immigration reform laws that were on the minds of many students.

It was common for my mostly Mexican students to describe significant differences among Latino cultures. As discussed previously, my students thought of themselves as Mexican, Brazilian, Guatemalan, Honduran or Ecuadorian before they thought of themselves as Latino or Latina. I was previously aware that some friction existed between Chicago's Puerto Rican and Mexican communities, but the welfare and immigration reforms had exacerbated an existing schism under the big tent of Latino coalition politics.[5] The direct attack on Mexican immigrants waged throughout the mid-1990s reforms weighed heavily on my Mexican students. I believe that Jacinta's interchanging of "Latina" with Mexican, or even undocumented Mexican, was primarily a sociolinguistic mistake. But it could also be understood as an assertion of Latina power specifically on behalf of Mexican women. Her message could be recognized as an elevation of the Mexican woman to a more prominent position, and assertion of a voice that needed to be heard more loudly in the Latino community.

Though I never asked, I am reminded that none of my students ever admitted to being undocumented—most or all were residents or citizens—and I believe they trusted me with such information. Moreover, none of them ever claimed to receive welfare benefits. Their constant attention to the impact of the welfare and immigration reforms, therefore, was clearly a stance in defense of community and culture. Under the extreme pressure of the reforms, the students knew they had to retrench in support of the subculture of undocumented Mexicans. That another Latino culture with political affiliations, Puerto Ricans, did not have to do so because their citizenship status guaranteed their rights and opportunities yielded resentment from the students. What my students seemed to miss, however, was that many provisions of welfare reform, those not targeted solely at immigrants, would affect the Puerto Rican community which, as our text *Latinas in Chicago* informed us, was the poorest and, according to its authors, most in need of public benefits.

I suggested that as we studied the rest of the text, the students should look for evidence of whether or not the report included undocumented Mexican women. In fact, while the report contained a section with census data regarding the percentages of non-citizen Latinas, it did not clarify whether data for non-citizens included undocumented people or just documented residents. The methodology section failed to mention any accounting for undocumented immigrants in its presentation of the several topics. Though another Latino Institute report (Paral, 1994) identified nearly five hundred thousand "non-citizens" in the Chicago area, it did not stipulate how many of these were undocumented immigrants as opposed to legal residents either.

Continuing the discussion, I asked what else from the tables and introduction was significant. Lucía and Olivia expressed concern over the numbers of teenage mothers in the Latina community.

Jacinta noted the rates of citizenship, "On the [table] they say to promote Latina citizenship."

I responded, "This one kind of troubled me because I know a lot of people are waiting a certain amount of time, or are choosing not to become citizens, because they may want to go back to Mexico or wherever. The authors of the report seem to think this is a problem."

Luis asked what happens if someone becomes a United States citizen but wants to return to his home country. I responded that it depended on the countries, whether they had a dual citizenship policy. I asked whether or not there was such a policy between Mexico and the United States.

Jacinta did not respond directly but explained her understanding of the rules, saying, "If you go to Mexico and you stay for six months, then you lose your citizenship here."

"You have to be for sure you going to live here the rest of your life," said Luis.

"So it's different for immigrants. So it's better to be immigrant, yes?" Olivia wondered.

While the immigration and welfare reforms were making it more difficult for noncitizens to stay in the United States, there were still particular advantages to not attaining citizenship status in the U.S. In the early 1990s, Mexico suffered a devastating recession that led many Mexicans to the United States in search of work, though many had little intention of remaining. Meanwhile, the North American Free Trade Agreement (NAFTA) made it easier for United States corporations to establish operations in Mexico and employ Mexican labor. Of course, such work would still pay dramatically lower wages than what could be earned in the United States, and important questions lingered over whether NAFTA would exacerbate the problem of sweatshops, particularly in the *maquilladoras* along the border. Still, the possibility existed that free trade would stimulate the Mexican economy and support Mexicans whose goal was to someday return to their country from the U.S. Becoming a United States citizen, therefore, did not seem to be the most beneficial course of action for many.

Attaining citizenship for many Mexicans was a defensive measure taken against the assault on their civil liberties delivered by the immigration reforms. Through

CHAPTER 14

NAFTA and the immigration reforms, the Clinton Administration was working at cross purposes and presenting a classic proletarian dilemma: Wealth, capital, and material goods could more readily move across borders, while workers could not. While hardly a new phenomenon, these policies presented conflicting, not to mention often dangerous, choices to those crossing the border in search of work.

HEARING LATINA VOICES

Seated at the head of the table, Jacinta, at my suggestion, had prepared notes from her previous Wednesday's Community Dialogues meeting and launched into her presentation,

> We decided to be united all the people from different places here from the community, to be meeting on Wednesday, to talk about the problems in the community, especially with education for the kids or to open programs to help them. And we talk about the homes. Some people are getting out of their apartments because they pay a lot of rent and they don't have a lot of money to pay that. So we decided to go to these meetings and resolve these kinds of problems, especially to get ideas for what we can do. And last week we talk about the homes—the new homes they are making in the community. We know already this community is Latino. One person say he has thirty years in the community. He grows up here. He went to school here. He went to college and he work downtown and he usually walked to work because he was poor. So he say he's not sure about security in the community. Some people say the white people are forcing the people to pay more. For example, when one people live in an apartment they usually pay $350 per month. So now the owners raise the bills so now you have to pay $400 per month. And what the people do—just working and working.

The longer Jacinta talked, the more confident she seemed. She grew more fluent in her delivery as she looked around and observed us in rapt attention. She continued, "So we decided that we should get new homes or an apartment for the people who has no money, who are not able to pay $400 or $450. That's why we want new houses. But we have another side." She looked around to make sure we were listening. "The white people want the new houses to live. The [current residents] should get out and the new people gonna come that is gonna be white people, rich people?" Jacinta posed the question before issuing her answer, "No!"

I asked if everyone understood. Justine asked for more explanation. "So I can understand better," she said.

Jacinta explained that with the low wages most of the local residents received they made only $160.00 per week or about $600.00 per month on average. The local rents would soon be approaching that. Most residents would have little left to support families.

Olivia asked, "But if you have the problem and if you have the solution do you have the place to go to find help?"

"No, that's why we're getting together." Jacinta said. "We are going to see that the rich people see that we are together. We are united and they can see that we can do this for us because all the communities are together."

As the discussion proceeded, Pablo realized that Jacinta was attending the same meeting his wife had been attending on Wednesday nights. Pablo and Jacinta exchanged pleasantries regarding the coincidence, but then Pablo challenged Jacinta's assertion that the rich, white people were the enemies of the community organizers. He reminded us of the story he told a month earlier regarding the assistance he received from white people when he first moved with his family to Chicago. He added that white people gave money to Erie for school supplies that we used.

The evening's assignment was to identify what more the students learned from the tables and introduction that were read in class. Jacinta led the discussion, identifying a statement in the book and then adding, "I put down that Latina voices are not heard," she said. "But I'm not sure because I read some more and think I'm wrong."

"I wrote that on my list, too. It's on page five," said Olivia.

"Yes, it says Latina voices are not heard. I think it is wrong. In the book it's about Latinas, the problems they got," Jacinta explained.

"So, then you supposed to say Latinas' voices are heard." Luis understood Jacinta's point.

"What I understood in the book was they said their voices are not heard," Olivia joined in. "But [in the book] has been promoted the visibility of them. So, somebody is looking for this."

I clarified that the students were declaring the fact of the publication as proof that Latina voices were being heard, at least in the book, and that there was even an audience for these voices.

"What do you think, huh, Pablo?" Jacinta looked Pablo's way, goading him in a good-natured way.

"Yeah, because my wife do that," he responded. "My wife do that. She's going everywhere. She's talking all the time about the problems. The thing is we need to learn more English."

"I agree with you, Pablo. I agree with you." Jacinta said.

"My wife, she is everywhere talking about the Latinas. She's on the council of the grade school and another agency, too." Pablo began thumping the table, adding that now his wife was attending the Wednesday meetings with Jacinta. "And she's at another training about what kind of food the kids need to eat."

"And they are all Latinas?" Jacinta asked, regarding the various groups.

"No, is American people. There only two or three Latina people there. Yeah, this is the reason I say, 'They are there!'" Pablo insisted.

"So, you are also saying that Latina voices are being heard?" I asked.

"Yes."

"Yeah, maybe because they know English," added Jacinta.

On a new overhead transparency titled "What am I Learning about Latinas in Chicago?" we listed the following:

CHAPTER 14

- Latina voices are not heard.
- But Latina voices are now being heard.
- Stereotypes about Latinas are wrong.
- Latinas have high rates of cervical cancer.
- Many, 26%, do not have health insurance.
- 11.1% of Latina teens have children. 46% of Latinas have children, compared to 29.2% of other women.
- 41% of Latina adults have completed high school.
- Domestic violence exists.
- 28.8% of Latinas are foreign born.
- If someone speaks, others will follow.

Some items yielded few comments while others prompted more discussion. The students first focused on the issue of health insurance. Olivia, who for weeks had been trying to understand the other students' concerns over the welfare and immigration reform legislation, was not sure why health insurance was a problem for Latinas. Jacinta explained that with public assistance many people also received government supported health services, but only if eligible for them, which, of course, many Mexican immigrants were not. Pablo explained that many people got health insurance through their jobs. But insurance was too expensive for people to purchase by themselves.

Olivia was puzzled. She asked, "If you are sick, you can't go to see a doctor if you don't have money to pay? You don't have free hospitals?"

Lucía, Jacinta and Luis responded unison, "No."

I explained that the United States is one of the only developed countries that does not have health coverage for all people. Olivia's jaw dropped as she looked around at her fellow students for confirmation.

Pablo offered some clarification, "There's Cook County."

"Yeah, but it's not too good," Jacinta responded immediately.

"It's not good?" Olivia asked, her brow furrowed as if she had been counting on Cook County Hospital to provide her with her medical care, but now was unsure.

I explained that Cook County was the poor people's hospital, and while it was vital to the city, the services were sometimes not good. "People show up at 6:00 in the morning and the doctors don't see them until—"

"2:00!" Jacinta announced.

"You say 2:00. It's more like 6, 7, or 8:00," Justine countered.

Olivia said, "It's worse than in Brazil. I thought they had—Oh, here it is worse. I thought we have hospitals, free hospitals that—"

Several voices interrupted in succession to discount Olivia's notion.

"Where people could go and be well treated." Olivia inserted.

"Just another thing you're learning about the United States," I said.

Olivia shook her head, smiling and said, "I think I go back."

"Just don't get sick while you're here," Luis warned.

We continued through the list of what we were learning from the text. After identifying the items regarding the birth rates of Latina teens and Latinas generally,

Olivia mentioned that she had recently attended Tim's ESOL class where many of the men, mostly Mexican, were discussing the numbers of children they hoped to have. Some wanted four, five, six or more. She added that according to Tim, it was part of the Mexican culture that the more children they had, the more pride the men felt.

Olivia did not understand. "I think they feel proud, but I don't know why. I think it is stupid. I don't agree with this."

"I think it was before," Jacinta said.

"But they said now," Olivia replied.

Pablo then launched into an explanation of the Mexican economy, the standard of living, and the ability of Mexicans in Mexico to support a family on less. When they came to the United States, they expected to have the same number of children, but the standards and cost of living were higher in the new country. Olivia and Jacinta agreed that the Mexican men in Tim's class needed to hear Pablo's argument. I asked whether or not it made a difference if the immigrant came from the city or the country, and if family sizes were larger for those who farmed for a living. Pablo, Lucía and Jacinta confirmed that families of farmers were larger.

"I think they are still thinking the same way as before, as when they were on the farm," Olivia then asserted. "They are not on the farm but they still are still thinking they are on the farm, so they have big families." Olivia turned to Jacinta. "Do you agree with me?"

"Yeah," Jacinta said, nodding her head.

A smile lit up across Olivia's face. "Hey, she agrees with me. She agrees with me!" Olivia exclaimed, betraying that she held Jacinta, the Latina with such a strong voice, in very high regard.

Luis agreed that Mexican men needed to be better educated. "If you are educated you will avade, or how you say—"

"Avoid," Lucía offered.

"You will avoid bringing children." Luis concluded.

There was general agreement that the more men and women knew about the costs of raising children, the fewer they would have. Education was critical. But Olivia added another dimension to the discussion. She announced that in China the government had policies to control the number of children each family could have. Perhaps that should be applied to Mexicans in the United States, she thought. A few students gasped. All eyes focused suspiciously on Olivia as she began flipping through the pages of *Latinas in Chicago* looking for the tables on birth rates and family. As she directed our attention to the tables, we saw that if we applied Olivia's recommendation we would likely be reducing family size for all of the races and ethnicities listed, with the possible exception of white s who were having the fewest children. Olivia countered the students' disagreements with the suggestion that family size could be controlled by economic status, if not race or ethnicity. She then started searching the pages for another table. I asked whether education or government control was the best way to achieve the objective of reducing family size. All of the students, including Olivia, were in agreement that education was the best approach.

CHAPTER 14

"But if education doesn't work?" Olivia began laughing, letting us know that she was not entirely serious about her proposal. She then turned to *Latinas in Chicago* again and started turning pages. Finding the page she was looking for, she announced: "I didn't understand this. What does this mean?"

Luis, seated next to Olivia, looked to where her finger pointed and read the quote from the book, a quote from a woman in one of the focus group interviews. *I feel like I need to apologize for not having children. What is wrong with a Latina who does not have a child?* (p. 11).

Olivia repeated the quote and then asked: "She's sad because she can't have babies?"

"She doesn't say she can't. . . . We don't know if she's married or not," Luis said.

"It's not necessary to be married to have a baby," Pablo said.

"Why, why is she apologizing?" asked Luis.

"Maybe she can't take care of children if she has children," Justine said.

"No, no. There is two different sentences," Olivia responded. "Here, she apologizes because she doesn't have a baby. On the other hand, she had: *what is wrong with a Latina who does not have a child?*"

"Nothing is wrong with that," Luis said.

Listening to the discussion, the ever-quiet Amalia squirmed in her seat. She understood something that the others did not. Slowly, almost painstakingly, she raised her hand, though few students ever raised their hands in class.

I looked her way: "Amalia?"

"It's because maybe everybody thinks the role for the woman is to have the children," Amalia said.

Jacinta understood Amalia's point, adding: "This includes the customs and traditions."

"If the woman don't have children, it's not a real woman," Amalia explained the dilemma that young Latinas face.

The students agreed that Amalia and Jacinta had it right. Culturally speaking, it might not be easy for a young Latina to pursue an education and career and put off having children.

"Long ago they used to talk about the Mexican man. They said, 'You are the machine to bring the baby,'" Pablo said.

"Yeah, years ago, right?" Jacinta responded quickly, glaring at Pablo, attempting to steer him and the discussion toward recognition that times were changing for Latinas.

"I'm talking years ago, no?" Pablo returned the look. "To clean the house, to make the food—"

"To stay with the children," Jacinta interjected, picking up where Pablo left off.

"Oh, no. Come on. I'm not gonna do that for a man," declared Justine.

"We are talking a long time ago," Pablo said.

"Years ago," Luis said.

"They think that the man is to make the money. But now, in this time, the head of the family are both," Jacinta said.

"It was a long time ago," Pablo repeated.
"But now they can do it, both," Jacinta insisted.
"Yes, now," Pablo agreed.

EDUCACIÓN

"The theme was violence and domestic violence," Jacinta announced. With her prepared notes in hand, she launched into another presentation of the information she obtained from her Wednesday Community Dialogues meetings.

> But all the people talk mostly about the police and the young people who are in the gangs. And the problem is the police see the young people like bad people, like gangbangers. And some of them are racist, the police. So they just stop the Mexican people. And one of the solutions is they should have one police in the neighborhood who knows all the community. And another thing, they say that the police should be more human, like more involved in the community. He can see all the problems there are in the community, and all the people. Also they make a resolution that there should be a club in the neighborhood, people who know each other. And also they decided to have phone numbers for neighbors to know. And they can call the police when they see problems.

Jacinta finished her presentation with the story of a woman who once called the police to report a juvenile crime. The police released the woman's identity and her home was subsequently vandalized.

Olivia, who walked to Erie House most days, mentioned that she saw several houses along her route with yellow signs stating, "We call the police." She wondered about this, surmising that the gangs knew whom to target.

"So this woman had a sign?" she asked Jacinta

"No, but her phone number was public." Jacinta explained that the police had released the woman's identity.

"Was she Mexican?" Olivia asked.

Nodding, Jacinta said, "And the gang was Mexican too."

"Probably not," Olivia reconsidered the possibility.

"Why not?" I asked.

Olivia looked at me quizzically: "Because Mexican against Mexican?"

"Yes," Lucía, Victoria and Jacinta replied in unison.

"When somebody is involved in a gang, they don't want to care that they are Mexican or Polish or whatever. They don't care," Victoria confirmed.

Amalia wanted to better understand Jacinta's motivations for attending the Wednesday meetings. She asked about her personal interests, about whether the community was changing suddenly, requiring such activism. Jacinta explained that things were different a few years earlier when she was in her mid-teens, but it had since become harder for the kids.

CHAPTER 14

Victoria attributed such problems, in part, to the increase in families with two working parents, leaving kids to fend for themselves. "In this country," she said, "it seems that the older people don't have time to talk to the kids. The parents are working. They need money and start leaving their kids when they are ten." She made a comparison to Mexico where, traditionally, that was not the case. But since the Mexican recession began it seemed that family units were unraveling in Mexico, too.

Lucía explained that in Mexico City, where she lived, kids were joining gangs at younger and younger ages. There was little difference as far as she could see.

Amalia asked if gangs existed only among the Hispanic people. "Because I've seen just Hispanic people—"

"No, we are Latin." Victoria attempted to correct Amalia.

Slowly, letting Victoria know that she chose her words carefully, Amalia responded, "I - see - just - Hispanic - people - in - gangs."

"Do you know a lot of black people or white people?" Victoria rebounded.

Amalia shook her head and looked my way.

"They are in gangs, too," Victoria retorted.

I nodded toward Amalia, confirming Victoria's statement.

Victoria continued talking about the change that Mexican families go through in the United States, focusing more on work and earning money and less on the children. The children, she explained, then become undisciplined. We discussed different options available to such children, identifying, for example, many of the services that Erie provided. But I noted that many of the local youth—gangbangers among them—walked past Erie every evening en-route to wherever else they were going. Victoria responded that such kids probably came from single or two-parent, working families in which discipline was lacking. This was compounded, she maintained, by an American social and legal system that granted children more rights vis-à-vis parents. She said that kids called the police to report parental abuse upon the smallest of disciplinary acts, such as spanking. I had heard this rumor from students and other ESOL teachers so often, without ever learning of a particular instance in which a child actually picked up the phone and called the police, that I had come believe it was more of an immigrants' urban legend. Before I could respond, however, Olivia launched into a condemnation of spanking or any physical discipline, exhorting her classmates to be patient and talk with children, to spend time teaching by example. Victoria noted that Olivia did not have children, but finally agreed that spanking was not good. Victoria said that she would, of course, never spank a child where she worked as a trusted childcare provider, where working parents dropped off their children every morning.

Though the students acknowledged Lucía's contention that gangs were also a problem in Mexico City, most of the students agreed that family dynamics changed when whole families moved to the United States and set down roots. The struggle for economic success led to the shake-up of many family units. Priorities shifted and families faltered as they attempted to maintain their values.

The students' concerns reminded me of Guadalupe Valdes's *Con Respeto* (1996), an ethnography of ten Mexican families living outside of El Paso, Texas where they contend with conflicting Mexican family values and American education values. I had been reading Valdes's book at the time and had marked a few passages in anticipation of a time when it might be informative to add Valdes's story to our ongoing discussions. When I presented the book to the students, they were surprised yet intrigued that an entire book might be written about Mexican immigrants and their social issues. The book was passed around the room while I explained one of Valdes's critical themes. The Mexican families in the book valued children's contributions to the family unit. Children were not the central focus of the family; rather, the entire family's well-being was the priority. But schooling in the United States situated the child's individual academic success and their working futures as the principle family value. I read aloud a passage from Valdes's book.

> ... in all 10 families in the study, children were not the central focus of the family. Rather, the energy of all family members was directed at the welfare of the household as a functioning unit. ... *Respeto* was a central value in the Mexican families and one that demanded that children honor their parents in a very old-fashioned sense of that word. The children were taught to be grateful for what their parents had done for them and they were encouraged to think about the father and mother and about their siblings before thinking about themselves. Selfishness was discouraged and children who began contributing to the household were seen as virtuous and responsible. (1996, p. 180)

I finished the passage, adding: "The main values in these families are that children are taught to be responsible and good people, and to be responsible to family and contribute to the family. Whereas, in the U.S. the family is set up to focus on the child and the child's success in school." I asked the students if these ideas had any relevance to our discussion, if any of it rang true to them.

Timoteo, who had left his parents in Mexico as a teenager, though had faithfully and consistently sent money home, responded that he saw no reason that children could not succeed in school but also learn respect from their families. However, he did not agree that too much focus should be placed on the family. "At the same time," he said, "they have to think about what are they going to do when they grow up, their futures, their own futures."

Victoria explained that Mexicans in Mexico had a lot of kids. It was part of the culture to have large, family-centered families in which the older children cared for the younger children and when older they worked and contributed financially to the family. She contrasted this to the United States where family sizes were smaller and children put their parents in retirement homes.

Olivia commented, "The person who wrote the book, she said that the schools have just to teach and prepare the person to have a better future. This part of school I agree with. This is the obligation of the school. But not to give the education. The education is in the house."

"You remember when I talk before," Victoria said, "knowledge and education are different."

CHAPTER 14

"Yes, yes," Olivia responded.

"You gonna get the knowledge at school," Victoria continued.

"How to be prepared for the future, you learn at school," Olivia said. "But education—"

"—Good manners—" Victoria inserted.

"Good manners and how to be a good person, all the feelings and behavior and everything. The parents have the responsibility," Olivia said.

"Yes!" Amalia punctuated the mounting assertions about the role of the family in educating their children.

I asked which is more important and several voices chimed in, "Both!"

"First, I think it is at home, it's more important," Olivia continued. "Because if you are well prepared at home—"

"Yeah!" Jacinta expressed her encouragement.

"You can go and face the world," Olivia said.

I noted that Valdes differentiated between the Mexican and American uses of the term "education." In the United States education typically refers to what takes place formally in schools. In Mexico education refers more to raising children to be polite and virtuous, with positive social values and sound moral character. The students agreed that their use of the term education was consistent with Valdes's explanation. That, Victoria explained, is why she differentiated between knowledge and education.

Timoteo, though, was concerned. If education took place at school, where and how were the children learning to be good people in this country? How did the United States culture employ language to identify that purpose? He asked: "How do you call it to respect somebody, to help somebody, to—"

"To be a good man?" Amalia interjected.

"What do you learn?" Jacinta wondered.

I responded that hopefully children in the United States learned all of those things. We simply didn't use the term education to refer to what took place in the home. As far as I knew there was no single term that captured the realm of responsibility and action that *educación* encompassed for the Mexican/Latino family culture.

Given the dilemma that the students described earlier regarding the influence of economic priorities on the family unit, the absence of an American English equivalent for *educación* resonates as significant. Perhaps the closest translation is "family values," a term that has been seized by conservatives in this country, a term that for some suggests a sense of tradition and for others an affinity for reactionary politics. *Educación* suggests that parents teach their children, whereas "family values" suggests a longing for a society that is slipping away or is perhaps already gone.

Mexican/Latino families, as my students described and as Valdes lamented, might have sacrificed traditional values in order to succeed in the United States, but my students still believed in their active responsibility to educate whole children. Conservatives in this country have long objected to the parceling out of traditional family responsibilities over to the schools. Clearly, my students agreed.

But this distribution of responsibility is, in part, a result of the economic demands placed on family units to succeed, or at least survive, in this country. Increasingly, there is little choice in most households regarding whether both parents will work. The drive to succeed in the modern economy is pitted against traditional family values.

But, as described earlier, my students envisioned an alternative to this dichotomy. They hoped to chart a new path, steering clear of the practices of "a long time ago," in which the woman had a defined role in the home. My young, immigrant Latina students wanted to attend college, wanted to work, and wanted to make the necessary changes in their community so that they and their families could succeed, so that they could educate their children to be responsible and successful.

With the term "education" clarified, our discussion turned to differences between schools in the students' home countries and the United States. Amalia complained that students in the United States were disrespectful. Timoteo compared the Mexican system of *secundaria* and *preparatoria* to the high school system in the United States. He questioned the value of completing high school, especially for those who Amalia described, but also for those who showed little promise in their early years of school. In Mexico, such students completed *secundaria* at a younger age and went off to work, usually to support their families. Victoria asked what happened to these students in the United States when they did not finish high school. I responded that we typically label them "dropouts" and consign them to a lower social and economic class. Employers are then reluctant to hire them and colleges tend to ignore them. On a more positive note, I added that in the United States there still existed the opportunity for such students and any student who performed poorly in their early years to complete high school and pursue a higher education in college.

Olivia had previously described the family as the provider of an educational foundation from which "you could go and face the world." In attempting to explain U.S. values to the students, I recognized the difficult choices that families faced. I explained that poverty, racism and gender discrimination also posed substantial barriers. I explained that in this country schools were more often viewed as the provider of that foundation from which "you could go and face the world." In fact, I proudly explained the American ideal that anyone could access the educational system, reap its benefits and climb higher.

Rather cynically, Victoria responded, "It's a dream, right?"

I agreed, though not with her cynicism. It was a dream that I earnestly believed in for her and the other students in the class. I believed that this group of young, immigrant, mostly Latina students could succeed through sound, relevant and responsive education.

THE GREAT DEBATE

As we neared the end of November, with the holidays offering more diversions and the students gravitating in different directions, I sought a successful completion of our study of *Latinas in Chicago*. Because the bulk of the report consisted of tables and graphs pertaining to the six topics of economic self-sufficiency, employment, education, immigration, health, and domestic violence, I first provided instruction in how to read such text, and then had each student select two of the topics to study and present to the class. In contrast to some research literature that describes the reading of graphs and charts as difficult, technical reading, my students learned the skills easily. Of course, it helped that each set of graphs was accompanied by bulleted sentences, highlighting key findings. The students selected their individual topics, forewarned that following our discussions about what each student learned about Latinas in Chicago, we would have a debate over which of the topics should receive priority in public policy considerations.

Jacinta studied the topic of Education, U.S.-style education. She presented a list of statistical data depicting language proficiency and school completion rates among different Latina groups. She paid particular attention to those groups who possessed the most education (South Americans) and those who possessed the least (Mexicans and Puerto Ricans) among Latinas. When I questioned her regarding her focus, she explained, "I think my point is that I want to see Mexicans someday as high as the other ones. For example, I would like to see the Mexicans at least higher than the Puerto Ricans, even if the Puerto Ricans have a lot of opportunities for education. If Puerto Ricans is lower than Mexican I would like to explore why Puerto Ricans didn't take much education." Jacinta explained that her greatest priority was to try and help the group at the bottom. Regarding completion rates, Jacinta and Lucía agreed the low rates could be explained by the numbers of Mexican immigrants in Chicago who had little opportunity for formal education, though they did not explain the low rates for Puerto Ricans.

Justine had selected the topic of domestic violence. However, she explained that there was no domestic violence in her family and, therefore, it was irrelevant. Besides, she explained, she didn't like domestic violence. Amidst some laughter, Olivia tried to explain that studying the topic was not a reflection on Justine. Olivia asked for a show of hands of those who liked domestic violence. After nobody came forward, she launched into her presentation on the topic. She informed us of the rates of incidence among different groups, identifying whites as having the lowest rates, African Americans the highest, and Latinos falling in between.

She repeated the high rates among African Americans, leading Justine to respond, "But sometimes the white people just abuse the black people."

Olivia continued, probing for a way to understand the phenomena. "If it was Hispanic instead of African, if it was the opposite I would say it is because Hispanic people have no money, so they were sad because they couldn't [support] the family. But it is not this problem because African Americans, they are citizens. They are not illegal. So probably they are in the same situation like white people to get things."

In two months, Olivia had spent so much time listening to the other students differentiating between the undocumented and documented, citizens and noncitizens, that she, too, viewed the new country as being divided accordingly. Of course, because she was in the United States on a tourist visa, she perceived her legal status to be the principal obstacle to future success in the country. In her travels about Chicago, especially downtown, she observed numerous employment opportunities for which, with a little more English, she considered herself qualified. But because of her tourist status, they were unavailable to her. Like the other students, she did not understand how citizens could fare worse than noncitizens.

Though I was not prepared to accept poverty as a cause for domestic violence, I challenged Olivia, asking how she knew that African Americans were not the poorest. Knowing that the information existed elsewhere in the report, I asked if there was evidence to be offered.

Jacinta responded first, "We have an idea. But we know that the African American makes money because they are legal, right? So we have an idea."

"But what if I told you that African Americans are not wealthier than Latinos, that they are more poor than Latinos?" I asked.

"But if they are poorer than Hispanics, it's not because they have no opportunities to work like white people," Olivia said.

"Do they?" I asked.

"I think so. They are citizens," Olivia replied.

"They speak English," Timoteo added. "They have the social security number. I think they all have residency and citizenship information."

I responded, suggesting that we continue examining the report for further information to confirm or disprove these opinions. I also added that we should never forget that Africans were the only race or ethnic group brought to the country involuntarily, as slaves. For hundreds of years, they were slaves, and for the last hundred, they too struggled against the political, legal, and racial discrimination. The students listened but offered no response.

We then heard reports from Lucía and Olivia regarding health. Justine was supposed to have reported on health also, but simply didn't do the work. Olivia joked that everyone in Justine's house was healthy, and, besides, Justine didn't like health. This comment drew a sneer that faded to a smile from Justine, an acknowledgment that she was again caught unprepared.

Amalia reported briefly on immigration issues. Following her report, the students decided they knew most of the issues and did not need to discuss them.

Jacinta and Amalia presented on economic self-sufficiency. They offered more details regarding the status of Puerto Rican women as the poorest of the poor among Latinas. Amalia told us that Puerto Rican women also received more public assistance than any other Latina group, providing the answer to a question previously raised by Jacinta. As we surveyed the pages focusing on economic self-sufficiency, I directed the students' attention to the table labeled "Percent of Women Who are in Poverty by Race/Ethnicity," and asked which had the highest rate of poverty.

Studying the table, Lucía responded, "African American."

"This gets us closer to some of our questions from earlier when we assumed that some people had more money because of citizenship status," I explained. "At least

CHAPTER 14

in terms of women and female-headed families, this table indicates that is not the case."

I waited approximately ten seconds—an interminable amount of time in a classroom—for a response, but none came. I then explained that we had a case in which we could find answers to questions previously raised by cross referencing the tables. I asked if anyone saw any other connections between the tables.

"The Puerto Ricans are the people who have the most poverty and who have less education. And I don't know why. Because if they have the opportunity to study. I think they don't take advantage," Lucía said.

"I think they just waste the money they receive from the government," Amalia said. "Traveling to Puerto Rico instead of making one house here. They have the opportunity to have more money but they don't want to."

Jacinta agreed, "I think because they have an easy way to get the money from public benefits. It's an easy way to get the money. It is an easy way to spend the money. They didn't work. People who work know how to spend the money. They know what they can do with the money. But when [Puerto Ricans] get the money they have more fun."

Amalia explained that she observed differences between Mexicans and Puerto Ricans. "The Mexican people they spend the money in their family and make a future for their children. But the Puerto Rican people don't think of the future. That's why they are poor?"

"Did we answer your question?" Jacinta asked Lucía.

"Yes," Lucía replied. "I don't think that [Puerto Ricans] are really the poorest group in the Latinas. They have the opportunity for Medicaid and they go and get the money. The don't care to look for a job. And the other groups they don't have documents. So they have to work."

"That's right," Jacinta said.

"I think so. Maybe that's what happens with the Puerto Ricans," Timoteo said.

"Do you base your opinions on your personal experience or on the information from the book, or both?" I asked.

"Both," Jacinta said.

"From both," Lucía said.

As I became increasingly bothered by the steady stream of negative characterizations of Puerto Ricans that the students presented throughout our reading and study of *Latinas in Chicago*, I also wondered about my complicity as a facilitator. I had brought the text to the class, viewing it, perhaps naïvely, as merely statistical data to interpret for its relevance to our interactions in the community. I had selected the KWL method that incorporated students' knowledge and opinions into the comprehension of the text. Moreover, I had previously laid a foundation for free response and interpretation that I also encouraged with this expository text. The authors of *Latinas in Chicago*, I assumed, did not perceive the potential of their report to unearth interethnic troubles. Nor did I. The feelings of alienation and the defensive posturing brought on by the immigration reforms were just surfacing. The effects of the all-out offensive on people's hopes, dreams, and livelihoods were as yet unclear but were still threatening. In recognizing my role, I am not faulting my efforts. Rather, I am claiming responsibility. I gave statistical data to the students and they used it to support existing beliefs. There was certainly nothing new in that.

Despite the students' choice of *Latinas in Chicago* and their dedication to my assignments, by the third week of reading and discussing the text, the students were ready to move on. Trying to bring our study to a close, I pushed forward with the idea of students debating each other regarding the public policy priorities. On a Wednesday during our third week, with Jacinta attending her Community Dialogues meeting, I entered the classroom where I found Olivia, Lucía, Justine, Amalia and Victoria quietly reading books selected from our classroom library. When I announced it was time for the debate, Olivia and Lucía indicated a preference to continue reading their novels. I then asked for a show of hands of those who liked the report. Only Lucía claimed to like it, though she would still have preferred to read her novel that evening. Amalia reminded me that she did not like to read about immigrant issues. Victoria complained that there was very little that she did not know already. It was probably written for white people, she stated. Moreover, she did not trust the statistics. She knew some people at *Mujeres Latinas en Acción* and did not believe they could possibly have counted and interviewed every Latina in Chicago. As she had missed a previous class session in which I explained the methodology used in the study, I directed her to that section of the report to review the census data and Public Use Microdata Samples (PUMS). I explained the use of statistical sampling and satisfied her concerns.

Following the students' earlier reports on the six topics, I had compiled all of their individually "What am I Learning about Latinas in Chicago" written responses, photocopied them, and provided a set for each student. Their assignment was to study the pages and determine the public policy issue that demanded the highest priority in the city. These positions were to be presented in a debate format. I informed the students that they would comprise a trusted advisory council on Latina affairs and would be presenting their findings to me, posing as Mayor Richard M. Daley.

Despite their protests, the students were prepared with their note cards. I had instructed each to put their comments on the front and back sides of a single 4 X 6 note card in order to deliver a clear, concise presentation that would prompt debate and discussion. On one side of the cards they were to identify the top public policy priority. On the other side, they were to identify solutions for addressing the priority.

"OK, my name is Richard M. Daley. Don't throw a turkey carcass at me," I announced as the students just stared at me blankly (none had attended the Thanksgiving protest). I continued, "There are important issues facing Latinas in Chicago and I don't know what they are. So I have gathered all of you, the most intelligent Latinas in the city, people who have studied the PUMS data, so that each of you can tell me what is the most critical issue facing Latinas in this city."

Justine responded immediately: "They need a good education to find a good job. And if they have a kid they can help with the homework. That is what I think."

CHAPTER 14

Before I, posing as Mayor Daley, could question Justine, Amalia began, "I have the same thing: Education." She then presented her rationale.

One by one, Victoria, Olivia, and then Lucía stated their agreement. Education should be the top public policy initiative for Latinas.

"So, we all agree," Olivia announced.

"It doesn't sound like we are going to have much of a debate," I noted, drawing laughter from the students. I sought and received clarification that each was referring to education as it is understood in the United States context and culture. The Mayor then explained that he needed to know how many Latinas were in need of educational services and what kind of services they should receive. Victoria explained that she knew at least ten women who fit the description she offered.

Olivia began flipping the pages of her report, then before finding any particular page, she announced, "I think at least one thousand."

Victoria declared, "We need to implement programs."

"That's a solution, but I'm not sure [what problems exist]," Mayor Daley said.

"OK, the problem is that people drop out of high school," Victoria clarified.

"Thank you. Let's hear from other trusted advisors," the mayor responded.

Softly at first, though increasingly more forceful, Amalia spoke. "I think the Mexican people is the persons who most need help in education. Because the statistics they show that they have lower levels of education. They don't have knowledge about education. Or maybe they don't have the time."

"So, I am understanding that it's not just learning English." Mayor Daley said, attempting to capture the most essential elements of Amalia's argument. "There's also a lot of dropouts And you're saying it's mostly Mexicans who have the biggest problem in the city. And you have statistics to support your –"

"Yes," Amalia interrupted.

"Let me ask you something. Why you think it's only Mexicans that need more education?" Justine asked Amalia.

"Because here the statistics show that the Mexicans they don't have too much education, college education or high school education," Amalia responded.

The data from *Latinas in Chicago* did indicate that Mexican women had lower rates of high school completion (36.2%) and slightly lower rates of completion of bachelors degrees (5.2%) than Puerto Rican women (42.2% and 5.4%, respectively), and far lower rates of education than any other Latina subgroup. At least by the measure of educational attainment, the students were correct— Mexican women might be the most in need. By focusing on education as the top priority in public policy considerations, the students possessed statistical evidence to support their assertions that Mexican women should receive the most attention. I am not suggesting that they searched among the topics to find a context in which Mexican women had the lowest position. They genuinely believed that education— schooling—provided the foundation for success. In asserting the priority of education as a public policy issue they were able to use the data to reach a different set of conclusions from the authors.

Mayor Daley turned to Justine, "Do you think it should not be just a focus on Mexican women? It's more than –"

"Yeah, it's more," Justine insisted. "It's not only Mexican. It's a lot of people."

"But my trusted advisor over here says she has statistics," Mayor Daley said.

"We don't have the same amount [of education as people] from Peru, Ecuador, Latina America as the people from Mexico. She say the Mexican people but how about the other race. I think the other teenagers don't drop out of school," Victoria said.

"Maybe because the Puerto Ricans they have more opportunities than Mexicans. That is why the Mexicans need more attention. The Puerto Ricans have more chances than the Mexican people," Amalia said.

"Why do you think the Puerto Ricans have more chance than the Mexican?" Justine asked.

Olivia answered, "They are allowed to come to the United States. But the Mexican people they are not."

"So, I should help only the Mexican people in the city?" Mayor Daley asked.

"No, but we are talking about the main issue of Latinas," Victoria answered.

"I think not only you should pay attention to Mexicans. I think Mexicans have a big group that needs help. But I think the other groups need help, too. So it's not fair that we just put attention to one group," Lucía said.

"But if they find solutions for the Mexican people then it is more easy to go for the next person, the rest," Amalia said.

"Excuse me, Steve. What do you think?" Justine asked.

"What do I think? I'm da mayor," I responded. Mayor Daley has never been known for his eloquence.

"Even though you the mayor you should say something," Justine said.

"OK, here's what I understand from my trusted advisors," the mayor responded. "The number one issue is education. That includes learning English and solving the dropout problem. And I should devote most of my attention to Mexican women."

"Men and women. The men need help too," Olivia inserted, perhaps reflecting on our earlier discussion about teaching men the importance of limiting family size.

"So when I do that, am I gonna lose votes in the Puerto Rican community? I got a lot of votes from the Puerto Ricans last time. I don't want to lose them." The mayor was growing concerned.

"That's why we don't focus in one group," Lucía said, showing her appreciation for the political context.

"I think we can take the Mexican people to see if the solution is good. Then help the Puerto Ricans and the others," Amalia offered.

Lucía liked Amalia's idea, "We are going to focus on the Mexicans, then Puerto Ricans, then the Guatemalans. We focus on all the groups. . . . The statistics, like she say, say that Mexicans need more help. But this is not the only group that needs help. We don't forget about the other groups."

"Now that you've convinced me what the most important issues are and where to focus my interests, what should I do? How should I do this?" Mayor Daley asked the group.

CHAPTER 14

"Put emphasis on the elementary school. Get people who want to teach, not only who want the money," declared Victoria.

"You can start by no more denying admissions to Latin persons," Amalia said. "Give them a chance to prove if they want to study. Give them a scholarship."

"Why do they need scholarships?" Mayor Daley asked.

"To go to college, for college and the university," Victoria responded.

"OK, trusted advisor?" Mayor Daley turned to Lucía.

"Stop denying education to the children of illegal people," Lucía demanded, referring to the recent federal welfare and immigration reform legislation.

"But I haven't been." Mayor Daley became defensive. In fact, Daley had vowed not to follow many of the new anti-immigrant polices of the federal government.

"You are denying education to the children of illegal people," Lucía repeated, this time more forcefully. "And try to have more schools like this for the parents. The parents need education too."

Olivia perked up. "For this kind of school. Oh, you put the same as I did here." She pointed to her note card. "I put that they have to have an opportunity to study—Latinas who don't speak English. One example is this school. This school is very important."

Victoria agreed, "One thing is you gotta have more sites like this."

Mayor Daley, still reeling from the accusation that he was denying education to anyone, clarified that it was the state and federal legislatures that were denying education to immigrant children and adults. Cowering before his increasingly assertive Latina advisors, he asked what to do if the laws were passed.

"Don't give them your vote," Lucía demanded, probably meaning his support, though the Mayor's influence with Illinois legislators could lead some of them to vote for pro-immigrant policies.

Olivia, still unsure of the new laws and the sentiment behind them, cautioned that a more reasonable position would prevail. "Probably they are not going to put this kind of law. They can't!" she exclaimed. "If they do this, many children are going to suffer!"

The mayor asked for additional ideas, but his request was met with silence. He continued, "Well, I'm gonna consider all of these things. Oh wait, what about curriculum? What should they teach at schools like this? I heard about a book called *Latinas in Chicago.* Do you think that I should get all the teachers in Chicago to teach that book?

"No," said Victoria.

"No," said Justine.

"No," said Amalia.

"Well do you think that I should have all the students in adult education programs in Chicago reading this book so that they will be as intelligent and well-informed about these issues as you are?" Mayor Daley asked.

"Nooo!" implored Justine and Amalia.

"Yes," Lucía and Olivia declared.

"Yes," Victoria added. "Even if I don't like too much this book, I think everybody should know about it."

PART VI

REFLECTIONS

CHAPTER 15

REFLECTIONS ON CONFRONTING INTOLERANCE

REFLECTIONS IN THE NEW MILLENIUM

In the fall of 1996 when our class was meeting, the new immigration policies of the antiterrorism, welfare, and immigration reforms had not yet been implemented. The students and I were only aware that difficult times lay ahead for many immigrants, documented and undocumented. Tim and the staff at Erie did their best to interpret the new legislation and present it to the students. But the possible scenarios that they could envision resulting from the new policies were still unclear. For some, the new provisions seemed unfathomable. Olivia, whose American dream was gradually slipping away and who had less at stake than many others in our class, declared at the end of chapter 14, "Probably, they are not going to put this kind of law. They can't! If they do this many children are going to suffer!" Unfortunately, Olivia's prediction proved inaccurate.

In the introduction to this book, I present stories from the nation's newspapers that identify the impact of the 1996 reforms on immigrant lives and families. Though they appeared with less frequency, alarming and tragic stories continued to emerge after the 2001 terrorist attacks amidst the debates that resurfaced in the middle of that decade. One story in particular stands out.

In 2007, National Public Radio aired a series of reports (Montaigne, 2007; Norris, 2007; Sanchez, 2007a, 2007b; Vasquez-Toness, 2007) following the Immigration and Customs Enforcement (ICE) raid of a garment and leather goods manufacturer in New Bedford, Massachusetts. The ICE was a new agency created as part of Homeland Security. Like the West Town neighborhood of Chicago, New Bedford had attracted immigrants to its manufacturing plants for over two hundred years, and many had settled there. The manufacturer, Michael Bianco, Incorporated, employed undocumented immigrants in its effort to fulfill a $200 million contract with the U.S. Defense Department to produce vests and backpacks for U.S. soldiers fighting in Iraq. A total of 361 employees were arrested and detained, most of them women working to support their families. Many were deported to their home countries. Although ICE representatives disputed the figures, a school representative claimed that between 200 and 300 citizen and non-citizen children were separated from at least one parent who was deported; 29 children ended up in foster care. Local, state-supported social service agencies took on the responsibility for caring for many of the children, some of whom were still being breastfed by their mothers when the women were arrested and detained. Local charities and the Catholic church stepped in to provide financial support and other material goods to the families. The local school system accepted the responsibility for counseling traumatized children. A crisis intervention team and school counselors attended to children who had lost one or both parents. Naturally, many of these children had been advised by parents not to discuss immigration matters with any adults outside of their families, and were therefore reluctant to speak with those who may have helped them to cope with parental loss. Numerous families, fearing interaction with any public entity, kept their children from returning to school.

Two of the radio reports from New Bedford describe the tragedy that struck the family of Dominga and her husband, Ricardo. Following the raids, Ricardo was detained in El Paso, Texas for six months before being deported to Guatemala. Ricardo's mother then sold her Guatemalan home to pay for his illegal return and eventual reunification with his family in New Bedford. Seven months after being deported, Ricardo made his way back to his family in Massachusetts, only to die in Dominga's arms on the very night of his return. At some point during his return trip, possibly while journeying though the desert, he developed an acute airway obstruction but he declined to seek health care and risk being discovered. The local director of the community economic development center, attending Ricardo's funeral, is quoted in the report as saying, "It's a story of the devotion of people to their family and to being united with their family. And it didn't matter whether he risked his life to cross the desert and then lost his life" (Sanchez, 2007b, ¶ 23).

In the first decade of the new millennium, tragic stories of border crossings, factory raids, and deportations appear to be of little importance to anti-immigrant proponents who rest on the argument that these people broke the law when they crossed the border. The elimination of constitutionally guaranteed protections for legal and undocumented immigrants and a retrenchment of entitlements for legal immigrants are insignificant to anti-immigrant proponents who argue that we have a border control problem and that immigrants in general will have to suffer the consequences. These positions have become more entrenched than they were a decade earlier before the 2001 terrorist attacks. Hearkening back to the brief period following the 1996 reforms and before the terrorist attacks, Tichenor offers a quote from Jonas and Thomas: "Taken together, what the most recent acts [1996] indicate is that the representatives of the American people want a low-paid, compliant and easily exploitable immigrant labor force, with no basic democratic rights" (in Tichenor, 2002 p. 296). These observations help to explain the reform policies and public sentiment of the 1990s. But a decade later, they are no longer adequate interpretations of the vehement anti-immigrant passion that has gripped many in the U.S. The denial of democratic rights is no longer enough for anti-immigrant activists. The loathing of undocumented immigrants ("illegals") is so robust that employers have also become targets of anti-immigrant ostracism. The New Bedford manufacturer who supplied backpacks and vests to U.S. soldiers in Iraq was forced to sell the company and the owners, at last report, faced a minimum of ten years imprisonment for employing the undocumented workers. In the new millennium, even the free market proponents who managed to preserve their interests during a century of vacillating immigration policies, have lost influence. Amidst the rhetoric and reality of a new global economy we have been willing to open our borders to free flowing commerce but have closed the doors to workers looking to take advantage of economic opportunities.

During the fall of 1996, as the new polices were just coming to light, my students were somewhat reluctant to identify racism or ethnic intolerance to be at the root of new immigration policies. When we read the story of Jesse Lopez de la Cruz and compared her struggles to students' contemporary struggles with workplace discrimination and the new reforms, the students identified employers, capitalism, and the government as their opponents. Most of the students were legal residents or citizens, and legally employed. Few of the students would have to directly confront the new policies. Because they were young, aware and determined, they would very likely succeed despite the atmosphere of intolerance. They did not want to believe that the society in which they were working so hard to achieve and gain membership could so easily turn on them because of their race or ethnicity. But, as we further discussed Jesse's story, the students determined that maybe white Americans feared an increase in the Latino population. The reforms, perhaps, were not just about preserving a way of life in America. They were also about preserving power, the students decided.

In more than a decade of monitoring immigration discussions and debates since I began teaching at Erie, I have come to believe the students were correct. The 1996 reforms and escalating intolerance of immigrants since then are responses to what Americans—white Americans, in particular—perceive as a threat to their culture and power. Responding, at least in part, from fear of an unknown future in which Spanish speaking, brown-skinned people would have an increasing influence in U.S. society, the country continues to implement tougher barriers and more difficult to obtain standards for admission. The U.S. has made it more burdensome for even legal immigrants to succeed. It has imposed significant roadblocks for people in their attempts to pursue and attain the American dreams we all embrace. In response to a fear of the other we have succumbed to manufactured fears and in turn given consent to repressive policies. There is a tremendous need for political, economic, labor, and immigration policies throughout the Western Hemisphere that will benefit working-class peoples and forestall the need to leave one's country in hopes of survival. Of course, our borders should be respected and monitored but not through the practices we have seen over the past decade, when absent a comprehensive immigration policy, enforcement has led to thousands of people dying while crossing the border. The anti-immigrant fervor that has taken hold in lieu of such comprehensive efforts and policies reveals heightened, extreme levels of anxiety and xenophobia among Americans. The severe intolerance that accompanies these conditions and has been unleashed upon immigrants must be confronted.

A HISTORY OF INTOLERANCE

The debate over the public policy priorities for Latinas in Chicago that was held during our last class session of the fall 1996 term was the last time that group of students met together. As discussed previously, most made new educational plans for the year. Justine continued in her morning GED class and resumed tutoring

CHAPTER 15

with me later in the spring. Lucía devoted more of her time to learning and working in Erie's technology center while occasionally attending my class in the spring. Olivia moved to a Chicago suburb with her new driver's license and, I assume, did some traveling before returning to Brazil. Jacinta joined the Pathways to Success program at Erie, expanded her geographic, economic, and personal horizons through a new job and a new church, and received tutoring from me later in the spring. Amalia enrolled in Wright College to begin her academic pursuit of a business career. Victoria registered for more classes at Harold Washington College to continue her studies in child development. Timoteo visited family in Mexico for two months before returning to Chicago, where he decided against participating in the union organizers' training institute. Instead he needed to work more and send more money home to his family. Cyntia continued working toward her GED in Spanish, and joined Jacinta in the Pathways class during the spring. Cyntia occasionally borrowed books from my classroom library, including Rigoberto Menchu's biography, which she reported on in her Pathways class. Luis worked more and more hours, and came to Erie less and less. Maya continued to study in the secure surroundings of her lower level ESOL class.

I continued teaching at Erie until June 1997. During the winter and spring of 1997, after the fall students had gone their separate ways, I was able to push the curriculum in directions I felt previously unable to with the fall students. While the students in the winter and spring semester have not been the focus of this book, a brief review of the curricular agenda in that class will serve readers of this book to better understand and critique the choices I made with the fall students.

As word spread that my approach to advanced ESOL instruction was an accessible one, many of Tim's level four ESOL students (including two Leadership students I had not taught previously) began attending my class in January 1997. Having come from Tim's class, many were already predisposed to accepting a politicized curriculum. As winter pushed on to spring, with April 1, 1997, the date planned for implementation of the first wave of immigration reforms, the political consciousness of these students was already piqued. Whereas I had needed to gently guide the curriculum with my combined group of Leadership students and advanced ESOL devotees in the fall semester, the new group of students was ready and willing to read and critique public policy. When a demonstration outside of the alderman's office was scheduled during our class time and announced as an option for us, the majority of these students voiced their desire to participate, declaring that to parade in below freezing weather would be a worthwhile use of our class time. April 1st arrived accompanied by a letter from the local alderman declaring his final decision not to sponsor the Erie Housing Coop in the City Council.

Meanwhile, July 1, 1997 was the date set for implementation of the new welfare reform, with its many provisions targeted at immigrants, to begin. In late April, the Illinois Department of Public Aid held a question and answer session regarding its interpretations of federal welfare reform. The spring students constructed a letter of complaint to read aloud at the public forum. A majority of the students decided it was an appropriate use of class time to board the Erie vans and travel to a predominantly Puerto Rican neighborhood a few miles away to present their letter.

As their political antennae were tuned into the latest public policy decisions that might affect their lives and those of friends and family, the defensive posturing of the mostly Mexican students in the winter/spring class also became more pronounced. We read several volumes of a locally published journal titled *The Journal of Ordinary Thought*[6] with stories, poems and essays written mostly by African Americans in Chicago. When reading, discussing, and responding to the readings, the students embraced the literature and described their identification with the various feelings of hope, determination, anxiety and defeat they encountered in the journal. Some wrote their own poems and stories in response. But when I pushed further, suggesting some identification and possible solidarity with the authors themselves, my students were reluctant to agree with me. Their stories were, of course, different. Yet, I think they also determined they could not look to the African American community for solidarity, for that community held little power itself.

When the students drafted a letter to the Illinois Department of Public Aid to protest the new policies, they were careful to employ a few rhetorical strategies. They acknowledged that many people abused the welfare system. But immigrants should not have to pay for the actions of others, they declared. When we assembled for class following the meeting with the public aid representatives, several students expressed their surprise at how many Puerto Ricans and African Americans also attended that meeting. For some reason, it had not been clear to the students that welfare reform would affect so many different people. Because the immigration reforms coincided with welfare reforms, the Mexican students assumed that they alone were the targets of all of the new laws. We had already been studying public policy research data regarding labor market projections, poverty levels, and livable wages. The students were now able to couple our studies with their realization that many people could be hurt by the welfare reform. They were then left with the question: If welfare reform was not aimed only at immigrants, but a larger portion of the population, why was it taking place? It was then that the students accepted my proposal to learn more about the history of intolerance the United States.

We ended the winter/spring semester by reading the *Declaration of Independence* and the *Constitution*, followed by a publication from the Southern Poverty Law Center titled *Us and Them: A History of Intolerance in America* (Carnes, 1995). The students (including Lucía, whose response is detailed in chapter 7) read several stories about intolerance covering a period beginning in the 1600's and continuing to end of the twentieth century. The students compared notes regarding the different stories and many decided there was a common factor throughout the history of the U.S.—white people. Whether or not race was the specific issue of a given story in the text—many stories pertained to intolerance based on religion, gender, and sexual orientation—somehow, it seemed, white people were always somewhere behind the hatred. These students, like the fall students had done, discussed the significance of whiteness in Latino identity and culture in Mexico and South America. In recognizing racism in the histories of their home countries, they more clearly understood the role of race at the crossroads of immigration and welfare reforms in the U.S. Their consciousness of the anti-immigrant zealotry was coupled with recognition that it was yet another episode in a long history of intolerance. The students plotted titles of the many stories on an historical timeline adjacent to different constitutional amendments. In doing so, they realized that constant vigilance and redress of social wrongs were required to satisfy our yearnings for the guarantee of life, liberty and the pursuit of happiness. Through our unit of study, the students realized that theirs was a historical struggle, and with that understanding they seemed a little more secure of their place and their futures in their adopted country.

During the previous fall semester, I had considered opportunities to present this history of the United States to the students. I thought they, too, might benefit from knowing their place in the troubled story of our country. A history of Puerto Rico and stories of Puerto Ricans struggling to assert their Latino identity in the United States might have helped the Mexican students to know more about this other Latino group in Chicago. While most were familiar with the fact of African American slavery, only a few were aware of an additional one hundred years of Jim Crow policies, not to mention the various types of continuing discrimination experienced by African Americans in Chicago. While I presented some of this information briefly before *La Marcha* and made some connections between *La Marcha* and the Civil Rights Movement, we did not read stories about the civil rights struggle. The scratchy black and white video of Dr. Martin Luther King Jr.'s speech at the Lincoln Memorial revved us up for our own exhausting journey. Though King's oratory is likely more inspiring than the same words on the page, one problem was that we still lacked a story to read. As a group we could not absorb King's words and contemplate their significance through his speech in the same way that this could be accomplished through the lingering presence of characters in a story. Jacinta felt the words come to life through her own reading about King, but we did not get to share those feelings based on her summary and presentation to us in class.

In one respect, the critical, responsive literacy instruction was inadequate during the fall semester. My quest to understand individual students' interests and ambitions, cultivate common points of inquiry, and construct a responsive curriculum kept us from examining the history that might have fostered more contemporary understanding and, possibly, cross-cultural solidarity. Through a response-centered pedagogy, I attempted to understand the cultural and political climate as seen through my students' eyes. I wanted to see how they were internalizing the issues of the day and then respond through the curriculum. In short, I hovered in and about the collective zone of proximal development and made pedagogical decisions accordingly. In so doing, I may have sacrificed what I believed to have been a right course of action. My field notes from the semester reveal that I was disturbed, particularly, by the comments made regarding Puerto Ricans. But as an interpreter of the entire milieu, I was also hampered by what I did not know. I had not yet developed my own understanding of the students' antipathy toward Puerto Ricans. At the same time, the psychological impact of the anti-immigrant movement on the students was still unclear to me. I recall during the spring 1997 semester wishing my fall students were still with me to continue my journey as I was learning more and more about how to help them with theirs.

CRITICAL, RESPONSIVE LITERACY INSTRUCTION

As described above, the picture of immigration reform was clearly emerging for the spring 1997 students. But that picture was only beginning to take shape during the previous fall. The fall students had a sense of the intolerant atmosphere that had drifted eastward from California. They comprehended the information that was presented in community forums and in the news regarding immigration reform, but it was still unclear how the new policies would affect them directly. The Leadership students were, of course, more aware of the new reform policies. The non-Leadership students who participated in the advanced English instruction were initially less aware, though increasingly they came to recognize the significance of the emerging state of affairs. While we attempted to make sense of all that was happening, it would still take another couple of years for the effects of immigration reform to be realized.

In our class we did not read the legislation that was being enacted in order to discuss and respond to it. Perhaps we should have. But, again, that information was being presented on a regular basis by Tim and others at Erie through community forums. Instead, we mostly read stories. We read about characters and their struggles. Through them we developed an appreciation for the various and interwoven contexts of immigration, work, activism, race, language, youth, history, cultural membership and local political priorities. We read stories and policy literature, responded to it and to each other, and set about determining who we wanted to be amidst the intense local and national debates.

Jesse Lopez de la Cruz helped us to see connections between the personal and the political, to recognize the array of forces that can be mounted to suppress the aspirations of a small but growing and vocal minority. My choice of Jesse's story had been made prior to our first class in response to my understanding of the Leadership students' interests. The Nicholasa Mohr and Gary Soto stories were more tentative choices, made in response to my perceptions of students' recent inclinations. I had hoped that Nicholasa Mohr's *An Awakening Summer 1956* would inspire the creative writings of the students. I hoped it would help them to recognize the passion that could be brought to the surface and inspire them to summon a good fight when they needed to do so in their own lives. In fact, the students recognized that passion in Mohr's story, though most were not motivated to compose stories of their own battles. Gary Soto's "Growing Up" offered us a gentle reminder of who we were during the rest of our lives when we relaxed, lowered our political antennae and filtered out the social tension, if only for a short time.

With David Gomez's "Yo Soy Chicano," I became more assertive in my teacher research role. During a year at Erie, I had learned much about the lives and ambitions of the young, adult immigrant students there. I had also become more acquainted with the educational research literature that pertained mostly to the children of immigrants and high school-age immigrant students. I had also read about and met older immigrant adults whose goal was to learn enough English language and literacy simply to get through daily life. But there was very little research regarding older adolescent and young adult immigrants (those ages eighteen to twenty five and not yet in college) who desire complete access to the opportunities that exist in the United States. I wanted to fill in the gap in the literature and learn how the young adults perceived their Latino identities amidst the dominant white culture. Therefore, I prepared a more carefully orchestrated approach to the lesson, involving an elaborate set of discussions that preceded our reading. As I have shown, the students' response revealed a very determined attitude toward achieving success. As young, first-generation immigrants, they stated that they would never be "American," but they were still determined to pursue their American dreams.

I followed up the careful construction of lessons surrounding the Gomez story with our study of *Latinas in Chicago*, the expository research text. By then, I had grown more comfortable in recognizing that responsive curriculum could include my accumulated understanding of students' interests and concerns. I had long ago dismissed a commonly held idea among community literacy educators that each session must begin with generative dialogue and only then could literacy instruction be offered in response. This makes it impossible to plan extended reading engagements, a necessity for students who desire participation in powerful literate discourses. Perhaps the requirement of having dialogue first is more suitable in writing groups, where reading of previously published material is given less emphasis (Heller, 1997). Again, I have not claimed to be a student-centered teacher. At Erie and elsewhere, I have endeavored to be a response-centered teacher with the belief that students are looking for experienced, caring teachers who possess the nerve to make some decisions on their behalf. That said, my stance with the students was still provisional. I waited to interpret students' actions and interests in the community before making decisions. I was certainly not teacher-centered, as made evident by my decision to invite Mayor Richard M. Daley into our classroom to hear and respond to the students' concerns over public policy and their futures in Chicago.

SUCCESSES AND SHORTCOMINGS

With regard to meeting students' stated interests, I consider the class to have been a success. We never read about or discussed roller-blading, but we did use language and literacy to explore all of the personal interests and community concerns identified by students during the first week of class (Table 2.1). I was successful in providing students with an entree to English literacy. The students were exposed to more English language and literacy than had ever been the case in their previous educational experiences. Most of the students had never experienced a literacy-oriented class that attempted to contextualize their interests and concerns for community as part of the curriculum. Many had not read books in their native language. Most had never read a book in English. They did in my class. Some of the Leadership students—Jacinta, Timoteo, Luis, Cyntia—learned to use literacy, literature, and biographies, in particular, to find continued inspiration for their activities in the community. Other students—Lucía, Amalia, Olivia, and even Justine—learned to use literacy to pursue their personal agendas with greater recognition of some of the obstacles that could besiege them.

In some respects, students' success in the fall class was mixed. The ongoing dilemma of adult literacy and adult ESOL education, and consequently, one of its most frequently used evaluative measures, pertains to retention of students. Adult literacy and adult ESOL attrition is so high that class completion alone is often recognized as a success. My principle determinant of success was whether or not our class made a contribution to students' ambitions. Of course, the students had to be present for me to claim a contribution to have been made. While attendance waned toward the end of the semester, of thirteen students who attended at least four class sessions, I would characterize eight as having completed successfully. Four of these—Jacinta, Victoria, Timoteo and Luis—were Leadership students. Four—Lucía, Olivia Amalia and Justine—were non-Leadership, advanced ESOL students.

Lytle (1990) and Mikulecky (1994) explain that significant changes in adults' literacy use is usually preceded or accompanied by significant changes in lifestyle. This was true of my Erie students. The course was most beneficial to those who were already determined to attend college and had arranged their lives accordingly. Such students included Jacinta, Lucía, Victoria and Amalia. Olivia, of course, was pursuing a different dream for what turned out to be a short period of time. She arranged her life in pursuit of that dream. The young men who had occasionally expressed the hope of attending college—Timoteo, Luis, Sergio—worked full time jobs and were unable to order their lives in accordance with that goal. Each had worked steadily since immigrating to the United States during their teenage years. Though Luis had completed high school, he did so while working full time. Despite their recognition that education was a way to escape the vicious cycle that kept them from achieving success, as Sergio described during our first week of class, it was too difficult for the young men to extricate themselves from working in what Sergio had referred to as "hands jobs."

It is clear that my class was best suited to the younger Latinas who had the background, time, and ambition to rise to the challenges presented in the curriculum. When we held the debate over public policy priorities for Latinas in Chicago, the students were unanimous in their opinion that education was the most pressing need. However, I do not overlook the fact that the debaters were the more highly educated, college-bound individuals. They had studied the data and arrived at reasonable conclusions. But they were also making claims about their own futures while projecting their values onto the aspirations of others. Sergio, who on the first night of class declared his unfulfilled dream of getting a college degree, would probably have agreed with the young Latinas. Pablo, who had completed *preparatoria* in Mexico where he owned his own print shop and was preparing his children for educational success in the United States, would likely have agreed. Had she remained in the advanced class and learned to read the statistical data along with the other Latinas, Maya might also have confirmed education to be the top priority. Like Pablo, her ambition rested with hopes and dreams for her children, one already in college. It is possible that all thirteen of the students might have agreed. But for a variety of reasons—most pertaining to the need to work, support family in Mexico, and raise children—many of the students did not make it to the end of the semester. They were not present to confirm education as a priority. Cyntia, Maya, Pablo and Brisa all left the class without, in my estimation, having derived much benefit. Their language and literacy, and their participation in the community, did not demonstrably improve from having spent time in my class.

DOMINANT DISCOURSES AND INDIVIDUAL PURSUITS

It is clear that the literacy emphasis of my critical, responsive pedagogy best served those whose existing discourse was compatible. Those who benefited the most had already completed high school, passed the GED test, or completed the equivalent in their home country. However, compatibility with or mastery of the dominant discourse, as described in the previous section, was not the sole determinant of success. While Luis, Sergio and Pablo had educational levels similar to the women identified here, they lacked the lifestyle that would have enabled them to take advantage of the literacy curriculum. The literacy activities we engaged in were significant for those Erie students who were able to participate in a more academically literate culture.

Among the Leadership students, Jacinta and Victoria benefited most from the course. Both had a high school level education through a Spanish language curriculum. Jacinta completed high school in Chicago, but more significantly, she returned to her childhood love of reading while in my class. She was a reader and accepted my emphasis on literacy. In particular, she liked reading novels. Given both her spiritual and political convictions she found that a more emotive or aesthetic stance to her reading best suited her interests in the literacy transaction. As described in chapter 13, if she could feel for the characters and believe in their struggles, then they could be of use in her daily, spiritual, and political life. They would help her to feel her way through and to seek out a future, quite possibly in service to the neighborhood.

Victoria had completed *secundaria* in Mexico and was already attending college in Chicago. Thus, she too had decided that it was through participation in literate discourse—academic literacy—that she could achieve her personal and political goals. Her interest in steering the younger generation toward heightened cultural awareness and respect would be served through her studies in child development education.

Among the non-Leadership, advanced ESOL students, Olivia, Amalia and Lucía benefited the most from the curriculum and instruction of our class. Olivia and Amalia had completed the equivalent of secondary education in their home countries. In addition, both had a middle class background, the expectation that they would continue their education, and the opportunity to do so.

Olivia attended a music conservatory in Brazil years earlier as a young adult. She had experience with a variety of literacy forms including poetry, novels, business correspondence, and travel literature. She was well versed in each and recognized how to use the different literate discourses to her advantage. When she wanted to extend her travels, expand her horizons, and look for the American dream that she still believed to exist, she buckled down and learned to read the *Rules of the Road.* Of course, she also had to learn where to take the test and how to offer a "tip" if necessary. For that, she was dependent on the Mexican students who had mastered a different discourse.

Amalia was going to college. Amalia was going to be a businesswoman. Amalia was going to be so wealthy that she would some day return to Ecuador and live the good life. Amalia, I also came to realize, was a very sensitive, young Latina who would likely use her literacy for all that she was determined to accomplish and, along the way, leave the world a little better off than when she arrived. She quietly observed the injustices of which her classmates spoke so often. She mulled it all over, and without asserting any leadership role among the older students in class, she surprised us with her essay, "The American Dream." Her essay exhibited serious thought about all that we had discussed, as well as genuine respect for the students who would likely not reach the educational level to which she aspired.

Lucía had to work harder than Olivia and Amalia, and she did. Since her childhood in Mexico, her academic ability had always been recognized. Unfortunately, her father derailed her ambitions when he prevented her attendance at *preparatoria* as a young adolescent. Fortunately, she had teachers at Erie who recognized her promise and encouraged her to keep moving on to the next English class, and eventually on to college. There was little doubt that she would work hard and succeed in mastering academic discourse. She read widely and sampled a variety of rhetoric. In response to her reading, she often claimed the participant or efferent stance and used it to explore the possibilities of her future. Likewise, she was tuning her rhetorical ability with greater confidence in her own passion and her own storytelling. Lucía, the aspiring poet-doctor, was ready for college. She just needed guidance.

CRITICAL EXPOSURES

It is disappointing to recognize that my critical, responsive pedagogy with its emphasis on literacy use best served those who were most ready to be served through literacy. There is always a hope, especially in community literacy programs, that through the activities of the classroom, students' lives will be transformed. The dream is that the students will embrace their literate futures, take full advantage of opportunities that literacy education avails, and do their part to change the world that we share. Of course, literacy success is often dependent upon the circumstances in which it is situated. Possession of literacy alone does not change people's lives.

When tutoring Justine, I tried to impress upon her that Frederick Douglass's turning point came when he decided to fight back against his master. His ability to read and write had already made him more conscious of his and his fellow-slaves'

CHAPTER 15

oppression. At times, he lamented his heightened awareness. The dreadful conditions of his slavery coupled with his knowledge of a seemingly unattainable human condition were more torturous than the physical abuse he received. But Douglass's coming to consciousness also awakened in him the need to fight back. His literacy alone did not provide his freedom, but his consciousness heightened through literacy led him to confront his master, to beat him down, to draw blood. From that point on, Douglass never turned back. He taught fellow-slaves to read and write, and he eventually escaped to fight for justice and freedom, and write his story.

I always welcomed Justine's passionate exclamations while reading *Frederick* during our tutoring sessions. "Damn!" she would exclaim when Frederick suffered another whipping. "That's good!" she would announce proudly when Frederick resolved once again to pursue his freedom. Even though we never finished the book together, she knew that by the end of the book he had beaten back the cruelty and the inhumanity. He had fought for his freedom and attained it.

As I reflect on my time reading about Frederick Douglass with Justine, I am compelled to reconsider some earlier estimations of success. Perhaps our activities in the classroom were more significant than course completion or college enrollment alone might suggest. Our readings heightened awareness of the fight for which many of the students had already enlisted. We marched on the Democratic National Convention and we drew inspiration from the story of Jesse Lopez de la Cruz. In Nicholasa Mohr's story we felt the passion of the woman who smashed a Pepsi bottle on the counter in a small Texas town and determined to fight back against intolerance. We then marched on Washington, D.C. to proclaim solidarity and advance a political movement. We recognized the angst and confusion of a young David Gomez trying to succeed in a white world that would not accept him. We protested at city hall, the mayor's residence, and later the alderman's office, declaring that gentrification was unacceptable, if not unavoidable. These were hard working students, going to school, learning the English language and striving for everything that could be expected of them. Yet, in the mid 1990s they found themselves under assault and, like Frederick Douglass and generations of Americans before them, they fought back, making use of their literacy and their heightened political consciousness.

The students learned to fight back and they did so with greater possession of literacy. Among them were those who would some day go off to college. It was just a semester in an educational life, but I have little doubt that the college-bound students were changed through exposure to their less academically successful classmates. They were forced to confront the critical and political contexts of their futures. I am proud to believe that the semester in my classroom contributed to their future success in college. It is too rarely that we see examples of older adolescent and young adult immigrants able to pursue such opportunities (Olivas, 1997). My dream is that those students embraced their literate futures and took full advantage of the education that awaited them. My dream is that a decade later they may have marched along with other Erie classmates and immigrants across the nation to confront anti-immigrant intolerance and continue in a united struggle to change the world we share.

REFERENCES

Acosta, C. (2007). Developing critical consciousness: Resistance literature in a Chicano literature class. *English Journal, 97*(2), 36–42.

Allington, R. L. (1997). *Why does literacy research so often ignore what really matters?* In C. Kinzer, K. Hinchman, & D. Leu (Eds.), *Inquiries in literacy theory and practice. Forty-sixth yearbook of the National Reading conference* (pp. i–iz). Chicago: National Reading Conference.

Allington, R. L. (2002). *Big Brother and the national reading curriculum: How ideology trumped evidence.* Portsmouth, NH: Heinemann.

Altwerger, B. (2005). *Reading for profit: How the bottom line leaves kids behind.* Portsmouth, NH: Heinemann.

Anzaldua, G. (1987). *Borderlands, La frontera: The new mestiza.* San Francisco: Aunt Lute Books.

Auerbach, E., & Wallerstein, N. (1987). *ESL for action: Problem posing at work.* Reading, MA: Addison Wesley.

Auerbach, E. R. (1992). *Making meaning, making change.* Washington, DC: Center for Applied Linguistics.

Auerbach, E., Barhona, B., Midy, J., Vaquerano, F., Zambrano, A., & Arnaud, J. (1996). *Adult ESL/literacy: From community to community: A guidebook for participatory literacy training.* Hillsdale, NJ: Lawrence Erlbaum and Associates.

August, D., & Hakuta, K. (Eds.). (1997). *Improving schooling for language minority children. A research agenda.* Washington, DC: National Academy Press.

August, D., & Shanahan, T. (Eds.). (2008). *Developing reading and writing in second-language learners: Lessons from the report of the national literacy panel on language minority children and youth.* Washington, DC: Center for Applied Linguistics/International Reading Association.

Avila, D., & Martinez, M. (2006). Immigrants at crossroads: Stakes are high for legalization campaign. *Chicago Tribune,* May 1, p. A(1).

Ayers, W. (1993). *To teach: The journey of a teacher.* New York: Teachers College Press.

Bailey, S., Eschbach, K., Hagan, J., & Rodriguez, N. (1996). *Migrant deaths at the Texas-Mexico border, 1985–1994.* Houston, TX: Center for Immigration Research, University of Houston.

Barry, T., Browne, H., & Sims, B. (1994). *Crossing the line: Immigrants, economic integration, and drug enforcement on the U.S.-Mexico border.* Albequerque, NM: Resource Center Press.

Bartolome, L. I. (1993). Effective transitioning strategies: Are we asking the right questions? In J. V. Tinajero & A. F. Ada (Eds.), *The power of two languages: Literacy and biliteracy for spanish speaking students.* New York: Macmillan/McGraw Hill.

Bauer, E. B. (2001). Using children's literature to shape identity: A bilingual, bicultural, and biracial perspective. *New Advocate, 14*(2), 143–152.

Beach, R. (1993). *A teachers' introduction to reader-response theories.* Urbana, IL: National Council of Teachers of English.

Berger, L. R. (1996). Reader response journals: You make the meaning... and how. *Journal of Adolescent and Adult Literacy, 39*(5), 380–386.

Bialystock, E. (1997). Effects of bilingualism and biliteracy on children's emerging concepts of print. *Developmental Psychology, 33*(3), 429–440.

Bloem, P. L. (1995). *Bringing books to adult literacy classrooms.* Kent, OH: Ohio Literacy Resource Center, Kent State University.

Bowles, S., & Gintis, H. (1986). *Schooling in capitalist America.* New York: Basic Books.

Boudin, K. (1993). Participatory literacy education behind bars: AIDS opens the door. *Harvard Education Review, 63*(2), 207–232.

Boyd-Batston, P. (2003). Reading with a hero: A mediated literature experience. In G. G. Garcia (Ed.), *English learners: Reaching the highest level of English literacy.* Newark, DE: International Reading Association.

Boyd-Batstone, P. (2006). *Differentiated early literacy instruction for English language learners: Practical strategies.* Boston. Pearson.

Bracey, G. W. (2004). *Setting the record straight: Responses to misconceptions about public education in the United States.* Portsmouth, NH: Heinemann.

REFERENCES

Britton, J. (1993a). *Literature in its place.* Portsmouth, NH: Heinemann.
Britton, J. (1993b). *Language and learning: The importance of speech in children's development.* Portsmouth, NH: Heinemann.
Carger, C. (1996). *Of borders and dreams: A Mexican-American experience of urban education.* New York: Teachers College Press.
Carlo, M. S., August, D., McLaughlin, B., Snow, C. E., Dressler, C., Lippman, D., et al. (2004). Closing the gap: Addressing the vocabulary needs of English-language learners in bilingual and mailstream classrooms. *Reading Researcg Quarterly, 39,* 188–215.
Carlson, D. (1996). Teachers as political actors: From reproductive theory to the crises of schooling. In P. Leistyna, A. Woodrum, & S. Sherblom (Eds.), *Breaking free: The transformative power of critical pedagogy.* Cambridge, MA: Harvard University Press.
Carlson, R. G. (1977). Professionalization of adult education: An historical-philosophical analysis. *Adult Education, 28,* 53–63.
Carnevale, A., & Desrochers, D. (2003). *Standards for what? The economic roots of K-16 reform.* Princeton, NJ: Educational Testing Service.
Chaiklin, S., & Lave, J. (1993). *Understanding practice: Perspectives on activity and context.* New York: Cambridge University Press.
Chang, J. S., & Krashen, S. D. (1997). The effect of free reading on language and academic development: A natural experiment. *Mosaic, 4*(4), 13–15.
Chapa, J. (1990). Population estimates of school age language minorities and limited English proficient children of the United States, 1979–1988.
Cho, K. S., & Krashen, S. D. (1994). Acquisition of vocabulary from the Sweet Valley Kids series: Adult ESL acquisition. *Journal of Reading, 37*(8), 662–667.
Cochran-Smith, M., & Lytle, S. (Eds.). *Inside outside: Teacher research and knowledge.* New York: Teachers College Press.
Coles, R. (1989). *The call of stories: Teaching and the moral imagination.* Boston: Houghton Mifflin.
Collier, V. P. (1995). Acquiring a second language for school. *Directions in Language and Education, 1*(4), 3–14.
Courts, P. (1991). *Literacy and empowerment: The meaning makers.* New York: Bergin and Garvey.
Crandall, J. (1993). Professionalism and professionalization of adult ESL literacy. *TESOL Quarterly, 27*(3), 497–515.
Cranney, A. G. (1983). Two decades of adult reading programs: Growth, problems, and prospects. *Journal of Reading, 26,* 416–423.
Crawford, J. (1994). *Chronology: Restrictions on immigration and naturalization.* Washington, DC: National Immigration Forum.
Crawford, J. (2004). *Education English learners: Language diversity in the classroom.* Los Angeles: Bilingual Education Services.
Cummins, J. (1984). The role of primary language development in promoting educational success for language minority students. In *Schooling and language minority students: A theoretical framework* (pp. 16–62). Los Angeles: California State University Evaluation of Dissemination, and Assessment Center (ERIC Document Reproduction Service No. ED249773).
Cummins, J. (1993). Empowerment through biliteracy. In J. V. Tinajero & A. F. Ada (Eds.), *The power of two languages: Literacy and biliteracy for Spanish speaking students.* New York: Macmillan/McGraw Hill.
Cyber Drive Illinois. (2006). Driver's license exams. In *Rules of the road* (Chap. 2). Retrieved December 22, 2006, from http://www.cyberdriveillinois.com/publications/rules_of_the_road/rr_chap02.html
Darder, A., Torres, R. D., & Gutierrez, H. (1997). *Latinos in education: A critical reader.* New York: Routledge.
Delgado-Gaitan, C. (1993). Researching change and changing the researcher. *Harvard Educational Review, 63*(4), 389–411.
Delgado-Gaitan, C. (1994). Socializing young children in Mexican-American families: An intergenerational perspective. In P. M. Greenfield & R. R. Cocking (Eds.), *Cross-cultural roots of minority child development.* Hillsdale, NJ: Lawrence Erlbaum Associates.
Delgado, R., & Stefanic, J. (2001). *Critical race theory: An introduction.* New York: New York University Press.

REFERENCES

Delpit, L. (1993). The politics of teaching literate discourses. In T. Perry & J. W. Fraser (Eds.), *Freedom's Plow: Teaching in the multicultural classroom*. New York: Routledge.

del Valle, M. (Speaker). (1996). *Speech at Erie neighborhood house* [personal recording]. Chicago.

Diekhoff, G. M. (1988). An appraisal of adult literacy programs: Reading between the lines. *Journal of Reading, 31*, 624–630.

Dewey, J. (1938). *Experience and education*. New York: Macmillan.

Edelsky, C. E. (1999). On critical, whole language practice: Why, what, and a bit of how. In C. E. Edelsky (Ed.), *Making justice our project: Teachers working toward critical whole language practice*. Urbana, IL: National Council of Teachers of English.

Eisner, E. W. (1991). *The enlightened eye: Qualitative inquiry and the enhancement of educational practice*. New York: MacMillan.

Ellingwood, K. (2004). *Hard line: Life and death on the U.S.-Mexico border*. New York: Pantheon Books.

Ellsworth, E. (1989). Why doesn't this feel empowering? Working through the repressive myths of critical pedagogy. *Harvard Educational Review, 59*(3), 297–324.

Enciso, P. E. (1997). Negotiating the meaning of difference: Talking back to multicultural literature. In T. Robers & A. O. Sotero (Eds.), *Reading across cultures: Teaching literature in a diverse society*. Urbana, IL: National Council of Teachers of English.

Erie Neighborhood House. (1996). *Annual report*. Chicago: Erie Neighborhood House.

Escamilla, K. (1993). Promoting biliteracy: Issues in promoting English literacy in students acquiring English. In J. V. Tinajero & A. F. Ada (Eds.), *The power of two languages: Literacy and biliteracy for Spanish speaking students*. New York: Macmillan/McGraw Hill.

Evans, K. S., & Walker, N. T. (2005). Reading first: Hidden messages, omission, and contradictions. In B. Maloch, J. V. Hoffman, D. L. Schaallert, C. M. Fairbanks, & J. Worthy (Eds.), *54th yearbook of the National Reading conference*.

Farr, M. (1994a). Biliteracy in the home: Practices among Mexicano families in Chicago. In D. Spener (Ed.), *Adult biliteracy in the United States*. Washington, DC: Center for Applied Linguistics.

Farr, M. (1994b). En los dos idiomas: Literacy practices among Chicago Mexicanos. In B. J. Moss (Ed.), *Literacy across communities*. Cresskill, NJ: Hampton Press.

Fingeret, H. A. (1992). *Adult literacy education: Current and future directions. An update*. Columbus, OH: ERIC Clearinghouse on Adult, Career, and Vocational Education. (ERIC Document Reproduction Service No. ED338863)

Foster, S. E. (1988). *Professionalization of the adult literacy workforce*. Southport, CT: Southport Institute for Policy Analysis. (ERIC Document Reproduction Service No. ED302680)

Frago, C. (1997, July 16–31). Development and displacement. *Streetwise*, p. 1.

Frank, R. (1993). *Critical cartography: Mapping teachers' journeys toward critical pedagogy*. Unpublished doctoral dissertation, Claremont Graduate School.

Freire, P. (1970). *Pedagogy of the oppressed*. New York: Continuum.

Freire, P. (1973). *Education for critical consciousness*. New York: Continuum.

Freire, P. (1985). *The politics of education: Culture, power, and liberation*. Boston: Bergin & Garvey.

Frerie, P., & Macedo, D. (1987). *Literacy: Reading the word and the world*. New York: Bergin & Garvey.

Gajdusek, L. (1988). Toward a wider use of literature in ESL: Why and how. *TESOL Quarterly, 22*(2), 227–257.

Gandara, P. (1995). *Over the ivy walls: The educational mobility of low-income Chicanos*. Albany, NY: SUNY Press.

Gay, G. (1993). Building cultural bridges: A bold proposal for teacher education. *Education and Urban Society, 25*(3), 285–299.

Gay, G. (2000). *Culturally responsive teaching: Theory, research, and practice*. New York: Teachers College Press.

Garcia, E. E. (1997). Effective instruction for language minority students. In A. Darder, R. D. Torres, & H. Gutierrez (Eds.), *Latinos in education: A critical reader*. New York: Routledge.

Garcia-Gonzalez, R., Mejia, P., & Porter, W. J. (1999). Si se puede! Teaching for transformation. In C. E. Edelsky (Ed.), *Making justice our project: Teachers working toward critical whole language practice*. Urbana, IL: National Council of Teachers of English.

Gee, J. P. (1987). The legacies of literacy: From Plato to Freire through Harvey Graff. *Journal of Education, 71*(1), 147–165.

REFERENCES

Gee, J. P. (1989). Literacy, discourse and linguistics. *Journal of education, 171*(1), 5–17.
Gee, J. P. (1992). What is literacy? In P. Shanon (Ed.), *Becoming political: Readings and writings in the politics of literacy education*. Portsmouth, NH: Heinemann.
Geertz, C. (1973). *The interpretation of cultures*. New York: Basic Books.
Genesee, G., Geva, E., Dressler, C., & Kamil, M. (2008). Cross-linguistic relationships in second-language learners. In D. August & T. Shanahan (Eds.), *Developing reading and writing in second-language learners: Lessons learned from the report of the National Literacy Panel on Language-Minority Children and Youth*. Newark, DE: International Reading Association.
Geva, E. (2008). Second-language oral proficiency and second-language literacy. In D. August & T. Shanahan (Eds.), *Developing reading and writing in second-language learners: Lessons learned from the report of the National Literacy Panel on Language-Minority*.
Gibson, M., & Ogbu, J. (Ed.). (1991). *Minority status and schooling: A comparative study of immigrant and involuntary minorities*. New York: Garland.
Giroux, H. (1981). *Ideology, culture, and the process of schooling*. Philadelphia: Temple University Press.
Gomez, D. F. (1973). *Strangers in our own land*. Boston: Beacon Press.
Gowen, S. G. (1992). *The politics of workplace literacy: A case study*. New York: Teachers College Press.
Greenberg, E., Macias, R. F., Rhodes, D., & Chan, T. (2001). *English literacy and language minorities in the United States: Results from the national adult literacy survey* (NCES 2001-464). Washington, DC: U.S. Department of Education Office of Educational Research and Improvement.
Greene, M. (1996). In search of critical pedagogy. In P. Leistyna, A. Woodrum, & S. Sherbloom (Eds.), *Breaking free: The transformative power of critical pedagogy*. Cambridge, MA: Harvard Educational Review.
Griffith, M., Jacobs, B., Wilson, S., & Dashiell, M. (1989). Changing the model: Working with underprepared students. *The Quarterly of the National Writing Project and Center for the Study of Writing, 11*(1), 4–9.
Grubb, N. W., Kalman, J., & Castellano, M. (1991). *Readin', writin', and 'rithmetic one more time: The role of remediation in vocational education and job training programs*. Berkeley, CA: National Center for Research in Vocational Education.
Guth, G. J. A., & Wrigley, H. S. (1992). *Adult ESL literacy programs and practices: A report on a national research study. National English Literacy Demonstration Program for Adults of Limited English Proficiency*. Washington DC: U.S. Department of Education.
Guthrie, J. T., & Wigfield, A. (2000). Engagement and motivation in reading. *Handbook of Reading Research, 4*(8), 402–433.
Guthrie, J. T., & Davis, M. H. (2003). Motivating struggling readers in middle school through an engagement model of classroom practice. *Reading and Writing Quarterly, 19*(1), 59–85.
Hansen, D. (1995). *The call to teach*. New York: Teachers College Press.
Heath, S. B. (1983). *Ways with words: Language, life, and work in communities and classrooms*. Cambridge, MA: Cambridge University Press.
Heller, C. E. (1992). *Until we are strong together: Women writers in the Tenderloin*. Unpublished doctoral dissertation, University of California, Berkeley.
Heller, C. E. (1997). *Until we are strong together: Women writers in the Tenderloin*. New York: Teachers College Press.
Hellwig, M., & Wilson, D. (1996). *Models of effective workforce preparation programs*. Chicago: Policy Research Action Group, Loyola University.
Hooks, B. (1991). *Yearning: Race, gender, and cultural politics*. Boston: South End.
Hooks, B. (1994). *Teaching to transgress: Education as the practice of freedom*. Boston: South End.
Hornberger, N. H., & Hardman, J. (1994). Literacy as cultural practice and cognitive skill: Biliteracy in an ESL class and a GED program. In D. Spener (Ed.), *Adult biliteracy in the United States*. Washington, DC: Center for Applied Linguistics.
Horton, M., Freire, P., Bell, B., & Gaventa, J. (1990). *We make the road by walking*. Philadelphia: Temple University Press.
Hull, G. (1991). *Hearing other voices: A critical assessment of popular views on literacy and work*. Berkeley, CA: National Center for Research in Vocational Education.

REFERENCES

Hull, G. (1992). *"Their chances? slim and none": An ethnographic account of the experience of low-income people of color in a vocational program at work.* Berkeley, CA: National Center for Research in Vocational Education.

Hull, G. (Ed.). (1997). *Changing work, changing workers: Critical perspectives on language, literacy, and skills.* New York: SUNY Press.

Hunt, S. M. (1982). The communicative effects of a rewritten driver manual. ED237941.

Hynds, S. (1992). Challenging questions in the teaching of literature. In J. Langer (Ed.), *Literature instruction: A focus on student response.* Urbana, IL: National Council of Teachers of English.

Ignatiev, N., & Garvey, J. (1996). *Race traitor.* New York: Routledge.

Illinois Community College Board. (1992). *Focused recognition visit:* Springfield, IL: Illinois Community College Board.

Ilsley, P. J., & Stahl, N. A. (1994). Reconceptualizing the language of adult literacy. In M. C. Radencich (Ed.), *Adult literacy: A compendium of articles from the Journal of Reading.* Newark, DE: International Reading Association.

Jackson, P. (1968). *Life in classrooms.* New York: Holt, Rinehart & Winston.

Jay, M. (2003). Critical race theory, multicultural education, and the hidden curriculum of hegemony. *Multicultural Perspectives, 5*(4), 3–9.

Jimenez, R. (2003). Literacy and Latino students in the United States: Some considerations, questions, and new directions. *Reading Research Quarterly, 38*(1), 122–128.

Jolliffe, D. (1994, January). *Problems of identity formation in work related contexts: Insights from discourse analysis and worker interviews.* Paper presented at the meeting of the Mid-Winter conference, NCTE Assembly for Research, Chicago.

Jurmo, P. (1987). *Learner participation practices in adult literacy efforts in the United States.* Unpublished doctoral dissertation, Center for International Education, University of Massachusetts, Amherst, MA.

Kaestle, C. F. (1988). The history of literacy and the history of readers. In E. R. Kintgen, B. M. Kroll, & M. Rose (Eds.), *Perspectives on literacy.* Carbondale, IL: Southern Illinois University Press.

Kazemek, F. E. (1988). Necessary changes: Professional involvement in adult literacy programs. *Harvard Educational Review, 58,* 464–487.

Kazemek, F. E. (1991). In ignorance to view a small portion and think that all: The false promise of job literacy. *Journal of education, 173*(1), 51–64.

Kincheloe, J. L. (2005). *Critical pedagogy primer.* New York: Peter Lang.

Kincheloe, J. L., & Steinberg, S. R. (1996). A tentative description of post-formal thinking: The critical confrontation with cognitive theory. In P. Leistyna, A. Woodrum, & S. Sherbloom (Eds.), *Breaking Free: The transformative power of critical pedagogy.* Cambridge, MA: Harvard Educational Review.

Kozol, J. (1992). *Savage inequalities: Children in America's schools.* New York: Crown.

Kozol, J. (2006, May). *Keynote address.* Annual meeting of the International Reading Association, Chicago, IL.

Kozol, J. (2007). *Letters to a young teacher.* New York: Crown.

Krashen, S. D. (1981). The "fundamental pedagogical principle" in second language teaching. *Studa Linguistica, 35*(1–2), 50–70.

Krashen, S. D. (1983). *The natural approach: Language acquisition in the classroom.* San Francisco: The Alemany Press. (ERIC Document Reproduction Service No. ED230069).

Krashen, S. D. (1989). We acquire vocabulary and spelling by reading: Additional evidence for the input hypothesis. *Modern Language Journal, 73*(4), 440–464.

Krashen, S. D. (1995). Immersion: Why not try free reading? *Mosaic, 3*(1), 3–4.

Krashen, S. D. (1997). Does free voluntary reading lead to academic language. *Journal of Intensive English Studies, 11,* 1–8.

Krashen, S. D. (2003). *Explorations in language acquisition and use.* Portsmouth, NH: Heinemann.

Kraver, J. R. (2007). Engendering gender equity: Using literature to teach and learn democracy. *English Journal, 96*(6), 67–73.

Kucer, S. B. (2005). *Dimensions of literacy: A conceptual base for teaching reading and writing in school settings.* Mahwah, NJ: Lawrence Erlbaum Associates.

Ladson-Billings, G. (1994). *The dreamkeepers: Successful teachers of African-American children.* San Francisco: Jossey Bass.

REFERENCES

Ladson-Billings, G. (1999). Just what is critical race theory, and what's it doing in a *nice* field like education? In L. Parker, D. Deyhle, & S. Villenas (Eds.), *Race is…race isn't: Critical race theory and qualitative studies in education*. Bolder, CO: Westview Press.

Ladson-Billings, G., & Tate IV, W. F. (2006). Toward a critical race theory of education. In A. D. Dixon & C. K. Rousseau (Eds.), *Critical race theory in education: All God's children got a song*. New York: Routledge.

Land, R., & Moustafa, M. (2005). Scripted reading instruction: Help or hindrance? In B. Altwerger (Ed.), *Reading for profit: How the bottom line leaves kids behind*. Portsmouth, NH: Heinemann.

Langan, M., & Orfield, G. (1991). *The revolving door: City colleges of Chicago*. Chicago: Metropolitan Opportunity Project, University of Chicago.

Langer, J. (1992). Rethinking literature instruction. In J. Langer (Ed.), *Literature instruction: A focus on student response*. Urbana, IL: National Council of Teachers of English.

Langer, J. (1995). *Envisioning literature: Literary understanding and literature instruction*. New York: Teachers College Press.

Lather, P., & Smithies, C. (1997). *Troubling the angels: Women living with HIV/AIDS*. Boulder, CO: Westview/Harper Collins.

Latino Institute. (1987). *Chicago's working Latinas: Confronting multiple roles and pressures*. Chicago: Latino Institute.

Latino Institute. (1993). *Does Chicago's Latino population mirror the national Latino population?* Chicago: Latino Institute.

Latino Institute. (1994). *Latstat: Latino housing*. Chicago: Latino Institute.

Latino Institute. (1994). *Latstat. Latino poverty*. Chicago: Latino Institute.

Latino Institute. (1995). *Latino origin groups*. Chicago: Latino Institute.

Latino Institute. (1996). *Latstat: Latino income*. Chicago: Latino Institute.

Lave, J. (1993). *Understanding practice: Perspectives on activity and context*. Cambridge, MA: Cambridge University Press.

Leistyna, P., & Woodrum, A. (1996). Context and culture: What is critical pedagogy? In P. Leistyna, A. Woodrum, & S. Sherbloom (Eds.), *Breaking free: The transformative power of critical pedagogy*. Cambridge, MA: Harvard Educational Review.

Leslie, L., & Caldwell, J. (1995). *Qualitative reading inventory II*. New York: Addison-Wessley.

Lesaux, N. K., Geva, E., Koda, K., Siegel, L. S., & Shanahan, T. (2008). Development of literacy in second-language learners. In D. August & T. Shanahan (Eds.), *Developing reading and writing in second-language learners: Lessons learned from the report of the National Literacy Panel on Language-Minority Children and Youth*. Newark, DE: International Reading Association.

Lewis, M., & Simon, R. I. (1986). A discourse not intended for her: Learning and teaching within the patriarchy. *Harvard Educational Review, 56*(4), 457–472.

Lewis, A. (2001, February 10). Abroad at home: Rays of hope. *New York Times*. Retrieved March 18, 2008, from http://query.nytimes.com/gst/fullpage.html?res=9807E5DC1331F933A25751C0A9679C8B63&scp=1&sq=Rays+of+Hope%2C+February+10%2C+2001&st=nyt

Lewis, C. (1999). The quality of the question: Probing culture in literature-discussion groups. In C. E. Edelsky (Ed.), *Making justice our project: Teachers working toward critical whole language practice*. Urbana, IL: National Council of Teachers of English.

Livdahl, B. S., Smart, K., Wallman, J., Herbert, T. K., Geiger, D. K., & Anderson, J. L. (1995). *Stories from response-centered classrooms: Speaking, questioning, and theorizing from the center of action*. New York: Teachers College Press.

Lohrentz, T. (1995). *The impact of the Chicago regional economy of operation jobs. Illinois Coalition for Immigration and Refugee Protection*. Chicago: Center for Urban Economic Development, University of Illinois at Chicago.

Lynch, J. (2000, November 15). York County Prison now has a wing designated for asylum seekers only. *York Daily Record*, p. (A)1.

Lytle, S., & Wolfe, M. (1989). *Adult literacy education: Program evaluation and learner assessment* (Information Series No. 338). Columbus, OH: Publications Office, Center on Education and Training for Employment. (ERIC document Reproduction Service No. ED315665).

Lytle, S. L. (1990, April). *Living literacy: The practices and beliefs of adult learners*. Presented at an invited symposium of the Language Development SIG, *Adult Literacy/Child Literacy: One World or Worlds Apart* at the annual meeting of the American Educational Research Association, Boston, MA.

REFERENCES

Lytle, S. L., Belzer, A., & Reumann, R. (1993). *Developing the professional workforce for adult literacy education* (PB92-02). Philadelphia: University of Pennsylvania, National Center for Adult Literacy.

Macias, R. F. (1994). Inheriting sins while seeking absolution: Language diversity and national data sets. In D. Spener (Ed.), *Adult biliteracy in the United States*. Washington, DC: Center for Applied Linguistics.

Manglesdorf, K. (1998). Literature in the ESL classroom: Reading, reflection, and changes. In T. Smoke (Ed.), *Adult ESL: Politics, pedagogy, and participation in classroom and community programs*. New Jersey: Lawrence Erlbaum Associates.

Martinez-Roldan, C. M. (2003). Building worlds and identities: A case study of the role of narratives in bilingual literature discussions. *Research in the Teaching of English, 37*(4), 491–526.

Matute-Bianchi, M. A. (1991). Situational ethnicity and patterns among immigrant and non-immigrant Mexican-descent students. In M. Gibson & J. Ogbu (Eds.), *Minority status and schooling: A comparative study of immigrants and involuntary minorities*. New York: Garland.

McDonnell, P. J. (2000, October 23). INS rules pose catch-22 for adoptee citizenship: A 10-year ban from U.S. is possible. The dilemma is common. *Los Angeles Times*, p. A-1.

McIntosh, P. (1990, Winter). White privilege: Unpacking the invisible knapsack. *Independent School*. Retrieved February 17, 2008, fromhttp://www.feinberg.northwestern.edu/diversity/uploaded_docs/UnpackingTheKnapsack.pdf

McKay, S. L., & Weinsein-Shr, G. (1993). English literacy in the U.S.: National policies, personal consequences. *TESOL Quarterly, 27*(3), 407–416.

Mikulecky, L., Albers, P., & Peers, M. (1994). *Literacy transfer: A review of the literature*. Philadelphia: University of Pennsylvania, National Center for Adult Literacy.

Mock, B. (2007, Winter). Immigration backlash. *Southern Poverty Law Center Intelligence Report*. Retrieved February, 20, 2008, from http://www.splcenter.org/intelreport/article.jsp?aid=845

Mohr, K. A. J., & Mohr, E. S. (2007). Extending English-language learners' classroom interactions using the response protocol. *Reading Teacher, 60*(5), 440–450.

Moje, E. B., & Hinchman, K. (2004). Culturally responsive practices for youth literacy learning. In T. L. Jetton & J. A. Dole (Eds.), *Adolescent literacy research and practice*. New York: The Guilford Press.

Moll, L. C., & Diaz, S. (1987). Change as the goal of educational research. *Anthropology and Education Quarterly, 18*, 300–311.

Moll, L. C. (Ed.). (1990). *Vygotsky and education: Instructional implications and applications of sociohistorical psychology*. Cambridge, UK: Cambridge University Press.

Moll, L. C., & Greenberg, J. B. (1990). Creating zones of possibilities: Combinant social contexts for instruction. In L. Moll (Ed.), *Vygotsky and education: Instructional implications and applications of sociohistorical psychology*. Cambridge, UK: Cambridge University Press.

Moll, L. C. (2005). Reflections and possibilities. In N. Gonzalez, L. C. Moll, & C. Amanti (Eds.), *Funds of knowledge: Theorizing practices in households, communities, and classrooms*. Mahwah, NJ: Lawrence Erlbaum Associates.

Montaigne, R. (Reporter). (2007). *Raid on illegal workers puts children in limbo* [Audio download]. Retrieved February 9, 2008, from http://npr.org/templates/story.story.php?storyId=16227353. Washington DC: National Public Radio.

Mulhern, M., Rodriguez-Brown, F. V., & Shanahan, T. (1994). *Family literacy for language minority families: Issues for program implementation*. Washington, DC: U.S. Department of Education, National Clearinghouse for Bilingual Education.

Nagy, W. E., Garcia, G. E., Durgunoglu, A., & Hancin-Bhatt, B. (1993). Spanish-English bilingual children's use and recognition of cognates in English reading. *Journal of Reading Behavior, 25*(3), 241–259.

National Immigration Forum. (2000). *Fix 96: Restore America's tradition as a nation of immigrants and a nation of just laws*. National Immigration Forum website. Retrieved June, 2001, from http://www.immigrationforum.org/fix96

National Public Radio/Kaiser Family Foundation/Kennedy School of Government. (2004). *Immigration in America*. Retrieved February 15, 2008, from http://www.npr.org/templates/story/story.php?storyId=4062605

Newman, D., Griffin, P., & Cole, M. (1989). *The construction zone: Working for cognitive change in school*. Cambridge: Cambridge University Press.

REFERENCES

Nieto, S. (1993). We speak in many tongues: Language diversity and multicultural education. In J. V. Tinajero & A. F. Ada (Eds.), *The power of two languages: Literacy and biliteracy for Spanish speaking students*. New York: Macmillan/McGraw Hill.

Nieto, S. (2005). Public education in the twentieth century and beyond: High hopes, broken promises, and an uncertain future. *Harvard Education Press, 75*(1), 43–64.

Nieto, S. (2000). Multiclturalism, social justice, and critical teaching. In I. Shore & C. Pari (Eds.), *Education is politics: Critical teaching across differences, K-12*. Portsmouth, NH: Heinemann.

Noddings, N. (1984). *Caring: A feminine approach to ethics and moral education*. Berkeley, CA: University of California Press.

Norris, M. (Reporter). (2007). *Immigration raid leaves schools scrambling* [audio download]. Retrieved February 9, 2008, from http://npr.org/templates/story.story.php?storyId=16227353. Washington, DC: National Public Radio.

Oakes, J. (1985). *Keeping track: How schools structure inequality*. New Haven, CT: Yale University Press.

Ogbu, J. (1978). *Minority education and caste: The American system in cross-cultural perspective*. New York: Academic Press.

Ogle, D. (1986). K-W-L: A teaching method that develop an active reading of expository text. *Journal of Reading, 39*(6), 564–570.

Olivas, M. (1997). Research on Latino college students: a theoretical framework and inquiry. In A. Darder, R. Torres, & H. Guierrez (Eds.), *Latinos and education: A critical reader*. New York: Routledge.

Orfield, G. (1990). Wasted talent, threatened future: Metropolitan Chicago's human capital and Illinois public policy. In L. B. Joseph (Ed.), *Creating jobs, creating workers: Economic development and employment in metropolitan Chicago*. Chicago: University of Illinois Press.

Padak, G. M., & Nixon-Ponder, S. (1995). *Adult literacy teachers as researchers: A report on statewide research and development sites*. Paper presented at the National Reading conference, New Orleans, LA, November 30, 1995.

Pang, E. S., & Kamil, M. L. (2004). *Second language issues in early literacy instruction*. Stanford University, Publication Series No. 1. Retrieved February 18, 2008, from http://people.ucsc.edu/~ktellez/kamil-L2.pdf

Paral, R. (1994). *Hopes and dreams: A statistical profile of the non-citizen population of metropolitan Chicago*. Chicago: Latino Institute.

Paral, R. (1996). *Estimate costs of providing welfare and education services to the native born and to immigrants in Illinois*. Chicago: Illinois Immigration Policy Project, Latino Institute.

Perez, S. M., & de la Rosa Salazar, D. (1997). Economic, labor force, and social implications of Latino educational and population trends. In A. Darder, R. D. Torres, & H. Gutierrez (Eds.), *Latinos in education: A critical reader*. New York: Routledge.

Peterson, J. (2000). Welfare a tangle for immigrants-legal and illegal. *Yakima Herald-Republic*.

Pew Research Center for the People & the Press. (2006, March). *No consensus on immigration problem or proposed fixes: America's immigration quandary*. Retrieved from http://pewhispanic.org/files/reports/63/pdf. Washington, DC: Pew Hispanic Center.

Pilgren, J., & Krashen, S. D. (1993). Sustained silent reading with English as a second language high school students: Impact on reading comprehension, reading fluency, and reading enjoyment. *School Library Media Quarterly, 22*(1), 21–23.

Power, K. (1995). Beyond history. *Race Traitor, 5*, 6–16.

Probst, R. (1992). Five kinds of literary knowing. In J. Langer (Ed.), *Literature instruction: A focus on student response*. Urbana, IL: National Council of Teachers of English.

Purcell-Gates, V. (1995). *Other people's words: The cycle of low literacy*. Cambridge, MA: Harvard University Press.

Purcell-Gates, V., Degener, S., & Jacobson, E. (2001). Adult literacy instruction: Degrees of authenticity and collaboration as described by practitioners. *Journal of literacy research, 33*(4), 571–593.

Purcell-Gates, V., Degener, S., & Jacobson, E. (2002). Impact of authentic adult literacy instruction on adult literacy practices. *Reading research quarterly, 37*(1), 70–92.

Purcell-Gates, V., & Waterman, R. A. (2000). *Now we read, we see, we speak: Portrait of literacy development in an adult Freirain-based class*. Mahwah, NJ: Lawrence Earlbaum Associates.

REFERENCES

Purcell-Gates, V. (2007). What's it all about? Literacy research and civic responsibility. In D. W. Rowe, R. T. Jimenez, D. L. Compton, D. K. Dickenson, Y. Kim, K. M. Leander, & V. J. Risko (Eds.), *56th Yearbook of the National Reading conference*. Chicago: National Reading Conference.

Quigley, B. A. (1997). *Rethinking literacy education: The critical need for practice-based change*. San Francisco: Jossey-Bass.

Rachor, G. (1995). *Practitioner inquiry: Model for adult education professional development*. Unpublished doctoral dissertation, Wayne State University.

Raines, A. S. (2005). Louise Rosenblatt: An advocate for nurturing democratic participation through literary transactions. *Talking Points, 17*(1), 28–31.

Raizen, S. A. (1989). *Reforming education for work: A cognitive science perspective*. Berkeley, CA: National Center for Research in Vocational Education.

Ramirez, A. G. (1994). Sociolinguistic considerations in biliteracy planning. In D. Spener (Ed.), *Adult biliteracy in the United States*. Washington, DC: Center for Applied Linguistics.

Ramsey, K., & Robyn, A. (1992). *Preparing adult immigrants for work: The educational response in two communities*. Berkeley, CA: National Center for Research in Vocational Education.

Ruiz, R. (1997). The empowerment of language-minority students. In A. Darder, R. D. Torres, & H. Gutierrez (Eds.), *Latinos in education: A critical reader*. New York: Routledge.

Rockhill, K. (1993). Gender, language and the politics of literacy. In B. Street (Ed.), *Cross cultural approaches to literacy*. New York: Cambridge University Press.

Rosenblatt, L. M. (1978). *The reader, the text, the poem: The transactional theory of the literary work*. Carbondale, IL: Southern Illinois University Press.

Rosenblatt, L. M. (1995). *Literature as exploration*. New York: Modern Language Association.

Sanchez, C. (Reporter). (2007a). *Town's immigrant students stay away from school*. Retrieved February 9, 2008, from http://npr.org/templates/story.story.php?storyId=16227353. Washington, DC: National Public Radio.

Sanchez, C. (Reporter). (2007b). *Immigration raid sets off tragedy for Mass. family*. Retrieved February 9, 2008 from http://npr.org/templates/story.story.php?storyId=16227353. Washington, DC: National Public Radio.

Schubert, W. (1986). *Curriculum: Perspectives, paradigm, and possibility*. New York: Macmillan.

Shanahan, T., Meehan, M., & Mogge, S. (1994). *The professionalization of the teacher in adult literacy education* (Technical Report TR94). Philadelphia: National Center on Adult Literacy, University of Pennsylvania.

Shankman, K. (1995). *Jobs that pay: Are enough good jobs available in metropolitan Chicago?* Chicago: The Working Poor Project. The Chicago Urban Leagues, The Latino Institute.

Shannon, P. (1992). Commercial reading materials, a technological ideology, and the deskilling of teachers. In P. Shanon (Ed.), *Becoming political: Readings and writings in the politics of literacy education*. Portsmouth, NH: Heinemann.

Shannon, P. (2000). *iSHOP, you shop: Raising questions about reading commodities*. Portsmouth, NH: Heinemann.

Sherman, R. Z., Kutner, M., Webb, L., & Herman, R. (1991). *Key elements of adult education teacher and voluntary programs*. Washington, DC: Pelavin Associates.

Shor, I., & Freire, P. (1987). *A pedagogy for liberation: Dialogues in transformative education*. New York: Bergin & Garvey.

Shor, I. (1987). Monday morning fever: Critical literacy and the generative theme of "work". In I. Shor (Ed.), *Freire for the classroom*. Portsmouth, NH: Boynton/Cook.

Shor, I. (1997). *Empowering education: Critical teaching for social change*. Chicago: The University of Chicago Press.

Shultz, K. (1997). Discourse of workplace education. In G. Hull (Ed.), *Changing work, changing workers: Critical perspectives on language, literacy, and skills*. New York: SUNY Press.

Simon, R. (1992). Empowerment as a pedagogy of possibility. In P. Shanon (Ed.), *Becoming political: Readings and writings in the politics of literacy education*. Portsmouth, NH: Heinemann.

Spener, D. (1993). The Freirean approach to adult literacy education. In J. Crandall & J. K. Peyton (Eds.), *Approaches to adult ESL literacy instruction*. Washington, DC: Center for Applied Linguistics.

Spener, D. (1994). Introduction. In D. Spener (Ed.), *Adult biliteracy in the United States*. Washington, DC: Center for Applied Linguistics.

REFERENCES

Spener, D. (1996). Transitional bilingual education and the socialization of Immigrants. In P. Leistyna, A.Woodrum, & S. Sherbloom (Eds.), *Breaking free: The transformative power of critical pedagogy.* Cambridge, MA: Harvard Educational Review.

Sperling, M. (1996). Revisiting the writing-speaking connection: Challenges for research on writing and writing instruction. *Review of Educational Research, 66*(1), 53–86.

Stairs, A. J. (2007). Culturally responsive teaching: The Harlem renaissance in an urban English class. *English Journal, 96*(6), 37–42.

Stasz, C., Ramsey, K., Eden, R., DaVanzo, J., Farris, H., & Lewis, M. (1992). *Classrooms that work: Teaching generic skills in academic and vocational settings.* Macomb, IL: NCRVE Materials Distribution Center.

Sticht, T. G. (1987). *Functional context education.* San Diego, CA: Applied Behavioral and Cognitive Science.

Sticht, T. G. (1988–1989). Adult literacy education. *Review of Research in Education, 15,* 59–96.

Suarez-Orozco, M. M. (1987). "Becoming somebody": Central American immigrants in U.S. inner-city schools. *Anthropology and Education Quarterly, 18*(4), 287–299.

Suarez-Orozco, M. M. (1991). Immigrant adaptation to schooling: A Hispanic case. In M. Gibson & J. Ogbu (Eds.), *Minority status and schooling: A comparative study of immigrant and involuntary minorities.* New York: Garland.

Suarez-Orozco, M. M. (2001). Globalization, immigration, and education: The research agenda. *Harvard Education Review, 71*(3), 345–365.

Suro, R. (1998). *Strangers among us: How Latino immigration is transforming America.* New York: Alfred Knopf.

Tate, W. F. (1997). Critical race theory and education: History, theory, and implications. *Review of Educational Research, 22,* 195–247.

Tatum, A. (2005). *Teaching reading to black adolescent males: Closing the achievement gap.* Portland, ME: Stenhouse Publishers.

Thomas, W. P., & Collier, V. P. *School effectiveness for language minority students* (NCBE Resource Collection Series, No. 9). Washington DC: National Clearinghouse for Bilingual Education.

Tibbets, J., Kutner, M., Hemphill, D., & Jones, E. (1991). *The delivery and content of training for adult education teachers and volunteer instructors.* Washington, DC: Offices of Vocational and Adult Education.

Tichenor, D. J. (2002). *Dividing lines: The politics of immigration control in America.* Princeton, NJ: Princeton University Press.

Torres, R. D., & de la Torre, A. (1997). Latinos, class, and the U.S. political economy: Income inequality and policy alternatives. In A. Darder, R. D. Torres, & H. Gutierrez (Eds.), *Latinos in education: A critical reader.* New York: Routledge.

U.S. Department of Education. (1993). *National education goals report summary guide.* Retrieved March 11, 2008, from http://www.ed.gov/pubs/goals/summary/goals.html. Washington, DC: United States Department of Education.

Valdes, G. (1996). *Con respeto: Bridging the distances between culturally diverse families and schools: An ethnographic portrait.* New York: Teachers College Press.

Van Maanen, J. (1988). *Tales of the field: On writing ethnography.* Chicago: University of Chicago Press.

Van Mannen, M. (1990). *Researching lived experience. Human science for an action sensitive pedagogy.* Albany, NY: SUNY Press.

Vasquez, M. J. T. (1997). Confronting barriers to the participation of Mexican American women in higher education. In A. Darder, R. D. Torres, & H. Gutierrez (Eds.), *Latinos in education: A critical reader.* New York: Routledge.

Vazquez-Toness, B. (Reporter). (2007). *Raid on illegal immigrants brings chaos to town* [Audio download]. Retrieved February 9, 2008, from http://npr.org/templates/story.story.php?storyId=16227353. Washington, DC: National Public Radio.

Vygotsky, L. S. (1978). *Mind in society.* Cambridge, MA: Harvard University Press.

Vygotsky, L. S. (1986). *Thought and language.* Cambridge, MA: MIT Press.

Wallerstein, N. (1987). Problem posing education: Freire's method for transformation. In I. Shor (Ed.), *Freire for the classroom.* Portsmouth, NH: Boynton/Cook.

Weinstein-Shr, G. (1993). Literacy and social process: A community in transition. In B. Street (Ed.), *Cross-cultural approaches to literacy.* Cambridge: Cambridge University Press.

REFERENCES

Weinstein-Shr, G., & Quintero, E. (Eds.). (1995). *Immigrant learners & their families.* Washington, DC: Center for Applied Linguistics.
Weiler, K. (1991). Freire and a feminist pedagogy of difference. *Harvard Educational Review, 61*(4), 449–474.
Wells, G., & Chang-Wells, G. L. (1992). *Constructing knowledge together: Classrooms as centers of inquiry and literacy.* Portsmouth, NH: Heinemann.
Whitmore, K. F. (2005). Literature study groups: Support for community building in democratic classrooms. *Talking Points, 17*(1), 13–22.
Wiley, T. G. (2005). *Literacy and language diversity in the United States* (2nd ed.). Washington, DC: Center for Applied Linguistics.
Willis, P. (1977). *Learning to labor.* New York: Columbia University Press.
Wolcott, H. F. (1988). Ethnographic research in education. In R. M. Jaeger (Ed.), *Complementary methods for research in education.* Washington, DC: American Educational Research Association.
Wolcott, H. F. (2001). *Writing up qualitative research.* Thousand Oaks, CA: Sage Publishers.
Wong, K. K. (1990). Toward a more effective job training policy in metropolitan Chicago. In L. B. Joseph (Ed.), *Creating jobs, creating workers: Economic development and employment in metropolitan Chicago.* Chicago: University of Illinois Press.
Worthman, C. (2006, May). *Building strength together: The literacy experiences of learners in different adult education contexts.* Paper presented at the annual meeting of the International Reading Association. Chicago, IL.
Young, R. (1992). *Critical theory and classroom talk.* Philadelphia: Multilingual Matters.
Zinn, H. (2005). *People's history of the United States: 1492 to the present.* New York: Harper Collins.
Zolberg, A. R. (2006). *A nation by design: Immigration policy in the fashioning of America.* Cambridge, MA: Harvard University Press.

Cited Classroom References

Anaya, R. (1972). *Bless Me Ultima.* New York: Time Warner.
Carnes, J. (1995). *Us and them: A history of intolerance in America.* Atlanta, GA: Southern Poverty Law Center.
Cisneros, S. (1989). *A house on mango street.* New York: Vintage Books.
de la Cruz, J. (1991). The battle for farm workers rights. In J. Gordon (Ed.), *More Than a Job.* Syracuse, NY: New Readers Press.
Douglass, F. (1963). *Narrative of the life of Frederick Douglass, an American slave.* New York: Anchor Press.
Gomez, D. (1993). Yo soy chicano. In V. Seeley (Ed.), *In Mexican-American literature.* New Jersey: Globe Fearon Company.
Illinois Secretary of State's Office. (1996). *Rules of the road.* Springfield, IL: Illinois Secretary of State's Office.
Mujeres Latinas en Acción & Latino Institute. (1996). *Latinas in Chicago: A portrait.* Chicago: Latino Institute.
Keller, R. (1992). *The kite flyer and other stories.* Syracuse, NY: New Readers Press.
Keller, R. (1993). *Orange grove and other stories.* Syracuse, NY: New Readers Press.
London, J. (1990). *The call of the wild.* New York: Mass Market Paperback.
Menchu, R., Burgos-Debray, E., & Wright, A. (1987). *I, Rigoberta Menhu: An Indian woman in Guatemala.* New York: Verso Books.
Mohr, N. (1993). An awakening summer 1956. In V. Seeley (Ed.), *In Latino-Caribbean literature.* New Jersey: Globe Fearon Company.
Perez, R. T. (1991). *Diary of an Undocumented Immigrant.* Houston, TX: Arte Publico Press.
Soto, G. (1993). Growing up. In V. Seeley (Ed.), *In Mexican-American literature.* New Jersey: Globe Fearon Company.
Stadelhofen, M. M. (1990). *Last chance for freedom.* Syracuse, NY: New Readers Press.
Stadelhofen, M. M. (1990). *The freedom side.* Syracuse, NY: New Readers Press.
Street, S. S., & Orozco, S. (1992). *Organizing for our lives: New voices from rural communities.* Portland, OR: New Sage Press and California Rural Legal Assistance.
Villasenor, V. (1991). *Macho!* Houston, TX: Arte Publico Press.

REFERENCES

NOTES

[1] Victor Villaseñor's book, Macho, which Luís later selected for personal reading describes the animosity that many undocumented Mexican farm workers felt toward César Chávez and the United Farm Workers Movement. Though a work of fiction, Villasenor intersperses historical accounts throughout his novel to highlight the divisiveness that existed.

[2] *Braceros* is from the Spanish word *brazos* (arms). Mexican workers who were encouraged to come to the United States and to California, in particular, to harvest the fields during the 1940s, 50s and early 60s were known as *braceros*. While the students knew the word, none knew of the hundreds of thousands of Mexican workers who preceded them in past decades.

[3] This is the story Jesse Lopez de la Cruz brings to her story. A difference of opinion exists regarding this issue.

[4] For further data specific to Illinois in the 1990s, see: "Taxes paid by Illinois immigrants: A technical paper produced for the Immigrant Policy Project." (1996) The Urban Institute and Illinois Immigrant Policy Project.

[5] U.S. Congressional Representative, Luís Guttierez, has represented the West Town community for many years. He is Puerto Rican and has been a leading advocate for Mexican immigrants.

[6] The Journal of Ordinary Thought was founded by a brilliant and compassionate man, Hal Adams, who led writing groups in several Chicago communities, always guaranteeing that writers' voices were expressed and presented with authenticity and determination. The motto of the journal is: "Every person is a philosopher." I presented the journals to my Erie students and told them, "Every person can read philosophy."